Organizing for High Performance

Organizing for High Performance

Employee Involvement, TQM, Reengineering, and Knowledge Management in the Fortune 1000

—The CEO Report—

Edward E. Lawler III

Susan Albers Mohrman

George Benson

JOSSEY-BASS
A Wiley Company
San Francisco

Published by

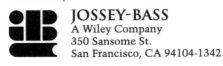

JOSSEY-BASS
A Wiley Company
350 Sansome St.
San Francisco, CA 94104-1342

www.josseybass.com

Library of Congress Cataloging-in-Publication Data

Lawler, Edward E.
    Organizing for high performance : employee
involvement, TQM, reengineering, and knowledge management in the
Fortune 1000 / by Edward E. Lawler III, Susan Albers Mohrman, and
George Benson.—Rev. and updated ed.
      p. cm.
Includes bibliographical references and index.
ISBN 0-7879-5689-9 (alk. paper)
  1. Management—Employee participation—United States. 2. Total quality management—United States. 3. Reengineering (Management)—United States. I. Mohrman, Susan Albers. II. Benson, George. III. Title.
  HD5660.U5 L385 2001
  658.4—dc21

2001000576

FIRST EDITION
HB Printing   10 9 8 7 6 5 4 3 2 1

Contents

List of Tables

Preface

Global competition, the explosion of the Internet, and rapid economic changes are among the many forces that challenge traditional approaches to management. There is no shortage of new ideas about how organizations should be managed in order to allow them to gain a competitive advantage in today's hypercompetitive markets. During the 1990s, employee involvement (EI), total quality management (TQM), and process reengineering were among the most frequently mentioned and used approaches to improving organizational effectiveness. Currently, organizations are placing increased emphasis on knowledge management and the Internet to achieve that end. Two questions are key with respect to any effort to improve organizational effectiveness: Does it work? and What is involved in introducing it in a complex organization?

Our interest in employee involvement dates back decades and includes considerable research and consulting. Nevertheless, despite great interest in the topic and much research, little systematic information exists on why companies are adopting EI programs, what types of practices they are using, whether the use of EI is increasing or decreasing, how effective companies think EI is, and how effective it actually is.

Much the same is true for total quality management. In many organizations, TQM is closely related to EI; studying one without the other is ill advised. Reengineering is newer still; consequently, less research has been done on it. It is increasingly part of organizational change efforts that install extensive corporate information systems, in most cases enterprise resource planning (ERP) systems, and adopt Internet-based information systems.

Knowledge management has recently become a critical issue in organizations, for a number of reasons. Perhaps the most important is an increase in the number of organizations in developed countries that are doing knowledge work. Further, in many instances, the development and distribution of knowledge is one of the major factors in organizational effectiveness. Because so little research has been conducted on knowledge management practices, it is important that we start to track the kinds of practices organizations use to manage knowledge and to determine their effectiveness.

Organizing for High Performance represents the fifth study of a continuing research program aimed at documenting how management practices in Fortune 1000 corporations are changing. The first study involved a 1987 survey that focused on which types of employee involvement practices were being adopted by Fortune 1000 corporations and on the firms' views of the effectiveness of these practices (Lawler, Ledford, and Mohrman, 1989). The second study involved a 1990 follow-up survey of the Fortune 1000 that focused on both employee involvement and total quality management (Lawler, Mohrman, and Ledford, 1992). A comparison of the 1987 and 1990 data showed inreased adoption rates for employee involvement practices among large U.S. firms. It also provided a benchmark of the degree to which TQM practices are actually employed by U.S. corporations.

The third study collected data in 1993; it provided much more extensive information on who adopts TQM and EI, as well as on the results of these efforts (Lawler, Mohrman, and Ledford, 1995). In the first two studies, we considered only the impact of EI and TQM on nonfinancial performance measures, whereas the third looked at their effect on such financial results as return on equity.

The fourth study collected data in 1996 (Lawler, Mohrman, and Ledford, 1998). It went beyond the first three studies. In addition to looking at employee involvement and total quality management, it studied process reengineering. It also focused on business and change strategies and on the employment contract.

The present study goes further than the earlier studies in a number of respects. Once again it looks at the adoption and effectiveness of employee involvement, total quality management, and reengineering, but it is not limited to these three areas. It also analyzes the adoption of practices that are intended to improve knowledge management in corporations and extends the work on process reengineering to include more information on the use of information technology and the Internet. It also continues the focus on the employment contract and the organizational change approaches that were studied for the first time in the 1996 survey.

This report should prove useful both to managers who are considering changing their management approach and to researchers looking for data on how management practices are changing in the United States. Managers who wish to compare their organizational change efforts with others' can use the data to measure their own organizations against the Fortune 1000. The results also provide important information about what changes are likely to be effective.

This report begins with a two-section introduction that reviews the past work on organization effectiveness and describes the study. Part One addresses the adoption rate of the major employee involvement practices—namely, those that focus on sharing information, building knowledge, rewarding individuals, and sharing power. In each case, we compare the use of these practices in 1987, 1990, 1993, 1996, and 1999.

Part Two focuses on the adoption of total quality management, reengineering, and knowledge management practices. It begins with an analysis of the rate of adoption of TQM and process reengineering practices. For TQM, we look at the adoption rates in 1990, 1993, 1996, and 1999; for process reengineering, we look at the adoption rates in 1996 and 1999; and for knowledge management practices, we look at only 1999. The final section in Part Two analyzes the degree to which companies adopt EI, TQM, reengineering, and knowledge management in conjunction with one another.

Part Three focuses on how organizations are changing in three areas. The first is the type of employment relationship or contract that they develop with their employees. The second comprises the new organizational approaches that they are using to improve their performance. The third consists of their change management strategies. These areas provide an interesting view of how organizations are changing. Our research clearly indicates that there is a "new deal" for employees. It also points out that organizations are doing a variety of things to improve their effectiveness. Finally, the results show that organizational change efforts are often led by senior managers and guided by a clear sense of direction and mission.

Part Four focuses on the effectiveness of EI, TQM, reengineering, and knowledge management programs. The results are consistently positive for all four programs as a whole, as well as for many of the specific practices they involve. Particularly interesting are the results that show a link between the adoption of EI, TQM, process reengineering, and the financial performance of corporations over time. Overall the data suggest that the most effective organizational change programs combine EI, TQM, and reengineering in ways that create a complete organizational change effort.

Part Five focuses on the factors that lead to the adoption of EI, TQM, reengineering, and knowledge management. There are a number of important relationships between the adoption of these practices and the characteristics of organizations and their environments. These relationships suggest that corporations choose these programs because they fit a firm's strategic agenda. The data also suggest that these programs are frequently combined with major structural changes in the way organizations operate.

The accompanying CD-ROM includes the entire text of the book, including all tables and resources.

Acknowledgments. Our study presents one focus of the research program of the Center for Effective Organizations. The center, which is part of the Marshall School of Business of the University of Southern California, is sponsored by a number of corporations interested in organizational effectiveness. Their financial support and that of the Marshall School provided the funding for this study. The Sloan Foundation provided financial support that allowed us to do the financial analyses presented in our earlier publications. The Association for Quality and Participation provided support for the 1990 and 1993 surveys.

A study like this requires that people in organizations take time to complete the questionnaires that we distributed. We are deeply appreciative of the time spent by members of the Fortune 1000 companies in responding to this survey.

Any research study of this magnitude requires a high level of staff support. We are fortunate at the Center for Effective Organizations to have a talented staff to assist our research activities. We would particularly like to acknowledge the excellent help we received in data collection and data analysis from Alice Yee Mark, Beth Neilson, and Nora Osganian. Sabrina Moreno did an outstanding job of preparing the manuscript.

Los Angeles, California　　　　　　　　Edward E. Lawler III
May 2001　　　　　　　　　　　　　　Susan Albers Mohrman
　　　　　　　　　　　　　　　　　　George Benson

The Authors

Edward E. Lawler III joined the faculty of Yale University as assistant professor of industrial administration and psychology after graduating from the University of California at Berkeley in 1964. Three years later, he was promoted to associate professor.

Lawler moved to the University of Michigan in 1972 as professor of psychology and also became program director in the Survey Research Center at the Institute for Social Research. He held a Fulbright Fellowship at the London Graduate School of Business. In 1978, he became a professor in the Marshall School of Business at the University of Southern California (USC). During 1979, he founded and became director of USC's Center for Effective Organizations. In 1982, he was named professor of research at USC. In 1999, he was named distinguished professor.

Lawler has been honored as a major contributor to theory, research, and practice in the fields of human resource management, compensation, organizational development, and organizational effectiveness. He is the author or coauthor of more than three hundred articles and thirty-two books. Recent books include *The Ultimate Advantage* (1993), *Organizing for the Future* (1993), *Creating High Performance Organizations* (1995), *From the Ground Up: Six Principles for Creating the New Logic Corporation* (1996), *Tomorrow's Organization* (1998), *Strategies for High Performance Organizations—The CEO Report* (1998), *The Leadership Change Handbook* (1999), *Rewarding Excellence* (2000), and *Corporate Boards: New Strategies for Adding Value at the* Top (2001), all published by Jossey-Bass.

Susan Albers Mohrman is senior research scientist at the Center for Effective Organizations in the Marshall School of Business at the University of Southern California. She received her B.A. degree in psychology from Stanford University and her Ph.D. degree in organizational behavior from Northwestern University.

She has published papers in professional journals and books on a great number of topics, including employee involvement and total quality management, innovative approaches to the design of organizations. organization development and change, high-technology organizations, team designs and lateral organizations, and innovative research and evaluation methodologies. She has been the editor or coauthor of numerous books, including *Research for Theory and Practice* (Jossey-Bass, 1985), *Large-Scale Organizational Change* (Jossey-Bass, 1989), *Self-Designing Organizations* (Addison-Wesley, 1989), *Designing Team-Based Organizations* (Jossey-Bass, 1995), *Strategies for High Performance Organizations—The CEO Report* (Jossey-Bass, 1998), and *Tomorrow's Organization* (Jossey-Bass, 1998). Mohrman has researched and consulted to a large variety of firms, in many different sectors of the economy, on redesigning their structures and systems to create high performance.

George Benson is a research associate at the Center for Effective Organizations. His current research focuses primarily on the role of training and development in the commitment and retention of employees. Benson is also interested in how human resource practices are viewed by financial markets and how employee involvement affects corporate financial performance. He previously conducted research on corporate human resource practices for the America Society for Training and Development in Alexandria, Virginia.

Introduction

SECTION 1

Improving Organizational Performance

Competing views of how organizations can most effectively be managed have characterized the field of management since its inception. Until the 1980s, much of the "action" took place in academic journals and inside corporations, so it was not a highly visible public activity. But during the eighties, the situation changed dramatically. Perhaps the defining event of this change occurred in 1982 when Peters and Waterman published their bestseller *In Search of Excellence.* Suddenly the debate concerning the best way to manage complex organizations became front-page news in the *Wall Street Journal, Fortune, Business Week,* the *New York Times,* the *Economist,* and virtually every other publication in the United States and Europe. Improving management effectiveness and organizational change became a major industry as consulting firms began billing companies millions of dollars a year for organizational improvement programs and a plethora of tapes, books, and seminars mounted by management "gurus" claiming to have found the key to effective management appeared.

Why has the effectiveness of different management approaches become a major concern? We believe the answer lies in the growing consensus that an effective approach to management offers corporations a powerful competitive advantage (Lawler, 1996; Mohrman, Galbraith, and Lawler, 1998). Prior to the 1980s, most executives, consultants, and researchers agreed that although being a well-managed corporation was helpful, it was not a particularly powerful way to gain a competitive advantage. Instead of competing by coming up with management innovations, companies competed on the basis of their ability to execute traditional management practices. They all generally accepted the bureaucratic, hierarchical organization model and varied simply in some of the methods they used and how well they executed them.

When the mass acceptance of the traditional bureaucratic paradigm began to break down in the 1980s, a major competition began among different paradigms. Unfortunately, this competition has generally lacked good data about what practices are being used and how effective they are. Three paradigms received the most attention during 1980s and early 1990s: employee involvement (EI), total quality management (TQM), and process reengineering. All three, perhaps because of their popularity, have been accused of being nothing more than fads. And in truth, like a fad, each has frequently been implemented as the program of the year, month or even week, with little understanding of their complexity on the part of the implementing companies. All three have been adopted, to at least a limited degree, by a wide range of major U.S. corporations. Our previous studies have documented the increasing implementation of EI, TQM, and reengineering practices (Lawler, Mohrman, and Ledford, 1998).

The 1990s saw interest increase in knowledge management as a formal organizational process. Like EI, TQM, and reengineering, knowledge management has been accepted by a number of companies despite the fact that there is very little evidence concerning which practices work and how knowledge management programs should be run. It has some of the faddish characteristics of the other three programs. It also clearly addresses an issue deemed crucial for organizations in the future: more and more organizations in developed countries are doing knowledge work and depend on knowledge development and use for competitive advantage. Thus it is critical to understand the effectiveness of knowledge management programs and how they should be structured.

The basic and very important question concerning EI, TQM, reengineering, and knowledge management is whether they represent part or all of a new management paradigm that can and should replace the traditional, bureaucratic one. It is also critical to establish who should use them and how effective they are. In this section, we will review all four, defining each and describing its potential impact on organizational effectiveness. We will also consider the issues involved in managing the organizational changes that occur when a company adopts one or more of them.

Employee Involvement. There is no single authoritative source or theory that defines employee involvement as a management approach. It has a long history dating back to early research on democratic leadership and participative management. It includes writings on leadership, job design, organizational design, pay systems, and organizational change. The research on democratic leadership that began in the 1930s emphasized the consequences of employee involvement in decision making. It shows that employees are more committed to decisions under certain conditions and that better decisions result if employees are involved.

An important part of the work on employee involvement concerns work design and its impact on intrinsic motivation and job satisfaction. The research on individual job enrichment, as well as that on self-managing work teams, forms a critical part of the historical thinking that has led to the development of management approaches stressing employee involvement.

Perhaps the most important overall focus in the work on employee involvement concerns locating decisions at the lowest level in the organization (Lawler, 1986). Employee involvement consistently advocates a bottom-up approach to management. Jobs at the lowest level are thought to be best designed when individuals or teams do a complete part of an organization's work process, such as making an entire product or providing a complete service (Hackman and Oldham, 1980). In addition, this approach argues that the individuals or teams need to be given the power, information, and knowledge they need to work autonomously, independent of management control and direction. The job of management is to prepare the individuals and teams to function in an autonomous manner. Management is an enabler, a culture setter, and a supporter rather than a director of employee action.

Some writings on employee involvement place a strong emphasis on reward systems. They suggest combining participation in decision making and democratic supervision with rewards for skill acquisition and for organizational performance. Gainsharing plans, profit-sharing plans, and employee ownership are important reward system practices associated with employee involvement efforts (Lawler, 2000).

Employee involvement programs lead logically to a flattening of the organization and in many cases to the elimination of substantial amounts of staff and support work. Such work is often seen either as moving out of the organization or as being done at lower and lower levels within the organization. Employee involvement programs also stress that a substantial amount of the work done by managers and supervisors is unnecessary because it simply supports a command-and-control approach to management that is not needed when employees are involved in their work and are capable of managing themselves.

Organizational change is given considerable attention in the literature on employee involvement. It stresses bottom-up change, and in most cases, it advocates the retraining of supervisors and the redesigning of work relationships at the first level of the organization. In many respects, employee involvement does not argue for a continuous improvement approach so much as for discontinuous change; it holds that substantial gains in organizational effectiveness are a result of moving to completely new work structures and new ways of organizing work.

The recent widespread adoption of information technology by organizations and the growing use of the World Wide Web has the potential to enable a great increase in the amount of employee involvement in business decisions. Most approaches to employee involvement emphasize the importance of employees having up-to-date business information and the knowledge to make operating decisions concerning the business. With the growing presence of information technology in organizations, it is substantially easier to move business information into the hands and minds of employees throughout large complex organizations. Indeed, it is possible, using company intranets, to create organizations in which updated business information is in the hands or on the desks of virtually every employee almost instantaneously.

The Web creates the possibility of much more on-demand training in organizations so that employees can receive training content that is immediately relevant to the decisions and challenges they face in their day-to-day work. The presence of as-needed or just-in-time training means employees no longer have to be as dependent on subject matter experts and supervisors to make many operating decisions. They can "skill up" as the need arises and as a result increase the range and scope of their decision making. They also can take more responsibility for managing their careers.

Total Quality Management. Just as with employee involvement, there is no single theoretical formulation for total quality management or any definitive shortlist of practices that are always associated with it (Cole, 1999). It has evolved out of the research and experience of such American quality experts as Deming, Juran, and Crosby and of an important Japanese expert, Ishikawa; their writings, as well as the application of their ideas in many Japanese, European, and American firms, allow us to identify the typical characteristics of most TQM programs.

Total quality management is best viewed as a management philosophy that combines the teachings of Deming and Juran on statistical process control and group problem-solving processes with Japanese values concerning quality and continuous improvement. The movement started to become popular in Japan during the 1950s as the country struggled to recover from World War II. During the 1980s, it became increasingly popular in the United States and Europe, probably as a result of the success of Japanese firms in a number of global markets (Womack, Jones, and Roos, 1990).

The definition of what constitutes quality in an organization's functions and activities is a major focus of TQM. Customer reactions are regarded as the best measure of quality. TQM uses internal customers (for example, employees in other departments) to substitute for external customers when no external customers are available. Focusing on quality is considered a way to gain competitive advantage. TQM advocates often argue that if quality is improved, costs will drop and organizations will respond more quickly and effectively to customer requests.

Total quality management programs usually emphasize the importance of top management acting as the main driver of TQM activities (Deming, 1986). There are many reasons for this, but the most important focuses on the view that TQM is a culture, not just a program. It is a culture in the sense that it tries to change the values of the organization and its employees as well as their behavior in multiple areas. Top management support is necessary to ensure that the right priorities are set and that commitment to the principles of TQM exists throughout the organization.

According to such TQM advocates as Deming, most quality problems in organizations are caused by managers and the systems they create. Managers are asked to improve these systems so that they do not lead to quality problems, particularly those that arise when functions are not properly interrelated. Estimates of the proportion of quality problems that can be traced back to worker performance problems range from 25 percent to less than 10 percent. Employees are seen as having good ideas on how to improve quality and as wanting to do a good job. In TQM programs, they are asked to contribute their ideas and are often given responsibility for monitoring quality.

The practices and methods that are used to support both quality measurement and quality improvement are highly visible elements of TQM programs. A typical program includes techniques that aid issue identification and problem solving. Most employees are trained in their use. They include statistical process control methods, measures of nonconformance, cost of quality measures, cause-and-effect analysis, and various group decision-making methods. These methods typically focus on creating and using accurate production and quality information and on the precise measurement and quantification of problems.

TQM places great emphasis on including all employees in the TQM culture. This is where employee involvement—or as it is usually referred to in the TQM literature, empowerment—comes in.

Employees are expected to take responsibility for quality in two important respects: they are expected to call attention to quality problems as they do their normal work, and perhaps more important, they are expected to accept the continuous improvement culture and look for ways to do their work better. They are also expected to look for ways to improve the overall operation of the organization. To do this, of course, they need skills and information as well as vehicles that allow them to implement change.

In most TQM programs, quality circles and improvement groups are the major vehicles that allow employees to make suggestions and change work processes. Employees work on problems of lateral coordination and make suggestions about how to improve managerial systems, work methods, and work procedures. In some cases, firms encourage employees to meet in their natural work groups to talk about improved approaches and new work methods. TQM programs usually emphasize work process simplification and codification. The objective is to create a simple workflow that carefully specifies work activities.

TQM programs typically call for employees to receive a substantial amount of quality information and training. In many instances, this is the first time employees have received training and valid information about quality. Also new may be the chance to influence work methods and procedures that influence quality. The implementation of TQM almost always marks the first time that employees have had a chance to monitor the quality of their own work and to make decisions about its adequacy.

As is true with employee involvement, the implementation of information technology in corporations and the growing use of the Web may greatly influence the implementation of total quality management programs and methods. They provide the opportunity to distribute and collect quality information much more effectively and rapidly in organizations so that employees can better monitor their own quality and respond to quality programs. The ability to put training on the Web can also facilitate the implementation of total quality programs by making training much more readily available and flexible. Finally, information technology can be used to make statistical process control and other technical aspects of quality programs easier to perform and more accessible to employees throughout the organization.

Reengineering. The term *reengineering* and the ideas associated with it burst onto the management scene in the early 1990s thanks to several articles in the *Harvard Business Review* (primarily

Hammer, 1990) and a spate of books (including Hammer and Champy, 1993) about its advantages. Few, if any, management approaches have enjoyed the almost instantaneous popularity of reengineering. Unlike employee involvement and total quality management, reengineering's popularity was driven primarily by a group of consulting firms that offered reengineering programs to major U.S. corporations. The names most associated with the reengineering movement are Michael Hammer and James Champy, both of whom have had long careers as consultants. Although reengineering is not firmly rooted in any particular discipline, its strongest roots are in information technology. Perhaps the most visible academic name associated with the movement is Tom Davenport, whose background is in this field. Many of the change activities involved in reengineering are driven by efforts to improve the utilization of computer systems by large organizations.

During the 1990s, consulting firms, notably Gemini, Index, and Andersen Consulting, signed multimillion-dollar contracts with major corporations to do corporate reengineering projects. For a while, it appeared that virtually every large U.S. corporation had a major reengineering project going on.

When first articulated, reengineering was primarily about improving the lateral processes of an organization and creating an organizational structure that focuses on processes more than functions; as a result, it is often referred to as *process reengineering*. It soon became associated with employee downsizing and headcount reduction. Downsizing often produced immediate cost reductions and had an initial positive impact on corporate performance. Many large corporations were and still are bloated bureaucracies with too many levels of management and too many managers, particularly middle managers.

Although each reengineering project differs somewhat in its features, most share some common elements. The change effort is almost always top-down, and it focuses on using information technology to improve the lateral processes of the organization. It usually places particular emphasis on reducing the cost and cycle time of routine transactions. Perhaps the most common part of an organization to be reengineered is the order administration area; information technology can help eliminate the often slow, labor-intensive production line process through which orders travel before they are executed. After reengineering, individuals or small groups with access to interactive on-line databases are typically able to execute an order quickly and respond intelligently to customer inquiries about where a particular order is in the production process, as well as integrate this with information concerning the state of a customer's account and credit.

Although total quality management programs and employee involvement programs address the issue of too much hierarchy, functional specialization, and overhead, they do it in a very gingerly fashion. They rarely recommend dramatic downsizing or the elimination of layers of management. Instead, they argue that over time, as employee involvement takes hold, fewer managers will be needed and that their numbers should be reduced gradually through attrition rather than through immediate and directive action on the part of senior management.

In many respects, employee involvement and total quality management set the stage for the popularity of process reengineering. Many employee involvement programs, particularly those that employed self-managing teams, demonstrated the advantages of organizing for lateral activities, showing that coordination can be improved when lateral relationships are established. They have also pointed out that teams can manage themselves, making fewer layers of management necessary. TQM programs have done a good job of showing how work can be made more customer-focused and how, with good process controls, quality can be dramatically improved, making it *much* less necessary to have extensive quality control functions and many levels of management. All of this information laid the groundwork for the realization on the part of many senior managers that tremendous reductions in management overhead could be realized if employee involvement and total quality management are used.

The rapid development of low-cost intrafirm computer networks was another major enabler of the process reengineering movement. Since the 1950s, articles have proclaimed that middle management would soon be obsolete because of the capability of computers to link people together and to make people more self-managing (Zuboff, 1988). In virtually every decade since, this prediction has been repeated. With the development of enterprise resource planning (ERP) information systems in the 1990s, the idea that information technology can in fact substitute for a substantial number of management layers started to take on a sense of reality.

The installation of ERP systems has proved to be a major challenge in many corporations. Such systems require the complete process reengineering of many corporations, and as a result, implementation is often very slow and extremely costly. Nevertheless, when ultimately implemented, these systems can provide a level of business transaction transparency that has never before existed in most major corporations. They also eliminate much of the transactional work that is done by employees and hence a number of corporate staff and business support jobs. By linking employees with databases directly and providing them with information and expertise, information technology was able to make certain staff and support operations unnecessary. Not only did this eliminate the need for middle managers to coordinate the work of individuals in microscopic jobs and functional silos, it also decreased the need for functional staff support specialists in areas like quality control, inventory control, order administration, and scheduling.

The late 1990s saw the development of the Internet and along with it the ability of companies to link with vendors and customers in new and efficient ways. In many respects, it increased the amount of information individuals can get, particularly in the purchasing and marketing areas. It also enabled companies to outsource work more easily because it eliminates much of the transactional work involved. Many analysts predict that business-to-business Web-based information systems will be the major way corporations deal with suppliers, vendors, and business customers in the future. Doing this requires major organizational changes, many of which have their roots in the process of engineering thinking that began in the early 1990s. In essence, individuals have to be organized and managed around processes, not around steps or functions.

Like total quality management and employee involvement, process reengineering got a tremendous push from the cost competition that global corporations faced in the 1980s and 1990s. It offered to make major corporations much more cost-effective, and it argued that it could speed up an organization's response to customers and to the rapidly changing competitive environment. With all these forces at work, it is hardly surprising that process reengineering became extremely popular and was widely implemented.

In the future, it is likely that reengineering will be driven not by a traditional downsizing emphasis but by the implementation of Web-based processes in organizations. Indeed, the term *reengineering* may well disappear entirely while many of its concepts and processes are used in conjunction with ERP systems that interface with the Web. The net result will be to allow much stronger instantaneous lateral processes that connect the manufacturing and supply functions of organizations directly with customers.

Knowledge Management. The recent emphasis on knowledge management stems from the realization that in the information economy, much of the value of many firms stems from knowledge assets rather than capital assets. Software firms and professional services providers are examples of firms that trade almost exclusively in knowledge. Technology firms of all kinds rely on research and development (R&D) to generate new knowledge and new knowledge assets, including patents and other intellectual property, that they can embed in new products, processes, applications, solutions, and services.

It is becoming evident that reaching customers through the Internet is not the only or maybe even the most important competitive capability that can be derived from e-commerce. The most important may come from being able to collect and interpret data and to use the resulting information to develop better products and services and more precisely target and reach individuals and market segments.

Companies such as General Electric have argued that in the knowledge economy, a major rationale for having multiple businesses managed by the same corporation is the potential for leveraging knowledge effectively across these businesses. The importance of this is evidenced by the fact that some corporations have created the position of chief learning officer to lead efforts in this area.

Just as total quality management provided a new lens through which to view the organization—focused on how to organize to achieve high quality and meet the requirements of customers—knowledge management provides a new lens. The knowledge management view addresses the new realities of the knowledge economy. It focuses on how to organize so that knowledge activities can be more effectively performed. Knowledge management improvement approaches have in common that they are intended to create an organizational context that enables the organization to generate and enhance, import, combine, apply, leverage and protect knowledge in order to achieve the organization's mission. These approaches may attend to the explicit or the tacit aspects of knowledge—or both. The explicit aspects are the knowledge that is embedded in the work processes of the organization and in its formal knowledge assets; the tacit aspects are the knowledge in the heads of individuals and collectives of people who have, through experience, learned routines, heuristics, and patterns of knowledge that enable superior performance.

Knowledge management is relatively new and has been the least programmatic of the four organizational effectiveness approaches we are studying. It is an assortment of approaches that build on and complement the foundation provided by employee involvement, total quality management, and business process reengineering. Traditionally, organizations have housed knowledge in functional and discipline departments. This has made it easy for individuals to learn from their coworkers, supervisors, and mentors. These functional groups were charged with ensuring that needed knowledge was developed or brought into the organization, and sometimes they promoted standard processes that were developed, improved, and enforced by the discipline.

Current organizational trends away from the traditional bureaucratic model make reliance on hierarchical, functional approaches to knowledge management inadequate. Knowledge work is increasingly decentralized and dispersed. Employee involvement emphasizes the autonomy of self-contained units and has moved decisions lower in the organization. Reengineered organizations are often composed of process-defined, cross-functional groups, such as customer service teams or new product development teams, rather than by discipline units. The increased reliance on temporary units and the global dispersion of work also limit the effectiveness of traditional approaches. All of these trends disperse talent and knowledge into multiple units and make it more difficult for discipline managers to rely on traditional knowledge management approaches.

Often the most important competitive knowledge in today's world pertains to cross-functional processes rather than to disciplines (Mohrman, Tenkasi, and Mohrman, 1999). For example, excellence in generating new products depends on knowledge about the processes of integrating knowledge from multiple disciplines. Building cross-functional knowledge into an organization often entails breaking up discipline knowledge-based groups and having people work with and learn an expanded knowledge set. At the same time, the speed of knowledge creation has accelerated geometrically and the cycle time for performance has decreased, making it harder for any given organization to keep up and stay at the forefront in key strategic areas. Given all these forces, traditional approaches to managing organizational knowledge have broken down, and new ones need to be developed.

Perhaps the strongest impetus for organizations to implement knowledge management activities is the power of modern information technology to make information broadly available across a dispersed organization (Davenport and Prusak, 1998). In this respect, knowledge management is similar to reengineering. Software applications are available for establishing shared data and information repositories, cataloguing knowledge, and providing user-friendly access. Groupware tools facilitate doing work in dispersed, multifunctional teams, and it can facilitate building electronic records of the knowledge of that group and its processes. Learning can be built into computerized work tools such as engineering design tools, and the parameters and assumptions built into the tools can be updated as more learning occurs. Lessons learned or information about particular customers can be entered into integrated information repositories or routed to everyone in the organization who needs to know. Information technology companies are developing and selling such applications, and services firms are developing practices based on helping companies adopt and implement knowledge management systems.

It is becoming increasingly evident, however, that the electronic tools are but enablers of knowledge activities: effective knowledge management depends on fostering and motivating new behaviors. Knowledge management builds on and subsumes the emphasis on organizational learning that was most prominently developed by Peter Senge (1990). He portrays learning as a discipline that can be established by emphasizing such processes as finding a common purpose, dialogue, and systems thinking. His work focuses primarily on person-to-person learning, as through learning circles and through rich accounts of organizational events from which learning can be derived. Related work by John Seely Brown and others has also emphasized interpersonal learning through communities of practice and the sharing of knowledge through stories (Brown and Duguid, 2000). These approaches emphasize connectivity between people across the organization, sharing of tacit knowledge, and relatively open-ended, divergent, qualitative thinking. They contrast with and complement the total quality management approach to learning through a systematic process improvement methodology that emphasizes measurement and statistical tools for root cause analysis.

Another dimension of managing knowledge is building the connections and relationships with external parties to ensure that the company has access to the knowledge it needs. In part because of the ease with which knowledge travels in today's electronically enabled world and also because of the speed with which knowledge is advancing, organizations can no longer be self-sufficient and self-contained in their knowledge management strategies. As the world moves toward open standards and Internet access, full reliance on a "cloak and dagger" strategy of secretiveness and proprietary knowledge is breaking down. Alliances and partnerships, co-development with customers and suppliers, connections with professional associations and universities, and benchmarking are examples of ways in which organizations are intentionally expanding their knowledge.

Using knowledge to accomplish company purposes requires that employees apply and share their knowledge. Competency management and motivational systems are key aspects of knowledge management that are just beginning to be considered part of the knowledge management agenda. The substantial emphasis on competency definition and talent management that has developed during the past decade has largely been occurring separately from the work on knowledge management. One aspect is defining needed knowledge competencies, knowledge sets, and behaviors and linking these definitions to human resource practices such as selection, career progressions, rewards, and feedback systems. A second aspect is building incentives for people to leverage the knowledge of the organization both by sharing and reusing knowledge and by further developing the competencies of others in the organization. Developing individuals with the right knowledge and behaviors and retaining them is a key challenge that requires a newly defined employment contract that addresses the realities of the highly skilled, educated, and mobile workforce of the knowledge economy. In its emphasis on development and motivation, knowledge management is similar to employee involvement.

The knowledge management organizational effectiveness framework is relatively new and at this point is a set of diverse approaches for which no overarching paradigm has evolved. Consequently, our examination of knowledge management will look at some representative practices, rather than trying to take an exhaustive look at all the numerous associated policies and practices.

Similarities and Differences. There are some obvious overlaps among the management principles and practices associated with employee involvement, total quality management, process reengineering, and knowledge management. All have employees taking on additional responsibility, improving and expanding their skills, and receiving more and better information. All emphasize the need for improvements and change in organizational systems and the need for managers to change their behavior and roles dramatically. They also emphasize the importance of culture and the idea that organizations are best viewed as complex, interrelated systems rather than as combinations of independent pieces. They all emphasize the advantages of lateral processes, including the fact that lateral management can make levels of management unnecessary and reduce the need for traditional, control-oriented supervision. Finally, they all call for a change in the employment contract from one that is based on loyalty and seniority to one that is based more on performance and skills.

Table 1.1 summarizes the major characteristics of EI, TQM, process reengineering, and knowledge management (see also Mohrman, Galbraith, and Lawler, 1998). As this table shows, the four differ in discipline base, age, and how they have affected the business community. Employee involvement has been around for a long time and has slowly grown in popularity. TQM is newer and enjoyed a dramatic spurt in popularity during the 1980s, but its growth was slow compared to the almost overnight popularity of process reengineering during the 1990s. Knowledge management is only now becoming an important focus in most companies.

All four approaches stress the importance of teams, but employee involvement stands out here. Through much of its early history, it focused on the development and use of self-managing work teams. Inherent in the idea of self-managing work teams is the concept of lateral process management, which was later to become the cornerstone of the process reengineering approach. Knowledge management proponents are more likely to stress the creation of networks across the organization, in part in reaction to the carving up of the organization into self-contained units.

Table 1.1	The Four Major Management Approaches.			
	Employee Involvement	Total Quality Management	Process Reengineering	Knowledge Management
Age	Young Adult	Teenager	Youth	Infant
Teams	Self-managing teams	Problem-solving work cells	Business process	Functional and cross-functional teams, networks
Feedback	Business unit performance	Customer feedback, quality levels	Process performance	Benchmarking, learning
Disciplinary Base	Social science	Quality engineering	Information technology	Systems thinking, organization learning, information technology
Implementation Process	Bottom-up	Top-down	Top-down	Top-down and bottom-up
Preferred Work Design	Enriched	Simplified, standardized	Mixed	Networks across work structures
Unique Contributions	Group processes, motivational alignment, well-being	Quality emphasis, worker tools (such as statistical process control)	Downsizing, process focus, technological change	Knowledge networks, communities of practice, leverage

Historically, employee involvement change efforts often looked at small processes, such as part of a production line; process reengineering has defined processes much more broadly and much more ambitiously. In fact, it has talked about entirely eliminating certain functions, such as marketing and sales, and building an organization around processes alone. This has happened in some companies; Harley-Davidson, for example, has only two processes: business development and order fulfillment. Whereas total quality management has emphasized techniques for improving the lateral processes in the organization, knowledge management has emphasized the sharing of learning across process teams no matter where they are in the corporation.

Employee involvement, total quality management, and process reengineering favor different organizational designs. Employee involvement tends to favor small business units that are in effect minibusinesses. Total quality management, by contrast, focuses heavily on groups that have clearly established customers and quality levels. Process reengineering tends to think more about how far processes extend and how a total corporation can be organized around them. Thus reengineering is likely to focus on feedback concerning cycle times for an entire process. Knowledge management addresses virtual and formal network connections but does not have a particular perspective on the appropriate core design for an organization.

One of the places where total quality management and process reengineering differ most from employee involvement is in the process for implementing change. Advocates of employee involvement have consistently argued that the process used to introduce EI should match the ultimate operating state; thus they believe that the change process itself should be highly participative. Employees are put on teams to redesign their work areas, design gainsharing plans, and so on. However, they often go on to argue that EI can be implemented only if there is strong support by top management.

Both total quality management and process reengineering are usually installed in a top-down manner. Both have extensively used outside experts and consultants; these experts, after studying the specific firm, simply tell the organization how the work should be reorganized, install new computer and information systems, and train employees how to operate within the new organizational structure.

The implementation of knowledge management approaches follows no recipe. Advocates stress the importance of engaging top management in an examination of the core processes of the organization from a knowledge management perspective and of championing a much greater focus on knowledge-oriented activities and behaviors. However, implementation is a complex mix of centralized attention to the information technology and human resource infrastructure and bottom-up participation in informal and formal networks.

More than total quality management and process reengineering, employee involvement has focused on creating rich, challenging, motivating work. Originally, the focus was on creating individually enriched jobs. An extensive literature developed on what makes a job motivating and how to enrich jobs (see, for example, Hackman and Oldham, 1980). Although individual job enrichment is still popular, our previous research has shown that self-managing teams are increasingly becoming the preferred work design for employee involvement programs (Lawler, Mohrman, and Ledford, 1998). There are a number of reasons for this, including the fact that teams are more likely to make supervision unnecessary and they can manage lateral relationships in ways that make layers of management unnecessary (Lawler, 1996).

Both total quality management and process reengineering are not clear about their preferred approach to work design. Total quality management talks of simplified, standardized jobs that make possible the use of statistical process control. It also stresses that individuals should be responsible for their own quality, thus moving more power into the hands of the employees. At times, TQM programs seem almost to be a throwback to the days of scientific management and simplified standardized jobs, with the difference that now employees can do some of the monitoring of their own performance. In many respects, process reengineering is similar to total quality management when it comes to work design. Its major emphasis is on integrating lateral processes through the use of information technology. It places little attention on whether and how individuals will be motivated to do the work that results from the intensive use of this technology. Knowledge management pays no explicit attention to work design but stresses the interconnectedness of knowledge and building knowledge and best practices into standard work processes to reduce the amount of human resource time spent reinventing the wheel.

Employee involvement, total quality management, reengineering, and knowledge management have all developed important new technologies and concepts. Since they have such different discipline bases, it is hardly surprising that they have contributed somewhat different technologies and approaches. The behavioral science focus of employee involvement, for example, seems to have led it to concentrate particularly on tools and approaches that promote the development and motivation of employees. Total quality management has focused more on tools that improve the reliability of work processes and the quality of the products that they produce. Process reengineering has been particularly powerful in developing organizational designs that fit well with modern information technology. Knowledge management has focused on learning from experience and on the importance of learning from others. It also has developed ways to use information technology to develop and spread knowledge.

Strategic Change. Increasingly, the literature on organizational effectiveness argues that reengineering, employee involvement, total quality management, and knowledge management make sense only if they fit the overall business strategy of an organization (Lawler, 1996). In many respects, they can be viewed as approaches that build key organizational capabilities; for example, TQM practices are intended to build customer focus into the organization, as well as, of course, to improve the quality of products and services. This is likely to have an important bottom-line effect for a corporation only if these capabilities are consistent with the organization's strategy and its overall position in the market. Thus we need to look at the adoption patterns for these programs in the context of how organizations are changing their business strategy.

The adoption of employee involvement, total quality management, or reengineering represents a major organizational change, and the effectiveness of these programs often depends on how well they are installed. This raises the whole issue of implementation strategy and process and of large-scale organizational change. In our earlier studies, we placed relatively little emphasis on the implementation process that companies use in installing TQM and EI practices. This has changed in our more recent studies, which have demonstrated the importance of the change process.

A number of key change strategy practices can be identified as important determinants of how effective an organizational improvement program will be. They include the role played by top management, the degree to which the program is companywide or business-unit-specific, and how long-term versus short-term its orientation is. Overall, most change theories argue that in order to be effective, a major organizational change program needs careful development and needs to adhere to a well-developed change process (see Nadler, Shaw, Walton, and Associates, 1995; Lawler,

Mohrman, and Ledford, 1998). Among the specifics mentioned are the need for a clear business strategy, a strong reason for change, a clear vision of where the organization is going, strong leadership by top management, broad involvement in defining the nature of the change, and a long-term orientation.

Because the change process may determine the impact of an organizational change, it is important to focus on what practices are adopted by corporations as well as how they are installed and how the overall change process is managed. When this information is combined with information on the effectiveness of EI, TQM, reengineering, and knowledge management programs, it can provide a complete picture of how organizations can be made more effective.

Employment Contract. Major change efforts such as EI, TQM, reengineering, and knowledge management call for changes in how employees are expected to behave, thus it is important to consider the employment deal or contract an organization offers. Typically, the key elements of the contract include issues such as employment security, the relationship between performance and rewards, and the degree to which an organization is committed to training and developing its employees. The growing literature on employment contracts suggests that they very much influence the kinds of relationships that individuals develop with their organization and hence how effective organizations are (Rousseau, 1995). Thus in focusing on the effectiveness of major changes, it is important to consider how strong a relationship exists between the characteristics of the employment contract and their effectiveness.

Adoption Patterns. It is important to the understanding of the impact and usefulness of any change effort to analyze its adoption pattern. Numerous factors can influence whether organizations adopt practices such as those associated with EI, TQM, reengineering, and knowledge management. Business strategists have pointed out, for example, that the external environment has a strong influence on the behavior of an organization. The environment often gets translated into specific business strategies and performance improvement strategies, which call for the adoption of specific practices in order to be successful.

The organization design literature has often focused on how the characteristics of the organization cause it to adopt certain management practices. One of the most powerful drivers of the adoption of management practices is organization size. Not surprisingly, larger organizations require different practices then smaller ones. In order to understand the usefulness and impact of EI, TQM, reengineering, and knowledge management, it is important to look at how significant features of an organization determine their rate of adoption. Such an analysis provides one clue, although only a partial one, as to where the specific approaches may be effective and evidence on how well they fit with particular issues that organizations face.

SECTION 2

The Study

In 1987, we conducted a study of the Fortune 1000 firms in order to determine whether companies had incorporated employee involvement practices into their approach to management (Lawler, Ledford, and Mohrman, 1989). In 1990, we repeated this study and added a series of questions on total quality management (Lawler, Mohrman, and Ledford, 1992). The 1990 study, while showing an increase in employee involvement activities, still indicated that a low percentage of employees in the largest U.S. corporations work in an environment that could be described as high involvement or high performance. Despite this, the companies surveyed generally reported that they were quite satisfied with the results of their employee involvement activities and that they planned to expand them.

Our third study of the Fortune 1000 was conducted in 1993 (Lawler, Mohrman, and Ledford, 1995). It too focused on the adoption of employee involvement and total quality management practices. This study, like the 1990 study, showed an increasing use of employee involvement activities but still indicated that a low percentage of employees in the largest U.S. corporations work in environments that could be described as high involvement or high performance. The 1993 study also showed an increasing use of total quality management practices. Analysis of the relationship between the use of employee involvement and total quality management practices and organizational effectiveness showed a significant relationship. The more that companies adopted total quality management and employee involvement practices, the better their performance became in a number of areas. Particularly important in the 1993 study was the significant relationship between company financial performance and the use of EI and TQM practices.

The results of our 1996 study clearly showed that more and more companies were using employee involvement practices (Lawler, Mohrman, and Ledford, 1998). The biggest change was in the area of power sharing; especially noticeable was the growing use of groups, particularly self-managing work teams. However, the data suggested that the growth of total quality management programs did not continue even though some TQM practices continued to grow in popularity. We studied reengineering for the first time in 1996; therefore, we could not reach any conclusions about growth, but we did find a very high adoption rate, with 81 percent of the companies having a reengineering program. The most popular practices were those leading to cost reductions. Companies consistently rated their EI, TQM, and reengineering programs as successful. This was supported by financial data, which showed that companies who adopt EI outperform other companies in a number of areas. Finally, we found that an organization's change strategy seems partly to determine how successful EI, TQM, and reengineering programs will be. Change strategies that emphasized integrated and clearly articulated reasons for change and that were led by top management were most likely to be successful.

Purpose of the Study. The present study continues our examination of the degree to which companies are using management practices, policies, and behaviors that are associated with employee involvement, total quality management, and reengineering. In particular, it assesses how much change occurred from 1987 to 1999. It also examines the effectiveness of these efforts.

For the first time, we look at the adoption of knowledge management practices and their relationship to EI, TQM, and reengineering. We also look at the degree of compatibility among the four approaches, and we examine how the environments that organizations face affect their adoption of all four types of practices. The study also identifies organizational policies and practices that are supportive of major organizational change efforts and how the adoption of EI, TQM, reengineering, and knowledge management relate to corporate strategies. Finally, it examines the changes that are occurring in the contract between corporations and their employees.

Study Method. The 1987 survey was conducted by the U.S. General Accounting Office (GAO). Michael Dulworth was the GAO project leader. At the inception of the study, the GAO brought together a panel of consultants to offer advice on the study's design. This panel included experts on employee involvement systems from both the federal sector and the private sector. A design team, including representatives from the University of Southern California's Center for Effective Organizations (Lawler, Mohrman, and Ledford) and Michael Dulworth from the GAO, developed the employee involvement survey questionnaire and analyzed the data. GAO collected the data.

The 1990 survey was designed and conducted by the Center for Effective Organizations at the University of Southern California; financial support was provided by the Association for Quality and Participation. It used many of the same questions that were asked in the 1987 study. In addition, it asked a series of questions about total quality management programs and practices. These questions were added because of growing interest in TQM programs and their close relationship to employee involvement.

The 1993 survey was a further refinement of the 1990 survey. The most significant changes involved adding questions about total quality management, both because of the increased interest in TQM programs and because of the continued focus on quality as a source of competitive advantage. A few new questions were added regarding employee involvement programs. They were intended to improve our understanding of organizational patterns concerning the use and impact of EI activities.

The 1996 survey was similar to the 1993 version but included some new sections. They focused on reengineering, the employment contract, business strategy, and organizational improvement strategies.

The 1999 survey contains most of the items from the 1996 survey and has an important new section on knowledge management. Some items were also added to the reengineering section. They focus on the Internet and information technology.

A glossary defining some of the terms used in the questionnaire has accompanied all surveys that have been done since 1987. The 1999 questionnaire is reprinted in Resource A, and Resource B reproduces the glossary that went with it.

Study Sample. The 1987 survey was sent by the GAO to 934 of the companies listed in the 1986 Fortune 1000 listing of the 500 largest service companies and the 500 largest industrial firms. The actual number of companies surveyed was fewer than 1,000 because of acquisitions and mergers. Responses numbered 476, a 51 percent response rate. The responding organizations employed almost nine million full-time employees.

The Center for Effective Organizations at the University of Southern California sent the 1990 survey to 987 organizations on the 1989 Fortune 1000 list. We received responses from 313 organizations, for a response rate of 32 percent. One hundred companies responded to both the 1987 survey and the 1990 survey.

The 1993 survey was sent to 985 companies from the 1992 *Fortune* listing of the 1,000 largest U.S. manufacturing and service companies. Responses were received from 279 companies, a response rate of 28 percent. A total of 135 companies responded to both the 1990 and 1993 questionnaires.

The 1996 survey was sent to all 1,000 companies from the *Fortune* listing. Mergers and other changes reduced the potential number of respondents to 994. We received responses from 212 companies, for a response rate of 22 percent. Eighty companies responded to both the 1993 and 1996 surveys.

The 1999 survey was sent to all 1,000 companies from the *Fortune* listing. Mergers and other changes reduced the potential number of respondents to 988. We received responses from 143 companies, for a response rate of 15 percent. The respondents included 44 companies that responded to the 1996 survey.

In 44 percent of the cases, responses to the 1999 survey came from managers responsible for human resources. The other 56 percent were completed by a wide variety of senior executives, typically someone in the corporate office two levels below the chief executive officer.

Our 1990, 1993, 1996, and 1999 surveys used many of the same mailing and follow-up procedures that the GAO used in 1987, but we did not obtain as high a response rate. Nevertheless, response rates of 32, 28, 22, and 15 percent are impressive given the large number of surveys being sent to companies today and the length of our questionnaire (fifteen pages for the 1999 survey). The high response rate to the 1987 survey was probably due in part to its sponsorship by the GAO, a credible government agency, and its brevity.

The declining response rate over the years is most likely due to the increased pressures individuals and organizations feel because of the very same competitive changes that are leading to the adoption of new management practices. When making follow-up calls to companies, we were consistently told that individuals simply did not have the time anymore to fill out such a "long and complicated" questionnaire. Fortunately, the response rates are high enough to allow us to make some interesting comparisons among the four surveys, as well as among the different types of companies represented in the 1999 sample.

Although all five surveys were sent to companies in the Fortune 1000 at the time of each study, they were not sent to the same companies each time. Changes in the Fortune 1000 also help account for the fact that we often did not receive responses from the same companies to each of the five surveys—for example, only 650 companies were on both the 1986 and 1992 Fortune 1000 lists. *Fortune* created more change when it dropped the distinction between manufacturing and service firms and simply identified the one thousand largest firms in 1996.

The samples represent a broad array of service and industrial firms. Approximately half of the 1987, 1990, and 1993 samples come from the service sector and approximately half from the manufacturing sector. The median size of the organizations in the samples is 9,200 employees in 1987, 10,000 in 1990, 11,000 in 1993, 14,749 in 1996, and 12,284 in 1999. The mean distribution of various types of employees in these organizations is almost identical in each sample, as Table 2.1 indicates.

Overall comparisons among the five samples suggest that the samples are generally comparable and representative of Fortune 1000 companies. This is an important point, as it means that any differences in results among the surveys are likely to be due to actual changes in how Fortune 1000 companies are managing their business rather than to the fact that different companies responded to the surveys. Where possible, we checked this by comparing the 1987, 1990, 1993, 1996, and 1999 survey data for the companies that responded to more than one survey, and we found the results to be generally consistent with those for the total sample.

Our data do have important limitations. They address only the thousand largest companies in the United States and thus say nothing about what is happening in the many smaller companies that constitute a large and growing part of the U.S. economy. Furthermore, they represent a view from the top. Senior managers completed most of the surveys. The views from middle

Table 2.1	Breakdown of Employees by Type (percentage).				
	1987	1990	1993	1996	1999
Hourly/Clerical	59	59	54	54	54
Technical/Professional	20	20	24	27	28
Supervisory/Managerial	14	14	15	14	15
Other	8	9	6	5	3

managers, front-line supervisors, production workers, and union leaders may be different.

Despite its limitations, this report is the most comprehensive accounting of practices and approaches to organizational improvement efforts in large corporations that is currently available. No comparable data set exists covering organizational practices and management activities in such a broad array of corporations. Particularly important is the possibility of comparing 1987, 1990, 1993, 1996, and 1999 data in order to determine how management approaches and practices are changing. Our data offer a unique opportunity to investigate major corporate change initiatives at various stages of implementation and in a variety of industrial and service organizations.

PART ONE

Employee Involvement: Information, Knowledge, Rewards, and Power

SECTION 3

Sharing Information

Basic to employee involvement in organizations is the sharing of information about business performance, plans, goals, and strategies. Without business information, individuals cannot understand how the business is doing, nor can they make meaningful contributions to its success by participating in planning and setting direction. Further, it is difficult for them to make good suggestions about how products and services can be improved or about how work processes in their area can be accomplished more effectively. Finally, without information, employees cannot effectively alter their behavior in response to changing business conditions.

Thus the absence of business information limits individuals simply to carrying out prescribed tasks and roles in a relatively automatic and bureaucratic way. They are prevented from understanding, participating in, and managing themselves and the business they are part of. For this reason, information is a key building block in most, if not all, organizational improvement efforts that stress the ability of individuals to add value through their involvement in the business.

Table 3.1 provides the responses to a question on the types of information that are shared. It shows that most organizations share information about the company's overall operating results with at least 80 percent of their employees. This was true in 1987, 1990, 1993, 1996, and again in 1999. The results also show little increase in the sharing of operating information from 1987 to 1999.

Every organization in the study is a public corporation and, by law, must provide financial information to shareholders. At a minimum, it seems that organizations would give their employees the same information they give their shareholders in their annual reports. So if anything is surprising about the results shown in Table 3.1, it is how many organizations do not share company financial results with all employees.

In 1999, some 20 percent of the companies still did not give most of their employees information about the company's operating performance, even though this information is public. The number is actually higher than the 1996 figure of 14 percent. Further, only 65 percent of the companies give all or nearly all of their employees

| | | | None or | | About | | All or Almost |
Information-Sharing Practice	Study	Mean (5-point scale)	Almost None[a] (0–20 percent)	Some (21–40 percent)	Half (41–60 percent)	Most (61–80 percent)	All[a] (81–100 percent)
Corporate Operating Results	1987	4.3	6	9	5	13	66
	1990	4.1	9	11	4	10	66
	1993	4.4	7	7	2	12	73
	1996	4.5	3	6	5	11	76
	1999	4.2	8	7	5	16	65
Unit Operating Results	1987	3.6	7	20	14	30	30
	1990	3.5	11	21	15	20	34
	1993	3.8	7	14	13	20	46
	1996	4.0	5	11	12	21	51
	1999	4.1	7	6	11	23	54
New Technologies	1987	2.7	17	37	21	17	9
	1990	2.4	28	35	13	16	9
	1993	2.8	17	36	16	15	16
	1996	2.8	15	36	17	15	18
	1999	2.7	23	26	20	21	11
Business Plans and Goals	1987	3.3	9	24	19	25	23
	1990	3.2	12	26	15	22	25
	1993	3.5	10	21	15	20	34
	1996	3.7	6	19	16	20	38
	1999	3.9	6	12	14	28	41
Competitors' Performance	1987	2.2	33	39	14	9	7
	1990	2.3	34	31	15	10	10
	1993	2.5	27	33	15	11	14
	1996	2.6	28	27	17	15	13
	1999	2.7	25	27	20	15	14

[a]For 1990, 1993, 1996, and 1999, responses were combined to convert a 7-point response scale to a 5-point response scale.

information about their overall operating results. This could be accomplished simply by distributing an annual report to all employees. The obvious conclusion is that in a significant number of companies, some employees are not treated as important stakeholders in or contributors to the company's performance.

Although important in helping employees view the business as a whole, information about the overall performance of a large company may, for practical purposes, be of limited utility to many employees. The corporate operating results are a considerable distance from their job activities and may not relate directly to what they do. Information on their unit's operating results is likely to be much more meaningful to most employees.

As can be seen from Table 3.1, a total of 77 percent of the companies share data on the performance of their work unit with more than 60 percent of their employees. However, more than one-third of all companies do not regularly share unit operating results with most employees. The results for 1987, 1990, 1993, 1996, and 1999 do show an increase over time in information sharing about business unit results. This is an encouraging trend. However, it will have to continue in order for most employees to receive the kind of information necessary for them to be involved in the business of their organization.

The data with respect to information sharing about new technologies show a low level of sharing. Only 32 percent of the corporations say they provide most of their employees with information about new technologies that may affect them. Information sharing in this area has not significantly increased since 1987. Without information about new technologies, employees cannot participate in the planning activities that are involved in the start-up of new technology, nor can they influence decisions about its adoption and acquisition. Lack of information concerning new technologies also prevents employees from knowing what skills and knowledge they need to develop in order to use a new technology and manage their careers.

Sixty-nine percent of companies provide most employees with information on the plans and goals of the business. This is obviously a key information area with respect to employee participation in problem-solving groups, self-managing work teams, and strategy or planning groups. It is encouraging to note that information sharing in this area has increased since 1987.

It is clear from the data in Table 3.1 that the typical employee gets extremely limited information about competitors' business performance. Only 29 percent of the organizations provide data on competitors' performance to most or all employees. This is an important point because it means that most employees cannot make informed judgments about whether their business is winning or losing in the market. It is encouraging to note that more employees get this information than they did in 1987.

To get an idea of the concentration of information sharing within companies, we counted the different kinds of information shared with at least 40 percent of employees. Table 3.2 shows the percentage of companies sharing from none to all of the five kinds of information listed in Table 3.1. The data from 1987, 1990, 1993, 1996, and 1999 show a trend toward sharing more information. The 1999 data show that 59 percent of companies share four or more of the five kinds of information with at least 40 percent of employees, and 31 percent share all kinds. This means that in 1999, a few more companies were broadly providing information than was true in 1996, and 15 percent more were doing it than in 1987. These results show a trend toward organizations sharing more kinds of information with their employees.

Overall, our results show that Fortune 1000 corporations still share only limited information with their employees. Further, a comparison between the 1999 and 1996 studies shows little change. Most of the growth in information sharing seems to have occurred from 1987 to the mid-1990s.

As a general rule, the farther information gets from the publicly reported results of the total corporation, the less likely it is that

Table 3.2	Percentage of Companies Sharing Information with More Than 40 Percent of Employees.				
Number of Kinds of Information Shared[a]	1987 (*n* = 323)	1990 (*n* = 313)	1993 (*n* = 279)	1996 (*n* = 212)	1999 (*n* = 143)
0	6	8	6	3	6
1	11	15	11	7	4
2	19	21	14	16	10
3	22	17	20	20	20
4	26	23	24	26	28
5	16	16	25	28	31

[a]Five possible kinds: corporate operating results, unit operating results, new technologies, business plans and goals, competitors' performance.

employees will be given the information. This is understandable in one respect: in many cases, organizations are not required to distribute information about how a business unit is doing or about new technologies to their employees or the public. However, not distributing this information to employees may have significant costs associated with it and may be a major obstacle to organizational improvement efforts.

The typical employee in companies that do not share information may not understand how well the business is doing and is likely to have little sense of what the company must do to be competitive. Information about the performance of business units is often the most important information for employees to have if they are to be involved in a business for which they have a "line of sight" with respect to the impact of their behavior. Awareness of corporate results helps employees understand the larger business context, but it is at the unit level where most of them can make a difference and can relate to performance results. Information at this level is also what they need in order to contribute ideas and suggestions and be involved in the business.

There was an increase in information sharing from 1987 to 1999, but it was limited to three kinds of information and fell far short of the amount of change that might be expected given the crucial importance of information to many employee involvement and total quality management programs. In essence, many organizations provide only what the law requires them to make available to shareholders: overall business results. Most employees do not get good information on the direction and success of the business. Given this, we find it hard to imagine most employees being meaningfully involved in decisions concerning the business of which they are a part. They are also not likely to be in a position to make informed decisions about their own development and careers.

Is the situation with respect to information likely to change in corporations? Perhaps—but for reasons unrelated to employee involvement programs. Corporations are increasingly being staffed by knowledge workers who are interested in the success of the business, understand financial data, and are much more likely to want a psychological and financial ownership position in the corporation. Thus they may want more information on the success of the business. Further, with the growing installation of company Web sites and electronic mail, it is becoming increasingly easy to distribute business information to employees. Indeed, with companies starting to provide employees with home Internet service and PCs, it may soon be possible for companies simply to post annual reports electronically, accessible to all employees, and to update them regularly in terms of the financial condition of the business and its prospects. It is therefore quite possible that thanks to the growing use of information technology, more business information may be available to employees.

SECTION 4

Knowledge and Skill Development

Organizational effectiveness increasingly depends on the skills and knowledge of the workforce. Without the right skills, individuals cannot do their jobs effectively, much less participate in a business and influence its direction, as employee involvement programs advocate. To be successful, total quality management programs demand that employees acquire a variety of skills. And since reengineering programs often lead to work that is more laterally integrated and based on information technology, they too require that employees learn new skills. The growing use of information technology creates the need for skill training in this area. Finally, as will be considered in Section 9, some companies have knowledge management efforts that require individuals to have a wide range of communication and analytical skills.

Table 4.1 reports on the prevalence of training for four of the skills frequently identified as necessary for effective employee involvement and total quality management (Commission on the Skills of the American Workforce, 1990). Three of these skills are essentially interpersonal and group skills. They are included because so many EI and TQM processes involve meetings, interpersonal interactions, group problem solving, and the ability to influence others.

The results for training in group decision-making and problem-solving skills show a general increase from 1987 to 1996. The increase from 1990 to 1993 is particularly impressive. The 1999 results show that little changed between 1996 and 1999 and that less than a majority of employees receive training in these skills.

The results for leadership training show an increase from 1987 to 1999. Even with the increase, however, only a small percentage of the companies trained more than 60 percent of their workforce in leadership skills. Indeed, only 32 percent trained more than 40 percent of their employees. In a traditional organization, this is to be expected, since hierarchical organizations see leadership as resting with a few

Table 4.1

Percentage of Employees Receiving Training in Interpersonal and Group Skills in the Past Three Years.

Training Area	Study	Mean (5-point scale)	None or Almost None[a] (0–20 percent)	Some (21–40 percent)	About Half (41–60 percent)	Most (61–80 percent)	All or Almost All[a] (81–100 percent)
Group Decision-Making and Problem-Solving Skills	1987	1.8	41	43	11	4	1
	1990	1.8	45	37	12	5	1
	1993	2.2	28	42	15	11	5
	1996	2.3	28	37	18	9	8
	1999	2.1	33	42	11	11	3
Leadership Skills	1987	1.8	37	51	10	2	1
	1990	1.7	46	42	8	2	1
	1993	2.0	33	45	14	4	3
	1996	2.1	31	42	16	8	3
	1999	2.2	24	44	18	11	3
Team-Building Skills	1987	1.8	45	36	13	4	1
	1990	1.9	44	34	14	6	1
	1993	2.4	26	36	21	9	9
	1996	2.5	21	33	23	14	8
	1999	2.4	24	36	19	14	7
Skills in Understanding Business	1987	1.7	48	39	8	4	1
	1990	1.5	61	34	4	2	0
	1993	1.6	59	33	4	4	1
	1996	2.0	39	40	12	6	3
	1999	2.1	36	37	14	7	6

[a]For 1990, 1993, 1996, and 1999, responses were combined to convert a 7-point response scale to a 5-point response scale.

employees at the top of the organization; therefore, training a large number of leaders is not cost-effective. In an organization that is encouraging individuals throughout the organization to take a role in its management, quite the opposite is true. Individuals throughout the firm need to lead teams, manage projects, and generally provide a sense of direction for the corporation (Mohrman, Cohen, and Mohrman, 1995; Lawler, 1996; Conger, Spreitzer, and Lawler,

1999). It follows logically that leadership training should be broadly spread throughout the organization and not be the exclusive purview of a small group of senior managers (O'Toole, 1999; Tichy, 1997).

Although there was an encouraging increase in training for team-building skills from 1990 to 1993, there was no increase from 1993 to 1999. Most individuals still are not being trained in the team and interpersonal skills needed for them to participate in problem-solving groups and team-based decision making.

The results for training individuals in the skills necessary to understand how businesses operate show a significant increase since 1993. This increase is particularly noticeable from 1993 to 1996, but overall the evidence clearly indicates that in the majority of corporations, most employees do not receive training in understanding business. Because basic business literacy is a precondition for almost any organizational improvement effort, the relatively low level of training in this area can be a particularly significant problem in businesses that wish to increase employee involvement. Clearly understanding the performance measures and operations of the business requires good financial skills. Without them, individuals will have a hard time participating knowledgeably in problem-solving groups, much less operating effectively in self-managing work teams or understanding a profit-sharing or stock option plan. Basic business literacy is a precondition for almost any organizational improvement effort.

Table 4.2 presents the results for training that is focused on more technical and job performance–related skills. The three technical skills—information technology (studied in 1999 only), quality and statistical analysis, and business understanding—are included because they are central to most organizational improvement and total quality management efforts. We also asked about job skills training (in all studies but 1987) and cross-training.

As can be seen from the table, during the three years prior to 1999, most employees were not trained in the quality and statistical skills necessary for an employee involvement or total quality management program to work effectively (Deming, 1986; Juran, 1989). Perhaps because of the national focus on total quality management and statistical analysis, training was greatest in 1993. The 1996 data show a slight decrease, and the 1999 results show a continuing decline.

The data are more positive with respect to job skills: 52 percent of the companies surveyed provide training to most of their employees. This is a significant increase from 1990 (34 percent) but not significantly

Table 4.2			Percentage of Employees Receiving Training in Technical and Job Performance Skills in the Past Three Years.				
Training Area	Study	Mean (5-point scale)	None or Almost None[a] (0–20 percent)	Some (21–40 percent)	About Half (41–60 percent)	Most (61–80 percent)	All or Almost All[a] (81–100 percent)
Quality or Statistical Analysis Skills	1987	1.6	58	28	7	6	1
	1990	1.7	57	25	10	5	3
	1993	2.3	38	28	12	13	10
	1996	2.1	45	22	15	9	9
	1999	1.8	54	27	9	9	2
Job Skills Training	1990	2.9	16	28	21	20	14
	1993	3.3	11	18	22	27	22
	1996	3.4	7	20	23	26	24
	1999	3.4	9	17	21	27	25
Cross-Training	1987	2.1	35	36	16	9	4
	1990	2.1	32	41	17	7	3
	1993	2.1	31	41	15	9	4
	1996	2.2	34	33	18	10	5
	1999	2.2	31	38	16	10	6
Information Technology Skills	1999	3.3	10	19	25	24	22

[a]For 1990, 1993, 1996, and 1999, responses were combined to convert a 7-point response scale to a 5-point response scale.
Note: Not all questions were asked in all studies.

higher than in 1993 and 1996. Sixteen percent cross-trained a majority of their employees, representing little change from earlier years.

Perhaps the most interesting results are with respect to training involving information technology skills. We asked about the training of IT skills for the first time in 1999. The results show a level of training that is close to job skill training. Ninety percent of the companies report that they did some IT training in 1999. Undoubtedly, this number reflects the growing use of IT in corporations. Since data are not available from previous years, it is impossible to determine how much training has increased in this area, but a good guess is that this represents a substantial upward trend. It is also one indicator that information technology is beginning to permeate most large corporations.

An analysis of how many types of training each company provides is provided in Table 4.3. It shows that in the three years prior to 1999, only 4 percent of the responding companies trained 40 percent or more of their employees in all five of the areas analyzed. This is a small decrease from the 7 percent who did this amount of training in 1996. In 1999, 39 percent did not train 40 percent or more in any of the areas, a significant decrease from 1993 (44 percent) and a large decrease from 1987, when 63 percent didn't train 40 percent or more of their employees in any of these areas. But it is slightly lower than the 1996 number, suggesting that the growth in training has slowed.

The results change significantly when job skills training is included (see Table 4.4). Then only 17 percent of the companies provided no training in any of these areas to 40 percent or more of their employees. This represents a small change from 1993 but a big change from the 1990 results. It clearly indicates that more training is being done than was done in 1990.

Overall, the data suggest that the situation with respect to the training of employees in U.S. corporations has improved since 1990. Most major U.S. corporations are making greater investments in training than they did in 1990, but the growth in training appears to have stopped, and this maybe a problem. It is difficult to determine just how much training organizations should do (see, for example, Kochan and Osterman, 1994; Pfeffer, 1994). Furthermore,

Table 4.3	Percentage of Companies Providing Five Kinds of Training to More Than 40 Percent of Employees in the Past Three Years.				
Number of Kinds of Training Provided[a]	1987 ($n = 323$)	1990 ($n = 313$)	1993 ($n = 279$)	1996 ($n = 212$)	1999 ($n = 143$)
0	63	59	44	35	39
1	16	22	15	17	22
2	12	8	19	20	16
3	6	7	11	15	10
4	2	2	7	6	9
5	1	1	3	7	4

[a]Five possible kinds of skills: group decision making and problem solving, leadership, team building, business understanding, quality or statistical analysis.

Table 4.4	Percentage of Companies Providing Six Kinds of Training to More Than 40 Percent of Employees in the Past Three Years.			
Number of Kinds of Training Provided[a]	1990 (*n* = 313)	1993 (*n* = 279)	1996 (*n* = 212)	1999 (*n* = 143)
0	34	20	15	17
1	32	28	25	27
2	19	14	15	19
3	6	19	19	14
4	6	10	15	9
5	2	6	6	9
6	1	3	6	4

[a]Six possible kinds of skills: group decision making and problem solving, leadership, team building, business understanding, quality or statistical analysis, job skills training.

the actual number of individuals who have been trained in a company at any point in time is undoubtedly larger than the number that have been trained in the past three years. Nevertheless, a strong case can be made that individuals need to be regularly trained in most of the areas we studied.

With the rate of change in many organizations, old training often amounts to no training. Work methods, technologies, and business systems now change at such a rapid rate that constant updating of the important skills in these areas is necessary in order for individuals to operate effectively. So even though training has grown, it most likely still falls short of the level needed for employees to keep up with the technological changes that are occurring and for employee involvement and total quality management to work—indeed, for most businesses to perform effectively, regardless of what management approach they use.

The lack of training certainly means that many employees do not have the necessary skills to become full business partners. Particularly disturbing is the lack of increase in training from 1996 to 1999. A positive interpretation of this is that training did increase but that the increase was in the IT skills area where we do not have longitudinal data. A more realistic interpretation is that companies are not making the investments in training they should be making.

Reward systems play an important role in determining the success or failure of any organizational improvement effort because they are a key driver of behavior. To support employee involvement, reward systems need to be designed in a way that encourages individuals to obtain more information about the business, add to their skills, take on more decision-making responsibility, and perform in ways that improve business performance (Lawler, 2000).

A key feature of reward systems is the degree to which pay is based on performance because when pay is based on performance, it has the potential to motivate improved performance. Two elements of pay-for-performance systems determine whether they do, in fact, motivate behavior that supports involvement and organizational effectiveness: the first is the kind of performance that is measured, and the second is the amount of money that depends on performance. For pay to be a motivator, a significant amount must be tied to measures of performance that are easy to understand and capable of being influenced by employees.

Table 5.1 shows the popularity of four approaches to basing cash payments on performance. It also presents information on the popularity of two stock plans and of recognition reward programs.

Individual incentive plans are usually not very supportive of employee involvement, total quality management, reengineering, or knowledge development and sharing. They focus on the performance of individuals and do not tie individuals to the overall success of the business; moreover, they can interfere with teamwork, group problem solving, process focus, sharing knowledge, and lateral integration (Zingheim and Schuster, 2000). Nevertheless, in situations where individuals hold jobs that can be done independently of others, individual incentive plans may be quite functional. They can motivate individuals to take charge of their particular area of responsibility and perform effectively. The pattern for individual incentives shown in Table 5.1 is interesting. All but 7 percent of the corporations report having some employees covered by individual incentives; however, these systems typically cover 40 percent or less of the workforce. The results from 1987 to 1999 show a significant increase in the use of individual incentive plans, most likely reflecting the increasing performance demands most organizations face.

Team incentives can be supportive of employee involvement activities such as work teams and problem-solving groups. They can also be supportive of reengineering efforts that focus on creating process teams and lateral integration. The results show that they are

Table 5.1

Percentage of Employees Covered by Performance-Based Reward Practices.

Reward Practice	Study	Mean (7-point scale)	None (0 percent)	Almost None (1–20 percent)	Some (21–40 percent)	About Half (41–60 percent)	Most (61–80 percent)	Almost All (81–99 percent)	All (100 percent)
Individual Incentives	1987	2.4	13	49	27	6	2	1	2
	1990	2.8	10	46	24	8	5	3	5
	1993	2.9	10	40	30	8	3	4	5
	1996	3.2	9	34	27	9	7	6	8
	1999	3.4	7	26	31	11	11	5	9
Work Group or Team Incentives	1990	2.1	41	38	10	6	1	2	3
	1993	2.4	30	40	14	6	3	3	5
	1996	2.8	13	45	21	8	2	4	6
	1999	3.0	20	31	19	9	5	5	10
Gainsharing	1987	1.5	74	19	4	1	0	1	1
	1990	1.6	61	28	8	1	1	1	0
	1993	1.8	58	26	7	2	3	2	2
	1996	1.9	55	26	9	3	1	2	4
	1999	2.1	47	30	9	4	3	4	4
Profit Sharing	1987	3.1	35	20	11	4	5	10	15
	1990	3.2	37	19	7	4	6	10	17
	1993	3.3	34	23	7	4	3	11	19
	1996	3.6	31	18	7	3	9	13	20
	1999	3.4	30	16	18	2	6	10	19
Employee Stock Ownership Plan	1987	3.8	39	8	4	4	6	10	28
	1990	3.8	36	9	6	3	5	13	29
	1993	4.1	29	9	9	4	6	14	30
	1996	4.1	32	9	4	3	5	15	32
	1999	4.2	29	8	9	3	5	13	33
Stock Option Plan	1993	2.6	15	56	15	2	1	2	10
	1996	2.9	13	46	21	2	3	5	10
	1999	3.3	9	42	18	7	3	6	15
Nonmonetary Recognition Awards for Performance	1990	4.0	9	23	18	10	13	10	17
	1993	4.3	6	22	17	7	10	17	22
	1996	4.5	4	17	17	10	16	12	25
	1999	5.0	4	14	12	10	10	19	32

Note: Not all questions were asked in 1987 and 1990.

increasingly popular. Eighty percent of the companies surveyed use them. The increase in their use matches the increasing use of teams, which will be discussed in Section 6. These incentive plans, when used, still tend to cover a minority of employees (40 percent or less). This finding makes sense, as many individuals do not work in teams or teamwork situations. Further, many employees in the United States prefer to be paid for their individual performance.

Basing rewards on organizational performance is one way to encourage employees to be involved in and care about the performance of their company (Lawler, 2000). It also helps ensure that they share in the gains that result from any performance improvement. Profit sharing, stock ownership, stock options, and gainsharing are approaches that can link employee rewards more closely to the success of the business. These systems are often cited as the reward approaches most supportive of employee involvement (Blinder, 1990; Lawler, 2000; Zingheim and Schuster, 2000). The results show that employee stock ownership is the most widely used and the most likely to be available to most or all employees.

Historically, gainsharing is the approach that has been most closely identified with employee involvement since it stresses involvement as a key to the success of its financial bonus system. As Table 5.1 shows, gainsharing is the least popular pay-for-performance approach. Forty-seven percent of responding companies say none of their employees are covered by a gainsharing plan. Of the corporations that offer some employees gainsharing, virtually all have a minority of their total workforce on it. Rare is the corporation that covers all employees with gainsharing: only 4 percent of companies that responded in 1999 do so.

The results from 1987 to 1999 show a significant increase in the use of gainsharing; however, the growth is slower then the growth for team and individual plans. One possible explanation for this is that gainsharing plans have already been installed in a significant percentage of the situations where they fit well. Future growth may depend on the development of new approaches to gainsharing that make these plans applicable to new settings.

Nineteen percent of the companies cover all employees with profit sharing, and 71 percent have a profit-sharing plan. Given its problems as a motivator (a poor line of sight from behavior to reward in large companies) and the number of employees that are covered by it, we think it is safe to conclude that profit sharing is not acting as an important motivator of involvement or performance in most companies. The results from 1987 to 1999 show a little increase in the use of profit sharing despite an increasing emphasis in the management literature on the use of variable or bonus-based pay (Zingheim and Schuster, 2000; Lawler, 2000).

Reward systems that use stock are generally consistent with employee involvement because they can help create an ownership mentality or culture. As is true with profit sharing, however, they are likely to have a poor line of sight and thus are not very effective motivators of performance in large organizations. Stock ownership plans are available to all employees in 33 percent of the corporations surveyed. It is likely that this result reflects the widespread use of employee stock purchase plans (Blasi, 1988; Rosen, Klein, and Young, 1986). In 29 percent of the corporations surveyed, stock ownership plans are not available to any employees. It is one of the few practices that companies tend to offer to all or none of their employees. There was a significant increase in their popularity from 1987 to 1999, but the increase is not as large as the ones for some of the other performance-based pay practices.

The results for stock option plans show that in most companies, they cover only a small percentage of the employees—probably the senior managers. There is evidence of an increase in the use of all-employee stock option plans. The implementation of companywide stock option plans by Pepsico, Bank of America, and other large companies has sparked considerable interest in such programs, so it is not surprising that they are becoming more popular. Our results, however, show that all-employee option plans are present in only 15 percent of companies.

The actual frequency of reward activities oriented toward employee involvement may not be captured by the data in Table 5.1 because profit-sharing, stock option, and employee stock ownership plans are included. Many profit-sharing plans have been around for years and are often best thought of as retirement benefits rather than incentives. Many employee stock ownership plans have been installed for tax advantages and are not tied to employee involvement (Blasi, 1988). We can also question the effectiveness of profit-sharing plans and stock plans because they have a poor line of sight in large corporations. In addition, the general lack of information and knowledge about the business that exists in many companies limits the line of sight even more. Without information and knowledge, variable rewards often appear capricious, rather than motivating and involving.

Nonmonetary recognition programs can be used to support employee involvement efforts. These reward systems are frequently advocated by proponents of TQM programs. Table 5.1 shows that most organizations have recognition programs and that they cover all employees in 32 percent of the firms. This suggests that they are typically targeted at special activities and groups. The data do show considerable growth in their popularity from 1990 to 1999.

Table 5.2 shows the concentration of the five pay-for-performance reward system approaches. Only 28 percent of companies are using none of them widely. A majority of companies use at least two of these reward practices. This reflects a significant increase from 1990.

Overall, the results show a continued strong increase in the use of pay-for-performance systems. Particularly noticeable is the growth in individual incentives, team incentives, stock option plans, and nonmonetary recognition awards for performance. This trend is probably not primarily caused by performance improvement efforts that are focused on employee involvement, total quality, reengineering, or knowledge management. It is more likely simply occurring because of a drive to improve performance through the increasing use of incentives and accountability. Despite the increased use of pay for performance, the opportunity still exists for many organizations to reward many more individuals for their performance.

Table 5.3 presents the results for five additional reward system practices that are considered supportive of employee involvement. The first of these practices, all-salaried pay, reduces the distinctions between exempt and nonexempt employees, thus creating a pay system more congruent with the notion of an egalitarian workforce. The

Table 5.2	**Percentage of Companies Using Performance-Based Reward Practices with More Than 40 Percent of Employees.**			
Number of Kinds of Rewards Provided[a]	1990 (n = 313)	1993 (n = 279)	1996 (n = 212)	1999 (n = 143)
0	29	24	18	21
1	38	41	30	28
2	24	21	32	26
3	8	8	16	17
4	2	5	3	6
5	0	1	1	2

[a]Five possible kinds of rewards: individual incentives, profit sharing, gainsharing, employee stock ownership, work group or team incentives.

Table 5.3 **Percentage of Employees Covered by EI-Supportive Reward Practices.**

Reward Practice	Study	Mean (7-point scale)	None (0 percent)	Almost None (1–20 percent)	Some (21–40 percent)	About Half (41–60 percent)	Most (61–80 percent)	Almost All (81–99 percent)	All (100 percent)
All-Salaried Pay Systems	1987	3.5	29	15	13	10	12	11	10
	1990	2.9	36	18	14	10	7	9	7
	1993	3.3	27	18	11	13	11	11	9
	1996	3.1	30	14	18	13	12	8	6
	1999	3.2	31	12	18	14	10	7	10
Knowledge- or Skill-Based Pay	1987	1.7	60	25	7	2	2	2	2
	1990	1.8	49	34	11	2	1	1	1
	1993	2.1	40	37	12	4	2	2	3
	1996	2.1	38	40	13	2	4	1	2
	1999	2.0	38	36	20	2	2	1	1
Flexible, Cafeteria-Style Benefits	1987	2.4	66	7	4	3	2	6	13
	1990	3.2	46	12	5	4	5	9	20
	1993	4.0	32	9	7	4	7	12	30
	1996	4.1	32	7	6	5	5	11	33
	1999	4.5	25	9	7	3	6	11	40
Employee Security	1987	3.0	47	14	6	2	6	8	18
	1990	2.6	47	20	6	4	6	9	8
	1993	2.2	63	13	5	2	3	5	9
	1996	2.0	65	15	4	3	5	3	6
	1999	1.9	66	16	5	3	2	4	5
Open Pay Information[a]	1993	3.4	34	17	8	7	6	9	20
	1996	3.6	30	18	6	7	8	10	21
	1999	3.7	31	14	7	5	12	10	22

[a]Not studied in 1987 or 1990.

table shows that over two-thirds of companies use this approach, but there is no evidence that it is increasing in popularity.

How the base pay of individuals is structured and set is crucial for employee involvement. For a pay system to support EI, it needs to send the proper messages about individual development, growth, learning, and the culture of the organization. When pay is based on knowledge and skill, it rewards individuals for their capability and flexibility in contributing to the organization. As a person learns more and can contribute more to the organization, his or her pay increases (Lawler, 2000). This approach fosters and rewards cross-training and permits the flexible deployment of people. It can also be supportive of teaming and can encourage individuals to learn the skills they need for their involvement in the business. Finally, it can promote a broader understanding of how the business operates, which can be useful in addressing complex problems. Table 5.3 shows that 62 percent of companies use this approach, although most with only a minority (1 to 20 percent) of their workforce.

A comparison among the 1987, 1990, 1993, 1996, and 1999 data shows significant growth in the use of skill-based pay from 1987 to 1993. However, there was no growth from 1993 to 1999. One possibility is that this practice has reached a saturation point. It seems to fit best in manufacturing and service situations where first-level employees in teams are cross-trained, and there are only so many of these situations. It may also be encountering significant resistance. Skill-based pay, after all, is not an easily added extra; it represents a major change in the way an organization determines base pay. Many base pay systems have been in place for decades and are not easily altered; they must be changed in a major way if skill-based pay is adopted.

There does seem to be increased interest in competency-based pay (Lawler, 2000). Like skill-based pay, it focuses on paying the person, not the job, but it is usually applied to managers and knowledge workers. Its use was not measured in our survey. A good guess is that if it had been, we would have found more growth in the trend of paying the person instead of paying the job.

Flexible benefits programs provide employees with some control over how the benefits portion of their compensation package is structured. This approach fits with the employee involvement philosophy of moving responsibility for decisions to the individuals who are affected by them. Seventy-six percent of companies used flexible benefits in 1999. Flexible benefits have increased tremendously in popularity from 1987 to 1999; they are the fastest-growing reward practice. Although flexible benefits programs fit with employee involvement because of their emphasis on employee choice in the reward mix, the increased adoption of this approach may have more to do with controlling benefit costs and meeting the needs of an increasingly diverse workforce than with supporting involvement. The cost of benefits, particularly health care, has been increasing dramatically, and many companies are using flexible benefits and cost sharing as ways to control these costs (Lawler, 2000).

The results concerning employment security are interesting. Some recent books and articles on organizational effectiveness argue that employment security is an important enabler of involvement and total quality management (see, for example, Pfeffer, 1994). Without job security, employees may fear that any improvement they make will threaten their jobs and those of others. As a result, individuals may feel hesitant to get involved in improvement activities. The results show a significant decline from 1987 to 1999 in the number of companies with employment security. Most noticeable is the increase in the percentage of companies covering no employees with job security—from 47 to 66 percent. The results for 1996 and 1999 suggest that the decline in employment security may be over, as the 1996 and 1999 results are essentially the same. Perhaps this is because companies have now reached a level of employment stability that fits their current business realities. We may, in effect, be seeing the development of employment security models that work on different levels: a high level of job security for "core employees" and a lower one for the rest.

Open pay information is one way to ensure that employees understand how they are paid, a necessary precondition to their participation in decisions about their pay and that of other employees. The results concerning openness show a slight increase from 1993 to 1999. They continue to show an interesting split among companies: 22 percent supply all employees with open information, while 31 percent supply none. Clearly, companies are operating with two quite different philosophies with respect to providing information about pay.

Overall, the data suggest that organizations are continuing to change their reward system practices. Particularly significant is the finding that organizations are increasing their use of certain pay-for-performance approaches. However, this may not have a powerful effect on motivation because some of the approaches that have been adopted, primarily stock and profit-sharing plans, have a poor line of sight. Still, they can contribute to employees seeing themselves as having a direct stake in organizational performance and ultimately lead to employees demanding more involvement in business decision making (Conger, Lawler, and Finegold, 2001).

Moving decision-making power downward in organizations is what employee involvement is all about. It also plays an important role in total quality management programs, since they emphasize empowerment. To get a sense of how active organizations have been in moving decision making to lower levels, the survey asked about the existence of a number of specific structural approaches to giving employees more decision-making power. These approaches can be divided into two basic types: parallel structures and work design approaches.

Parallel structures involve special meetings or problem-solving activities that are separate from the normal day-to-day work processes; as a result, they are often referred to as parallel organizational structures (Lawler and Mohrman, 1985; Lawler, 1992). Although problem-solving activities do move some power downward, they are limited in their impact (Ledford, Lawler, and Mohrman, 1988). Typically, employees provide only input and recommendations; they do not make substantial decisions, nor do they have the resources or power to implement decisions.

As can be seen in Table 6.1, four of the five forms of parallel structure are used by most companies. However, the use of each parallel structure is limited to fewer than half of the employees in most organizations that use them.

Quality circles are used in 54 percent of all companies, a percentage that has declined slightly since 1987. Participation groups are used by 84 percent of all companies, up from 70 percent in 1987, but showing a decline since 1996. The trend from 1987 to 1999 shows an increase in the use of employee participation groups, with most of the increase occurring from 1987 to 1993. This increase is significant and provides a contrast to the slight decrease in the use of quality circles. Apparently, companies are adopting employee participation groups instead of expanding their use of quality circles.

Union-management quality-of-worklife (QWL) committees have been tried in a much smaller percentage of the companies. This finding, of course, follows from the relatively low level of union membership in the United States in general and in the surveyed companies in particular (less than 50 percent have union members). From 1990 to 1999, there has been virtually no change in the use of these committees.

Survey feedback is an activity that does not necessarily entail the creation of a parallel structure, since it often takes place in

Table 6.1 **Percentage of Employees Covered by Parallel Structure Practices.**

Parallel Structure Practice	Study	Mean (7-point scale)	None (0 percent)	Almost None (1–20 percent)	Some (21–40 percent)	About Half (41–60 percent)	Most (61–80 percent)	Almost All (81–99 percent)	All (100 percent)
Quality Circles	1987	2.1	39	32	18	7	2	0	1
	1990	2.2	34	36	19	7	4	1	1
	1993	2.3	35	32	19	6	5	3	1
	1996	2.1	40	28	20	6	3	1	2
	1999	1.9	46	29	18	4	3	1	0
Employee Participation Groups Other Than Quality Circles	1987	2.4	30	33	21	9	3	2	1
	1990	2.8	14	35	30	11	5	3	3
	1993	3.2	9	26	31	14	13	5	3
	1996	3.4	6	28	28	17	9	7	5
	1999	3.1	16	23	25	19	10	4	3
Union-Management Quality-of-Worklife Committees	1987	1.4	70	20	7	2	1	1	0
	1990	1.5	65	23	9	2	0	0	1
	1993	1.6	65	22	6	3	2	2	1
	1996	1.6	64	23	9	2	2	0	0
	1999	1.5	66	22	9	3	0	0	0
Survey Feedback	1987	3.0	32	22	17	6	7	6	10
	1990	3.3	23	26	20	5	4	7	16
	1993	4.1	15	19	15	8	9	10	25
	1996	4.5	9	15	15	8	8	20	26
	1999	4.8	11	8	16	8	7	15	35
Suggestion Systems	1987	4.0	17	17	16	7	11	11	21
	1990	3.9	14	24	14	7	10	12	19
	1993	3.5	15	26	19	11	7	9	14
	1996	3.5	11	29	23	7	9	7	15
	1999	3.5	15	25	19	9	11	8	14

established work groups. However, it is often seen as an extra or special activity. As can be seen in Table 6.1, fully 89 percent of companies use it for at least some employees, and 35 percent use it for all employees. Survey feedback shows a very large increase in popularity from 1987 to 1999; it is the one parallel structure practice that increased from 1996 to 1999 and is the most widely used of all power-sharing practices.

Finally, our survey asked about the use of suggestion systems. Typically, these involve one or more employees submitting a written improvement suggestion. In 1999, 85 percent of the companies reported using them; their rate of use declined from 1987 to 1993 and was essentially unchanged from 1993 to 1999. So even though they are among the oldest and perhaps least powerful approaches, suggestion systems continue to be popular.

Table 6.2 looks at the prevalence of programs that use work design practices to move power downward. Job enrichment, self-managed work teams, and minibusiness units (defined as partly autonomous units operating much like small businesses) all involve a substantial change in the basic structure of the organization and are aimed at moving important operating decisions into the hands of individuals and teams performing basic manufacturing or service work. Finally, employee committees are a way to give employees more say in policy and strategy decisions.

As shown in Table 6.2, job enrichment is used widely and gained in popularity from 1987 to 1996. However, this trend did not continue from 1996 to 1999. Still it is the most widely used work design power-sharing practice. The broad acceptance of job enrichment probably results from the fact that this approach has been around for decades and has been widely publicized (see, for example, Herzberg, 1966; Hackman and Oldham, 1980).

The use of self-managing work teams increased substantially from 1987 to 1996 but did not continue to increase from 1996 to 1999. They are still used less frequently than job enrichment. Self-managing work teams are used in 72 percent of the corporations, but in most organizations, they involve only a small percentage of the workforce. One possible explanation for the slowdown in their growth may be that they have reached a saturation point with respect to situations where they fit well. Furthermore, they are not simple to install, and the management literature is increasingly focusing on their limitations.

Minibusiness units are used less frequently than any of the other power-sharing practices and tend to affect a small percentage of an

Table 6.2

Percentage of Employees Covered by Work Design Power-Sharing Practices.

Power-Sharing Practice	Study	Mean (7-point scale)	None (0 percent)	Almost None (1–20 percent)	Some (21–40 percent)	About Half (41–60 percent)	Most (61–80 percent)	Almost All (81–99 percent)	All (100 percent)
Job Enrichment or Redesign	1987	2.0	40	38	12	6	2	2	1
	1990	2.2	25	43	23	6	2	0	1
	1993	2.6	18	40	25	8	4	3	3
	1996	2.9	13	31	31	14	8	1	2
	1999	2.6	21	35	25	9	7	1	3
Self-Managing Work Teams	1987	1.4	72	20	6	1	0	0	0
	1990	1.6	53	37	9	1	0	0	0
	1993	1.9	32	49	15	3	2	0	0
	1996	2.3	22	46	23	4	3	2	0
	1999	2.2	28	45	15	8	4	0	1
Minibusiness Units	1987	1.3	75	18	4	1	1	0	0
	1990	1.4	72	23	3	1	0	1	0
	1993	1.8	56	23	14	3	4	1	0
	1996	2.1	40	35	14	5	4	2	1
	1999	2.0	47	29	12	4	5	2	1
Employee Committees Concerned with Policy or Strategy[a]	1993	2.0	35	45	13	5	2	1	0
	1996	2.1	26	50	19	3	1	1	0
	1999	2.1	24	50	18	6	1	0	1

[a]Not studied in 1987 or 1990.

organization's employees. Since this approach involves more power sharing and change than self-managing teams do, it is not surprising that it is used less frequently. Simply stated, it represents the most significant departure from traditional management. The results show a significant increase in the use of minibusiness units from 1990 to 1996 but no increase from 1996 to 1999. This finding is not surprising given the lack of increase in other power-sharing approaches, particularly work teams.

The data show a small increase in the number of companies (from 65 percent in 1993 to 76 percent in 1999) that have employee committees that focus on policy and strategy issues. Implemented effectively, this approach can give employees input on organizationwide policy and effectiveness issues.

Additional analysis of the data suggests that companies with job enrichment, self-managing work teams, and minibusiness units are more likely to have parallel structure activities such as quality circles. In other words, companies that engage in one of the popular employee involvement activities are also more likely to use the others. However, as Table 6.3 shows, the use of multiple approaches on a large scale is not widespread.

Only 37 percent of companies use two or more of the seven possible approaches with over 40 percent of their employees. Even though this represents a significant increase from 1987 (when it was 20 percent), it is still a low figure. The most significant change may be the large decrease in the percentage of companies that do not cover 40 percent or more of their employees with any power-sharing practices (from 58 percent in 1987 to 21 percent in 1999). Finally, it is important to note that as of 1999, a high percentage of Fortune 1000 companies were using one or more power-sharing practices on a wide scale.

Overall, the data on the use of practices designed to move power downward in organizations show that suggestion-type programs continue to be widely used, particularly survey feedback. Most corporations have tried this approach somewhere. This is probably because these programs are the easiest to install and effect the least change in the power relationships in organizations.

We have no data that show why the use of all parallel structure practices with the exception of survey feedback is stable or declining

Table 6.3	Power-Sharing Approaches Used with More Than 40 Percent of Employees.				
Number of Approaches[a]	1987 ($n = 323$)	1990 ($n = 313$)	1993 ($n = 279$)	1996 ($n = 212$)	1999 ($n = 143$)
0	58	52	33	21	21
1	23	28	30	36	42
2	11	13	17	19	19
3	6	4	12	11	7
4	3	3	5	9	6
5–7	0	1	3	3	5

[a]Seven possible approaches: survey feedback, job enrichment, quality circles, employee participation groups, union-management quality-of-worklife committees, minibusiness units, self-managing work teams.

from 1996 to 1999. In the case of quality circles, QWL committees, and suggestion systems, the findings are not surprising. They indicate a continuation of a long-term trend. It is a bit surprising, however, with respect to the use of employee participation groups since they have been experiencing long-term growth. Perhaps the best explanation for the plateauing of their growth is saturation. They are limited vehicles that are best used on a selective basis and may have reached their optimal utilization level.

The biggest surprise in the data is the lack of continued growth in the use of work design power-sharing practices. All of them, particularly job enrichment, work teams, and minibusiness units, have been increasing regularly since our first survey in 1987. However, none of them showed an increase from 1996 to 1999. One obvious explanation is that they too have reached the saturation point. Another is simply that they have been pushed aside by other change initiatives such as those based on information technology and as a result are no longer an increasing focus of change efforts. This seems the most likely explanation.

Finally, it is important to note that none of the power-sharing practices in Tables 6.1 and 6.2 are employed throughout most companies. Typically, they cover less than 40 percent of the employees in the companies that use them. This finding strongly suggests that companies are still piloting these practices or using them selectively rather than adopting them as their only approach to organizing and managing work. For some practices and companies, this decision is undoubtedly appropriate because the various approaches to power sharing are not universally applicable. Nevertheless, it suggests that many companies are still not committed to creating high involvement organizations.

PART TWO

Total Quality Management, Reengineering, and Knowledge Management

Total Quality Management

Total quality management (TQM) is a set of organizational strategies, practices, and tools for organizational performance improvement. Although TQM enjoyed its greatest initial popularity in Japan, it is now a worldwide movement with international groups offering quality certifications. A variety of practices are included under the general rubric of TQM (Cole, 1999). At the operational level, it includes the application of systematic approaches to the measurement and improvement of work processes to ensure that they are adding value and meeting customer needs. Work simplification is often part of TQM as organizations focus on eliminating steps that do not add value and on combining tasks to reduce the number of interfaces.

Many companies are collaborating with their suppliers as part of their efforts to improve quality. They recognize that quality problems often result from the delivery of supplies and raw material that do not meet specifications and that supplier interfaces often include steps that do not add value. Although the focus in TQM is primarily on *quality,* defined as meeting customer needs, this management approach also has cost, service, and schedule implications. The practice of monitoring the cost of quality links the quality- and customer-focused aspects of TQM to the financial or cost aspects of the organization. To create customer focus, TQM incorporates systematic customer satisfaction monitoring and direct exposure of employees to customers to ensure an understanding of their needs.

TQM was first applied in manufacturing settings, where it typically includes training front-line employees to use statistical process control methods to monitor and improve work processes and to inspect their own work (Cole, 1999). It also often includes just-in-time deliveries from suppliers to reduce inventory costs. Some organizations have redesigned the workplace into work cells that apply TQM techniques and that in many cases have the characteristics of self-managing teams. Some of the more production-oriented administrative and service parts of organizations have also adopted these TQM techniques and practices.

TQM includes strategic elements—namely, the involvement of management in quality councils that link TQM activities to the key strategic focuses of the organization and cross-functional planning that explicitly acknowledges and plans for interdependence among functions. Process reengineering is often linked to total quality management (see, for example, Hammer and Champy, 1993; Davenport, 1993). Reengineering may result in the introduction of substantially different work processes. But instead of taking the process improvement approach that is common in TQM, reengineering focuses on reconceptualizing what and how work is done, often by incorporating the capabilities of information technology. In practice, reengineering often equates to process simplification and lateral integration with a primary focus on downsizing. However, because, as noted in Section 1, it has developed its own identity, reengineering will be treated separately in this book, in Section 8.

The use of the TQM approach was on an upward trajectory in U.S. companies from the early 1970s to the mid-1990s. In our 1993 survey, 76 percent of companies reported having a TQM program (see Table 7.1). This compares with 73 percent in our 1990 survey and 74 percent reported in a 1993 survey of human resource and quality respondents (Moran, Hogeveen, Latham, and Ross-Eft, 1994). Our 1996 data showed a significant drop in the percentage of companies with TQM programs, to 66 percent. The 1999 data show a further decline to 55 percent.

The 1999 data also show a drop in the percent of employees covered by TQM programs. In our 1993 survey, TQM programs on average covered 50 percent of employees, compared with 32 percent in our 1999 survey, a smaller percentage than was covered in 1990. Finally, 11 percent of companies (compared to 18 percent in 1990, 25 percent in 1993, and 19 percent in 1996) report that all employees are covered by TQM programs. Overall, the results suggest that TQM efforts are in decline and have fallen below their 1990 levels. It now appears that 1993 was the high water mark for TQM programs. Interestingly, this is the same time when Cole (1999) reports that quality programs such as the U.S. Baldrige National Quality Award program peaked.

Table 7.1	Total Quality Management Coverage.			
	1990	1993	1996	1999
Percentage of Companies with a TQM Program	73	76	66	55
Average Percentage of Employees Covered	41	50	41	32
Percentage with All Employees Covered	18	25	19	11

Tables 7.2 and 7.3 present data on the usage patterns for a number of common TQM practices. These tables include data from only companies indicating that they have TQM programs (55 percent of all companies in 1999). The practices are presented in three groupings that resulted from a statistical analysis to determine common usage patterns. The six practices in Table 7.2 are the core practices that tend to be adopted by most companies as they become

| Table 7.2 | Percentage of Employees Covered by Core TQM Practices. |

TQM Practice	Study	Mean (7-point scale)	None (0 percent)	Almost None (1–20 percent)	Some (21–40 percent)	About Half (41–60 percent)	Most (61–80 percent)	Almost All (81–99 percent)	All (100 percent)
Quality Improvement Teams	1993	3.9	3	21	20	22	14	15	5
	1996	3.7	1	25	28	16	13	8	8
	1999	3.8	3	21	31	9	21	9	8
Quality Councils	1993	3.0	20	35	14	12	5	8	5
	1996	2.7	22	33	23	12	5	2	4
	1999	2.9	19	30	28	9	4	5	5
Cross-Functional Planning	1993	2.8	13	38	26	8	10	4	2
	1996	2.6	21	34	24	9	7	2	2
	1999	3.1	9	33	32	12	4	5	5
Work Simplification	1990	3.0	13	26	33	12	7	7	0
	1993	3.2	8	28	28	17	8	6	4
	1996	3.4	8	23	28	18	15	5	4
	1999	3.4	4	31	23	21	15	4	3
Customer Satisfaction Monitoring	1993	4.2	1	15	25	18	13	18	10
	1996	4.0	2	16	24	21	15	18	4
	1999	4.1	0	20	18	26	12	15	9
Direct Employee Exposure to Customers	1990	3.1	4	32	31	16	4	4	0
	1993	3.3	2	31	33	16	11	6	2
	1996	3.4	1	28	35	15	12	7	2
	1999	3.3	4	24	40	13	10	6	3

Notes: Questions were not asked in 1987. Not all questions were asked in 1990.

Table 7.3 — Percentage of Employees Covered by Production and Other TQM Practices.

TQM Practice	Study	Mean (7-point scale)	None (0 percent)	Almost None (1–20 percent)	Some (21–40 percent)	About Half (41–60 percent)	Most (61–80 percent)	Almost All (81–99 percent)	All (100 percent)
PRODUCTION-ORIENTED PRACTICES									
Self-Inspection	1990	3.2	10	25	31	14	7	7	0
	1993	3.4	7	27	27	14	15	8	3
	1996	3.6	8	24	21	13	20	8	6
	1999	3.5	7	20	35	12	17	7	4
Statistical Control Method Used by Front-Line Employees	1993	2.8	12	38	27	11	7	5	1
	1996	3.0	16	30	23	14	10	5	2
	1999	3.1	10	35	20	17	8	9	1
Just-in-Time Deliveries	1990	2.6	24	31	22	11	4	4	2
	1993	2.9	17	29	26	13	8	6	1
	1996	3.2	10	33	19	16	12	7	3
	1999	3.3	12	27	24	13	7	13	4
Work Cells or Manufacturing Cells	1990	2.1	41	27	19	9	2	2	0
	1993	2.2	35	33	14	14	3	2	0
	1996	2.5	30	29	21	10	5	5	1
	1999	2.7	27	25	23	14	3	6	3
OTHER PRACTICES									
Cost of Quality Monitoring	1990	2.7	18	35	24	11	4	4	3
	1993	2.8	17	37	20	13	6	5	2
	1996	2.8	19	32	22	14	6	4	4
	1999	2.9	12	40	19	12	11	4	3
Collaboration with Suppliers in Quality Efforts	1990	2.8	13	37	27	11	3	3	2
	1993	3.4	5	28	27	16	13	8	3
	1996	3.5	4	31	22	16	13	10	3
	1999	3.2	1	36	30	14	10	4	4

Note: Questions were not asked in 1987.

increasingly involved in TQM. The four production-oriented practices in Table 7.3 constitute a related set of practices that tend to be used where the work is routine and measurable. Most often this means that they are used in manufacturing settings and in white-collar output-oriented operations. The patterns of adoption for each of the last two practices in Table 7.3 (cost-of-quality monitoring and collaboration with suppliers) do not relate to each other or to the preceding two clusters of practices. For that reason, they are treated as individual practices in all analyses.

The two most heavily used core practices are quality improvement teams and customer satisfaction monitoring. Both of these practices showed little change in their use from 1993 to 1999. Four-fifths of companies use customer satisfaction monitoring in areas employing more than 20 percent of the workforce, and 24 percent cover more than 80 percent of all employees with this practice. Three-fourths use quality improvement teams with more than 20 percent of the workforce, and 8 percent cover all employees.

The use of work simplification and direct exposure to customers was measured in 1990, 1993, 1996, and 1999; a comparison shows that the use of both in companies with TQM programs has increased slightly since 1993. Two-thirds of the companies with TQM programs use these practices in areas employing more than 20 percent of the workforce.

The least frequently used core practices are quality councils and cross-functional planning. Fewer than half of the companies with TQM programs use them with more than 20 percent of the workforce. There is a slight increase in the use of cross-functional planning from 1996 to 1999. It is significant that these less frequently employed practices are more strategic and involve higher-level direction and involvement.

The four production-oriented practices in Table 7.3 all experience increases from 1990 to 1999. However, the increases for self-inspection and statistical control are small. The most frequently used practice by companies with total quality programs is self-inspection, a practice that covers more than 20 percent of employees in two-thirds of the companies. Statistical process control by front-line employees and just-in-time deliveries are used by over half of the companies with more than 20 percent of their employees.

The least frequently used practice is work cells; they are not used at all by 27 percent of companies, and less than half of the companies use them with more than 20 percent of their employees. Their use has consistently increased since 1990, however.

The relatively low usage pattern of the production-oriented practices no doubt reflects the fact that they are applicable only to the production-oriented areas of a company. These practices may in fact cover a large percentage of the appropriate employees, given that less than 35 percent of the employees in these companies are involved in manufacturing operations.

The use of cost-of-quality monitoring shows little increase. Fewer than half the companies with TQM programs use it with more than 20 percent of their employees. In contrast, collaboration with suppliers in quality efforts experienced the largest and most significant overall gain of any practice from 1990 to 1996; however, it showed a slight decrease from 1996 to 1999. Almost two-thirds of companies with TQM practices used it in 1999 with more than 20 percent of their employees, up from one-half of the companies in the 1990 survey. The increased implementation of this practice is particularly interesting because it always involves two or more organizations. It provides evidence of how strongly TQM thinking is affecting the way manufacturing organizations are operating today.

Overall, the 1999 survey results suggest some interesting conclusions about what is happening to total quality management programs. On the one hand, fewer companies seem to have formal TQM programs. Given the overall decline in the number of companies with TQM programs, this means that fewer employees overall are covered by TQM practices than were covered in 1990, 1993, and 1996. On the other hand, the results suggest that companies that do use TQM are using some TQM practices more frequently than they did in 1990. This is particularly true of the production-oriented practices we studied. The usage patterns for particular practices vary considerably, with only a few companies employing any of the practices for all employees. Quality improvement teams and customer satisfaction monitoring remain the most extensively employed. In general, the operational aspects of TQM are the most widely used. The strategic approaches that require top management involvement, such as the creation of quality councils and cross-functional planning, are used less frequently.

One way of summarizing what seems to be happening with the total quality management approach is that as a program it is in decline but some of its practices continue to be used and may be gaining in popularity. At this point, there is little reason to suspect that in the future more companies will have total quality management programs. This is not to say, however, that the specific practices associated with TQM are going to be used less frequently. Some of them are likely to be used not only by companies that remain committed to total quality management efforts but also by companies who simply find them to be approaches that offer support for their way of managing. Thus it is possible that TQM programs will eventually disappear but that many TQM practices will continue to be used.

Process Reengineering

Process reengineering became a popular approach to improving organizational performance in the mid-1990s (Hammer and Champy, 1993). As our discussion in Section 1 highlighted, it is a newcomer compared to employee involvement and total quality management. Judging by the attention reengineering received in magazines, journals, and books during the 1990s, it is not surprising that our 1996 survey found that many corporations have used it. The big question at this point concerns how much use is still being made of it in light of the criticism it has received. It is also important to find how much it now involves the use of e-commerce practices.

Our 1996 survey was the first to include a series of questions on reengineering. Our intention in including these items was simple: to gather data that might shed some light on this popular and frequently debated management approach. Table 8.1 shows the results of a question that asked companies to indicate what percentage of their employees are in work units that have experienced process reengineering efforts. The results confirm the widely held view that process reengineering was indeed used in many American corporations in 1996. More surprising is the finding that it was still widely used in 1999. In 1996, 81 percent of the companies reported that at least some of their employees were affected by reengineering. This number declined slightly to 76 percent in 1999. In most cases, reengineering efforts affect less than half of the employees in the companies with reengineering efforts (36 percent on average), but in

Table 8.1 Process Reengineering Coverage.	1996	1999
Percentage of Companies with Program	81	76
Average Percentage of Employees Covered	38	36
Percentage with All Employees Covered	10	8

8 percent of the companies, they affect 100 percent of the employees. In many ways, these are astoundingly high impact levels for a new organizational improvement method that first received attention in the early 1990s.

We also asked the companies that reported having process reengineering efforts to identify the changes that were made as a part of these efforts. A statistical analysis of our 1996 study clustered the items into two groups, work structures and cost reduction. As is shown in Table 8.2, the results for 1996 and 1999 are almost identical for both groups.

Given the close tie between process reengineering and the adoption of information technology, we were not surprised that one of the most common work structure changes in companies with process reengineering efforts was the redesign of a company's information systems. The three other most common changes were generally consistent with the cost reduction image of process reengineering efforts: doing the same work with fewer people, doing the same work with less supervision, and an overall lower cost structure. Lower costs, of course, follow directly from having less supervision and fewer people.

Process reengineering efforts are moderately likely to create cross-functional units. It is somewhat surprising that this result is not stronger, given the heavy emphasis on multifunctional units in the literature on process reengineering. Like process simplification, it is frequently called a key component of reengineering.

It may be a little surprising to see that reengineering efforts frequently result in having less supervision, since reengineering is not particularly associated with employee involvement and self-management. It is impossible to tell whether the reduction in supervision is a result of information technology making fewer supervisors necessary or restructuring the work so that less coordination is necessary on the part of supervisors. It is also impossible to say whether it is done to involve employees in decision making and improve the quality of worklife of employees. A good guess, however, is that the reduction in supervision is more likely associated with a desire to reduce overhead costs than with a desire to create more involvement and a better quality of worklife for employees. This conclusion is generally supported by the finding that enriched, multiskilled jobs and multiskilled teams are not common changes in process reengineering efforts.

Questions concerning information technology and e-commerce were asked for the first time in 1999. Electronic transactions with

Table 8.2 **Percentage of Companies Adopting Reengineering Practices.**

Reengineering Practices	Study	Mean (7-point scale)	Little or No Extent	Some Extent	Moderate Extent	Great Extent	Very Great Extent
WORK STRUCTURE							
Process Simplification	1996	3.2	3	22	34	36	6
	1999	3.1	3	24	36	31	7
Creation of Cross-Functional Units	1996	3.0	12	24	30	25	9
	1999	2.9	7	27	40	23	4
Major Information System Redesign	1996	3.3	8	22	19	32	19
	1999	3.2	8	22	27	29	15
Enriched Multiskilled Individual Jobs	1996	2.7	12	32	37	16	3
	1999	2.6	11	36	38	12	3
Multiskilled Teams	1996	2.7	13	32	32	18	5
	1999	2.7	13	33	30	21	3
COST REDUCTION							
Doing Same Work with Fewer People	1996	3.4	4	16	30	34	17
	1999	3.4	4	11	42	31	13
Doing Same Work with Less Supervision	1996	3.3	6	19	32	30	13
	1999	3.2	5	19	43	26	8
Lower Overall Cost Structure	1996	3.2	5	23	31	27	14
	1999	3.3	2	21	36	32	9
E-COMMERCE							
Installation of an Enterprise Resource Planning (ERP) System	1999	2.2	45	19	16	12	9
Electronic Transactions with Suppliers	1999	2.8	11	28	32	24	5
Electronic Transactions with Customers	1999	2.9	12	26	31	24	8

Notes: Questions were not asked in 1987, 1990, and 1993. Not all questions were asked in 1996.

suppliers and customers are reported to be used to a moderate or greater extent by more than 60 percent of the companies undertaking reengineering efforts. Least common is the installation of ERP systems. This finding is hardly surprising since ERP systems typically require an enormous commitment on the part of the corporation and are suitable in only a limited number of organizational situations. The adoption rate for electronic transaction activities suggests that significant numbers of companies are moving toward a strong e-commerce orientation. Because this question was not asked in previous surveys, it is impossible for us to estimate when the growth of electronic transactions began. It is likely, however, that their use is a relatively new development in most companies. In light of the growth of the Internet and e-business, it is highly likely that e-commerce transactions with suppliers and customers will increase dramatically in the near term.

Because data on reengineering were not collected prior to 1996, we cannot make any definitive statements about the growth of process reengineering before then. In our 1993 study, we did ask whether organizations had engaged in process reengineering as part of their total quality management programs. A significant number of companies responded that they had. Ninety-two percent of the companies that had TQM programs had engaged in some process reengineering. At that point, 76 percent of all corporations had a TQM program. Thus we can deduce that around 70 percent of the companies in 1993 had a reengineering effort. But at that time it was more common for companies to adopt other TQM practices than to adopt process reengineering. For example, quality improvement teams and customer satisfaction monitoring were used by a higher percentage of the companies than reengineering was. In any case, the data from 1993 suggest that some process reengineering was already going on, though certainly not to the extent suggested by our 1996 data. It is hard to imagine that much process reengineering activity would have been reported in 1990 if we had asked about it. Process reengineering was clearly a 1990s event in American business that affected most corporations and many of the people in them.

Overall, the developments with respect to reengineering from 1996 to 1999 show less change than might have been expected. Reengineering has been heavily criticized in recent years, and few companies seem to be launching new reengineering programs. Nevertheless, our 1999 data suggest that most companies still have reengineering programs and that they are still using the same practices that were used in 1996. It is therefore far too early to declare reengineering obsolete. It is most probably being transformed into e-commerce programs that emphasize the use of information technology to improve processes, enable cross-functional work, and achieve cost reductions. As this occurs, the use of the term *reengineering* will undoubtedly disappear but many of the concepts and some of the practices associated with it will survive because they fit well with an e-commerce orientation.

SECTION 9

Knowledge Management

Knowledge management can take place through practices and behaviors that may or may not be the result of a specific program. For this reason, our survey asked both about whether there were a number of knowledge management practices in place and about whether there was someone formally in charge of a program focused on learning and knowledge management.

When asked whether they had an executive in charge of learning and knowledge management, 33 percent of the companies said they did. This number is somewhat higher than the one reported in a recent study of 158 companies by the Conference Board (Hackett, 2000), which found that 25 percent had an executive in charge. In our study, the companies that responded yes said, on the average, that they created this position in 1996. Hence most organizations do not have someone formally in charge of learning and knowledge management, and those that do have only relatively recently created this position. Clearly, the idea of a formal knowledge management effort is still relatively new and is not a dominant practice in most organizations.

To understand precisely how organizations are positioning knowledge management, a question was asked concerning whether knowledge management was the responsibility of the human resources (HR) function. In 74 percent of the organizations that had an executive in charge of knowledge management, the individual was in the HR organization. The other 26 percent had their knowledge management executive in a variety of other functions and departments. It therefore appears that learning and knowledge management are regarded more as an HR activity than as a general business issue. It is understandable that knowledge management would be given to the HR function because of its historical focus on training and individual development, but there is an obvious danger in relegating it to the HR function. Doing so may mean that knowledge management fails to receive the kind of senior management involvement that will effectively tie it to business strategy and business outcomes. This may in turn end up making it nothing more than a series of training programs rather than a true organizational capability that permeates the organization.

Table 9.1 presents the results with respect to specific knowledge management practices that are in place. Two different groupings of questions appeared when the data were analyzed. The first concerned general management practices that either transferred knowledge or developed it, and the second concerned reward system practices.

The results concerning management practices reveal one overwhelmingly popular activity: more than half of companies report that to a great or very great extent, they give their employees access

Table 9.1   **Percentage of Companies Using Knowledge Management Practices in 1999.**

Knowledge Management Practices	Mean (5-point scale)	Little or No Extent	Some Extent	Moderate Extent	Great Extent	Very Great Extent
MANAGEMENT PRACTICES						
Knowledge-Sharing Conferences	2.0	40	35	16	8	1
IT-Enabled Knowledge Storing and Transfer	2.4	18	37	30	13	2
External and Internal Benchmarking	3.0	8	26	35	26	6
Visits to Customers, Suppliers and Others for Learning	2.9	6	30	37	21	6
Lessons Learned or Postmortem Reviews	2.8	11	29	33	24	4
Communities of Practices or Networks	2.2	29	33	29	8	0
Internet Access for Obtaining Information and Knowledge	3.5	3	17	27	36	18
External Partnerships to Develop New Knowledge	2.6	19	29	34	15	3
Rotational Assignments for Development	2.4	18	41	27	12	2
REWARDS						
Rewards for Developing Knowledge Assets	1.8	45	36	15	3	1
Rewards for Sharing Knowledge	1.8	47	36	14	3	1

to the Internet. This result clearly points to the growing importance of the World Wide Web and its use by companies for knowledge purposes. Three other practices show a relatively high level of use. They all have to do with learning from experience. In the case of external and internal benchmarking, it is learning from a particular technique that allows organizations to capture best practice information. The two other kinds of learning—visits to customers, suppliers, and others and postmortem reviews—allow organizations to gather information and learn from experience.

The next most popular practices involve knowledge transfer and development. They include the use of information technology, communities of practice, rotational assignments, and external partnerships. The least frequently used form of knowledge management is conferences.

The two questions concerning rewards show that organizations do little in the reward system area to support the developing or sharing of knowledge. A similar finding is reported in the Conference Board study of knowledge management (Hackett, 2000). Given that a considerable amount of research has shown that individuals focus their attention on those things that are rewarded, this is not a positive situation with respect to the degree to which individuals are likely to focus on either developing or sharing knowledge (Lawler, 2000). Because these activities are not rewarded, individuals are unlikely to regard them as a high priority.

Overall, the result suggests that organizations engage in a number of activities that are likely to develop and share knowledge. However, they do not particularly reward either the development or the sharing of knowledge. Instead they use management practices that are designed to gather knowledge and information from a variety of sources; the web, other organizations and their own experience. Missing from the knowledge management activities of most companies is a focus on developing knowledge assets. Rather than focus on creating new knowledge, organizations seem to be more inclined to gather information from others. An exception to this is that some use is made of external partnerships to develop knowledge and of postmortem reviews of programs.

Relationships Among Employee Involvement, Total Quality Management, Reengineering, and Knowledge Management

The similarities and differences among employee involvement, total quality management, reengineering, and knowledge management were discussed in Section 1. There we pointed out that the employee involvement and TQM literatures share an emphasis on the use of participation groups that use problem-solving and decision-making tools (see also Lawler, 1994, 1996; Mohrman, Galbraith, and Lawler, 1998). They both also emphasize performance feedback and information sharing. TQM tends to focus primarily on process feedback and customer information, whereas the employee involvement literature focuses more on business results and other business information. TQM provides management tools that emphasize the control and improvement of work processes and gears activities to customer requirements. Employee involvement emphasizes the motivational systems in an organization, including the design of motivating jobs and ways of setting goals and reviewing and rewarding performance. It also focuses on the design of teams and business units to enable employee involvement in the business.

Reengineering shares some characteristics with both EI and TQM. For example, it focuses on the importance of lateral relationships and on decreasing the number of management levels. But it typically places less emphasis on employee participation and teams than either EI or TQM does.

Effective knowledge management can be a crucial underpinning to employee involvement, total quality management, and reengineering. All of them require the development of new knowledge and the movement of knowledge from outside to inside an organization and among users on the inside. Effective knowledge management can therefore in many ways be seen as the foundation on which successful employee involvement, total quality management, and reengineering programs should be built.

EI, TQM, and reengineering can also support knowledge management. By moving decision making to units, EI can encourage the kind of experimentation that leads to new knowledge. The focus of TQM programs on problem analysis and process control can create new knowledge. Finally, reengineering, particularly with the growth of e-commerce, has the potential to spread information and learning throughout organizations.

It is one thing to point out the similarities and differences among EI, TQM, reengineering, and knowledge management; it is quite another to combine them effectively in an organization. Here we will look at the degree to which corporations combine them in practice. In Part Four, we will examine how their effectiveness is altered when they are combined.

Employee Involvement and TQM. There is a strong correlation between the adoption of some employee involvement approaches and the use of TQM practices by companies with TQM efforts (see Table 10.1). The extent to which companies employ the core TQM practices, the production-oriented practices, collaboration with customers, and cost-of-quality monitoring is strongly related to the overall employee involvement index in 1996 and to a lesser degree in 1999. The relationship of TQM to the development of knowledge and skills is particularly strong in 1996 but is not significant in 1999. TQM's relationship to power sharing is very strong in 1996 and in 1999, reflecting the focus on problem-solving and decision-making groups in TQM in general and on work cells and teams.

Work simplification is strongly related to power sharing (1996 and 1999) and to knowledge and skills development (1996 only). This suggests that work simplification is not leading inexorably to simple, unenriched jobs; quite the opposite appears to be true. Self-inspection, often a part of work simplification, is also associated with knowledge and skills development (1996 only) and with power sharing (1996 and 1999).

An interesting finding is the strong relationship of cross-functional planning to many of the EI indices. The creation of planning processes that extend across the organization is associated with more opportunities for people to be informed about their company, develop knowledge and skills, and participate in empowered decision-making forums. Most of the other TQM practices show some statistically significant relationships to the EI indices. Finally, the percentage of employees covered by TQM practices is related to the EI indices.

There is no overall strong relationship in either 1996 or 1999 between the use of TQM practices and the use of involvement-oriented reward practices. The lack of a relationship with reward practices suggests that companies that employ more TQM practices are not more likely to make employees stakeholders in business performance.

Overall, the relationship between the use of total quality management practices and employee involvement is clearly weaker in 1999 than it was in 1996 (and in 1993; for 1993 data, see Lawler, Mohrman, and Ledford, 1998). This suggests that companies have become less inclined to use both of them together. Despite the fact

	EMPLOYEE INVOLVEMENT OVERALL		INFORMATION SHARING		KNOWLEDGE AND SKILLS DEVELOPMENT		REWARDS		POWER SHARING	
TQM Practices	1996	1999	1996	1999	1996	1999	1996	1999	1996	1999
CORE PRACTICES OVERALL	.49***	.36**	.23*	.14	.47***	.23	.23*	.25*	.54***	.42***
Quality Improvement Teams	.30***	.21	.13	.09	.36***	.10	.13	.28*	.45***	.16
Quality Councils	.22*	.19	.18*	−.03	.30***	.05	.01	.30*	.20*	.21
Cross-Functional Planning	.38***	.33**	.25**	.10	.42***	.21	.18*	.18	.39***	.40***
Work Simplification	.44***	.34**	.12	.12	.42***	.22	.30***	.13	.48***	.51***
Customer Satisfaction Monitoring	.35***	.36**	.20*	.23*	.28***	.24*	.12	.20	.36***	.29*
Direct Employee Exposure to Customers	.34***	.26*	.26**	.26*	.28***	.01	.15	.15	.32***	.18
PRODUCTION-ORIENTED PRACTICES OVERALL	.48***	.15	.29**	.01	.54***	.02	.18	.17	.53***	.27*
Self-Inspection	.49***	.26*	.22*	.10	.48***	.08	.26**	.13	.47***	.47***
Statistical Control Method Used by Front-Line Employees	.30***	.06	.21*	−.04	.50***	.02	.04	.02	.38***	.25*
Just-in-Time Deliveries	.35***	.10	.24**	.06	.35***	−.03	.14	.21	.34***	.03
Work Cells or Manufacturing Cells	.36***	.05	.31***	−.07	.36***	.02	.03	.05	.40***	.15

Table 10.1   Relationship Between EI Indices and TQM Practices.

Table 10.1 (Continued)

TQM Practices	EMPLOYEE INVOLVEMENT OVERALL		INFORMATION SHARING		KNOWLEDGE AND SKILLS DEVELOPMENT		REWARDS		POWER SHARING	
	1996	1999	1996	1999	1996	1999	1996	1999	1996	1999
OTHER PRACTICES										
Cost-of-Quality Monitoring	.24**	.20	.18*	.02	.31***	.19	.05	.08	.35***	.31**
Collaboration with Suppliers in Quality Efforts	.40***	.21	.24**	.20	.32***	.04	.15	.17	.39***	.12
PERCENTAGE COVERED	.31***	.32***	.14*	.20*	.35***	.25**	.12	.23**	.34***	.35***

Correlation coefficients: * = weak relationship ($p \leq .05$);
** = moderate relationship ($p \leq .01$);
*** = strong relationship ($p \leq .001$).

that they may be complementary in many respects, it seems that companies are selectively using practices from each orientation rather than simply using all the practices that are part of both employee involvement and total quality management.

Employee Involvement and Reengineering. Table 10.2 shows the relationship between the EI indices and the adoption of reengineering practices for companies with reengineering efforts. There are a number of significant relationships. EI overall is related particularly strongly to the adoption of work structure changes and e-commerce. For instance, multiskilled teams are associated with the EI indices as might be expected since they are also often part of EI efforts. Employee involvement is less strongly but still significantly related to the adoption of several cost reduction practices.

Information sharing, knowledge development, and power sharing tend to be related to the use of reengineering practices, but rewards are not. The rewards result suggests that reengineering efforts typically do not change reward systems or that at least they do not change them in ways that reward performance and skills.

The results for the work-restructuring practices are not surprising. To operate successfully, these approaches require employees to be more involved in their work and to take more responsibility for how it is done. The results for power sharing, which, like knowledge and skills development, showed strong correlations with work restructuring

Table 10.2 **Relationship Between EI and Reengineering Practices.**

Reengineering Practices	EMPLOYEE INVOLVEMENT OVERALL		INFORMATION SHARING		KNOWLEDGE AND SKILLS DEVELOPMENT		REWARDS		POWER SHARING	
	1996	1999	1996	1999	1996	1999	1996	1999	1996	1999
WORK STRUCTURE	.40***	.37***	.27***	.34***	.39***	.31***	.08	.10	.37***	.30**
Process Simplification	.31***	.18	.23**	.15	.28***	.13	.01	.07	.25***	.12
Creation of Cross-Functional Units	.35***	.11	.23**	.07	.33***	.05	.08	.04	.33***	.17
Major Information System Redesign	.27***	.25*	.17*	.30**	.22**	.23*	.10	.03	.26***	.14
Enriched Multiskilled Individual Jobs	.30***	.32**	.19*	.33***	.31	.32***	.08	.02	.27***	.25*
Multiskilled Teams	.29***	.33***	.22**	.25**	.36***	.28**	.01	.16	.31***	.30**
COST REDUCTION	.24**	.25*	.02	.22*	.32***	.14	.01	.15	.31***	.18
Doing Same Work with Fewer People	.22**	.11	.01	.11	.29***	.06	.00	.02	.28***	.10
Doing Same Work with Less Supervision	.19	.32**	.00	.22*	.30***	.24*	−.06	.15	.30***	.27**
Lower Overall Cost Structure	.24**	.21*	.04	.23*	.28***	.06	.08	.21*	.25***	.10
E-COMMERCE	—	.40***	—	.33***	—	.23*	—	.17	—	.37***
Installation of an Enterprise Resource Planning (ERP) System	—	.34***	—	.30**	—	.12	—	.16	—	.35***
Electronic Transactions with Suppliers	—	.30**	—	.26**	—	.26**	—	.10	—	.23*
Electronic Transactions with Customers	—	.29**	—	.20*	—	.19	—	.17	—	.26**
PERCENTAGE COVERED	.24***	.34***	.10	.29***	.24***	.25**	.07	.12	.31***	.31***

Correlation coefficients: * = weak relationship ($p \le .05$);
** = moderate relationship ($p \le .01$);
*** = strong relationship ($p \le .001$).

in 1996, support this conclusion. These results clearly confirm that activities like creating multiskilled teams and redesigning information systems are associated with the use of greater sharing of power and the development of knowledge and skills. The adoption of reward system practices is not significantly related to work structure changes. This is a bit surprising since some of the reward system practices (such as skill-based pay) fit with the work system changes.

The results for cost reduction follow the same general pattern as those for work structure. Cost reduction was strongly associated with knowledge and skills development in 1996 and with the adoption of power-sharing practices in 1996 but not in 1999. It was not associated with the adoption of reward system practices oriented toward employee involvement or with the adoption of information-sharing practices in 1996 and only weakly associated in 1999. The underlying explanation would appear to be that when cost reduction is the major target, organizations feel that they have to train the remaining workers to be more flexible and capable. They inevitably have to share more power with them because there is less supervision available to "control them."

It is somewhat surprising that organizations do not change their reward systems in order to reinforce people for operating successfully in a lower-cost environment. This raises the obvious issue of why everyone in reengineering efforts doesn't participate in the financial gain that comes from whatever cost reduction savings are realized. It also suggests at least one reason why reengineering efforts are seen as having a negative effect on employees: the workers experience the reductions but do not participate in the gains.

The results for the e-commerce questions show significant relationships to EI overall. They also show generally significant relationships with information sharing, knowledge and skill development, and power sharing. Like other reengineering practices, they show little relationship to rewards. The relationship between e-commerce and EI is not surprising. EI practices inevitably create more information sharing in an organization, and they require knowledge and skill development in order to work effectively. Finally, by their very nature, they often require the use of power-sharing practices, and they are frequently used with knowledge workers who work most effectively when they are able to manage themselves, work in teams, and influence the way work is done.

EI and Knowledge Management. The relationships shown in Table 10.3 between EI and knowledge management practices are consistently positive and very strong. The adoption of EI and

Table 10.3 — Relationship Between EI and Knowledge Management Practices.

Knowledge Management Practices	EMPLOYEE INVOLVEMENT OVERALL 1999	INFORMATION SHARING 1999	KNOWLEDGE AND SKILLS DEVELOPMENT 1999	REWARDS 1999	POWER SHARING 1999
MANAGEMENT PRACTICES	.57***	.43***	.51***	.28***	.53***
Knowledge-Sharing Conferences	.38***	.27***	.35***	.23**	.37***
IT-Enabled Knowledge Storing and Transfer	.38***	.32***	.24**	.27**	.28***
External and Internal Benchmarking	.33***	.21*	.36***	.10	.38***
Visits to Customers, Suppliers, and Others for Learning	.39***	.24**	.37***	.20*	.39***
Lessons Learned or Postmortem Reviews	.39***	.24**	.34***	.23**	.38***
Communities of Practice or Networks	.51***	.36***	.48***	.24**	.47***
Internet Access for Obtaining Information and Knowledge	.40***	.40***	.25**	.22**	.28***
External Partnerships to Develop New Knowledge	.31***	.31***	.30***	.10	.32***
Rotational Assignments for Development	.47***	.34***	.50***	.20*	.42***
REWARDS	.47***	.33***	.51***	.23**	.43***
Rewards for Developing Knowledge Assets	.41***	.30***	.48***	.20*	.34***
Rewards for Sharing Knowledge	.45***	.31***	.46***	.23**	.45***

Correlation coefficients: * = weak relationship ($p \leq .05$);
** = moderate relationship ($p \leq .01$);
*** = strong relationship ($p \leq .001$).

knowledge management seems to be much more closely inter-twined than the adoption of EI and total quality management or EI and reengineering. In many respects, this is not surprising since EI very strongly emphasizes creating a knowledge base that can facilitate employees' effectively using the power and the information that they are likely to receive. Further, many employee involvement programs have emphasized knowledge management practices in order to create a workforce that has an understanding of how EI works and can best be practiced. Thus it is not surprising that practices like benchmarking visits and communities of practice are particularly strongly associated with EI programs. Finally, several knowledge management practices, such as rotational assignments for development, are important parts of many EI programs since they lead to individuals' understanding the business and therefore contributing to it in ways that capitalize on their involvement.

The strong relationship between rewards for knowledge management and employee involvement is somewhat surprising. Perhaps it reflects the recognition in employee involvement programs that knowledge management, development, and sharing are critical to any employee involvement program. In any case, it is clear that organizations that practice employee involvement are particularly likely to reward the development and transfer of knowledge.

Reengineering and Total Quality Management. Table 10.4 shows the relationship between the adoption of TQM practices and reengineering practices for companies that have these programs. The relationships are consistently positive, and many are significant. They tend to be strongest for the work structure items, indicating a high degree of overlap between what are regarded as reengineering practices and those considered TQM practices. In the work structure area, the weakest relationships are with major information system redesign, which is not a major theme in TQM. Thus it is not surprising that it is relatively unrelated to the adoption of a number of TQM practices. In contrast, particularly in 1996, the adoption of process simplification and cross-functional units was strongly related to all of the TQM practices that we studied.

The cost reduction reengineering items showed a number of significant relationships with TQM practices in 1996 but fewer in 1999. Apparently, the core TQM practices, the production-oriented practices, cost-of-quality monitoring, and collaboration with suppliers all tend to be included among the activities that are combined with most reengineering practices. In many respects, this is not surprising; quality consultants often emphasize that improving quality leads to an overall lowering of the cost structure of the business. It can also lead to organizations doing the same work with

	CORE PRACTICES OVERALL		PRODUCTION-ORIENTED PRACTICES		COST-OF-QUALITY MONITORING		COLLABORATION WITH SUPPLIERS IN QUALITY EFFORTS		PERCENTAGE COVERED	
TQM Practices	1996	1999	1996	1999	1996	1999	1996	1999	1996	1999
WORK STRUCTURE	.45***	.38**	.50***	.23	.41***	.36**	.33***	.14	.06	−.09
Process Simplification	.45***	.29*	.32***	.22	.37***	.18	.43***	.11	.07	−.12
Creation of Cross-Functional Units	.41***	.44***	.50***	.37**	.43***	.28*	.33***	.16	.10	−.13
Major Information System Redesign	.33***	.21	.21*	−.02	.23*	.25*	.18*	.09	.07	.07
Enriched Multiskilled Individual Jobs	.31***	.20	.44***	.20	.29**	.28*	.22*	.02	−.04	−.15
Multiskilled Teams	.24	.37**	.44***	.29*	.29**	.43***	.12	.18	.04	.04
COST REDUCTION	.36***	.13	.37***	.33**	.23*	.23	.29**	.16	.06	−.02
Doing Same Work with Fewer People	.29**	.07	.31**	.20	.19*	.11	.29**	.07	.06	.09
Doing Same Work with Less Supervision	.29**	.20	.31**	.35**	.20*	.34**	.21*	.19	.00	−.04
Lower Overall Cost Structure	.38***	.07	.38***	.31**	.24**	.14	.30***	.16	.09	−.11
E-COMMERCE	—	.13	—	.18	—	.22	—	.16	—	−.05
Installation of an Enterprise Resource Planning (ERP) System	—	.03	—	.11	—	.15	—	.15	—	.06
Electronic Transactions with Suppliers	—	.22	—	.13	—	.15	—	.14	—	−.04
Electronic Transactions with Customers	—	.13	—	.16	—	.24	—	.11	—	−.07
PERCENTAGE COVERED	.31***	.32**	.17	.22	.03	.07	.10	.21	.18**	.39***

Correlation coefficients: * = weak relationship ($p \leq .05$);
** = moderate relationship ($p \leq .01$);
*** = strong relationship ($p \leq .001$).

fewer people because of a reduced need for rework. And it can lead to less supervision if individuals become better at monitoring their own work and at managing themselves.

The e-commerce items show no significant relationships to total quality management practices. Though the relationships are generally positive, none of them reached statistical significance, indicating that information technology practices and use of the Web are not related to total quality management programs. In some respects, this is not surprising, since they are from different eras, TQM being the older. However, they do share a common focus on business processes and might in some cases be used jointly.

Overall, as was true in earlier data, the relationships are stronger for the 1996 data than for the 1999 data. The 1993 data (not included in the table) are very similar to the 1996 data (Lawler, Mohrman, and Ledford, 1998). What this suggests is that organizations are perhaps more selective in their use of practices and programs. Instead of simply installing everything, organizations are carefully picking the practices that fit their particular situation and that fit with each other.

TQM and Knowledge Management. The relationship between TQM and knowledge management practices is shown in Table 10.5. The results show relatively few significant relationships between these two approaches in companies that have TQM efforts. The strongest relationship is for communities of practice and benchmarking. This is not surprising since many total quality management programs have emphasized building networks in order to share learnings about total quality methods and approaches. In a similar vein, it is not surprising that external and internal benchmarking and visits are related to the use of core TQM practices. TQM programs often emphasize the importance of benchmarking and of visiting customers and suppliers.

Overall, the results suggest that the use of TQM practices is much less likely to be associated with knowledge management practices than with employee involvement practices. This most likely reflects the different philosophies and orientations of TQM and EI. EI places a great emphasis on the importance of knowledge and learning so that people can self-manage and be involved in the business. TQM certainly emphasizes learning, but primarily about TQM and what it takes to create an effective TQM program.

Reengineering and Knowledge Management. The relationship between reengineering and knowledge management practices in companies with reengineering efforts is shown in Table 10.6. The

	CORE PRACTICES OVERALL	PRODUCTION-ORIENTED PRACTICES	COST-OF-QUALITY MONITORING	COLLABORATION WITH SUPPLIERS IN QUALITY EFFORTS	PERCENTAGE COVERED
Knowledge Management Practices	1999	1999	1999	1999	1999
MANAGEMENT PRACTICES	.34**	.22	.19	.16	.18*
Knowledge-Sharing Conferences	.12	.21	−.01	.02	.11
IT-Enabled Knowledge Storing and Transfer	.21	.06	.04	.10	.14
External and Internal Benchmarking	.34**	.06	.17	.06	.25**
Visits to Customers, Suppliers, and Others for Learning	.31**	.21	.17	.13	.24**
Lessons Learned or Postmortem Reviews	.28*	.10	.14	.06	.10
Communities of Practice or Networks	.39***	.28*	.33**	.19	.17*
Internet Access for Obtaining Information and Knowledge	.12	.10	.01	.10	.07
External Partnerships to Develop New Knowledge	.24*	.32**	.29*	.20	.08
Rotational Assignments for Development	.29*	.21	.20	.21	.09
REWARDS	.13	.05	.07	−.09	.07
Rewards for Developing Knowledge Assets	.13	.03	.09	−.09	.06
Rewards for Sharing Knowledge	.10	.06	.04	−.07	.06

Correlation coefficients: * = weak relationship ($p \leq .05$);
** = moderate relationship ($p \leq .01$);
*** = strong relationship ($p \leq .001$).

Table 10.5   Relationship Between TQM and Knowledge Management Practices.

Table 10.6	Relationship Between Reengineering and Knowledge Management Practices.			
Knowledge Management Practices	WORK STRUCTURE 1999	COST REDUCTION 1999	E-COMMERCE 1999	PERCENTAGE COVERED 1999
MANAGEMENT PRACTICES	.52***	.45***	.47***	.28***
Knowledge-Sharing Conferences	.24*	.32***	.31***	.18*
IT-Enabled Knowledge Storing and Transfer	.37***	.36***	.29**	.18*
External and Internal Benchmarking	.39***	.34***	.30**	.24**
Visits to Customers, Suppliers, and Others for Learning	.36***	.40***	.41***	.21*
Lessons Learned or Postmortem Reviews	.36***	.25*	.26**	.03
Communities of Practice or Networks	.47***	.32***	.39***	.21*
Internet Access for Obtaining Information and Knowledge	.22*	.23*	.31***	.26**
External Partnerships to Develop New Knowledge	.43***	.33***	.41***	.15
Rotational Assignments for Development	.48***	.32***	.33***	.24**
REWARDS	.37***	.21*	.23*	.13
Rewards for Developing Knowledge Assets	.34***	.20*	.14	.11
Rewards for Sharing Knowledge	.34***	.18	.27**	.12

Correlation coefficients: * = weak relationship ($p \leq .05$);
** = moderate relationship ($p \leq .01$);
*** = strong relationship ($p \leq .001$).

results show a generally strong relationship between these practices. All of the relationships with work structure are significant, and all but one of the relationships is significant with respect to cost reduction and e-commerce. The pattern of relationships is similar to the one that was found between EI and knowledge management practices. Apparently, knowledge practices are commonly combined with the kind of change that is involved in a major reengineering effort. This is somewhat surprising, since reengineering is not particularly known to emphasize knowledge transfer and development, but in many respects, the two approaches are complementary. The installation of a major reengineering program is a significant knowledge management challenge as learning needs to be transferred, best practices identified, and ultimately individuals trained to use new information technology and methods. It is therefore important that knowledge management practices be used.

Conclusion. Table 10.7 summarizes the relationship among the four efforts: EI, TQM, reengineering, and knowledge management. It shows that as a general rule, they tend to be adopted together. This is particularly true of EI and knowledge management practices as well as of reengineering and knowledge management practices. The weakest relationship is between knowledge management and TQM. This is a bit surprising, since knowledge management is an activity that can support TQM and TQM itself includes some knowledge management practices. EI, TQM, and reengineering all seem to be moderately related. If an organization uses the practices that are associated with one of them, it is also likely to use some that are associated with the other two. This of course raises the question of what the effect is of combining them. This will be explored further in Part Four, which looks at the effectiveness of these four efforts.

Table 10.7	Relationships Among Practices.			
	Employee Involvement	Total Quality Management	Reengineering	Knowledge Management
Employee Involvement	—	Moderate	Moderate	Strong
Total Quality Management	—	—	Moderate	Weak
Reengineering	—	—	—	Strong

PART THREE

Organizational Change: Practices and Strategy

The Employment Contract

One key element of all work organizations is the employment relationship between individuals and the organizations they work for. We are not speaking here of a legal document to which an individual and an organization agree but rather of the psychological commitment that an organization makes to an individual and that an individual makes to an organization (Rousseau, 1995; Rousseau and Schalk, 2000). William H. Whyte's book *The Organization Man,* which was published in 1956, does a good job of outlining the traditional contract between large organizations and individuals. Whyte focuses on IBM, but similar contracts existed at AT&T, Exxon, and a host of other large companies in the United States at the same time. This "loyalty contract," as it has often been called, promises individuals a lifetime paternalistic relationship with their organization in return for their commitment to that organization and for doing what they are told. In most companies, this contract applied primarily to management and technical employees. Production and nonmanagement employees typically enjoyed less job security and fewer opportunities for development.

Many of the practices that are part of employee involvement, TQM, reengineering, and knowledge management efforts run counter to the traditional employment contract. Not only do they require individuals to learn new skills and competencies, they fundamentally change the conditions of the employment relationship in a number of other areas. Overall, individuals are expected to be more responsible for themselves and their careers and to add value in ways that justify their continued employment. Much of the paternalism of the traditional employment contract is gone, and individuals are valued more for skills, competencies, and performance than for loyalty. In addition, much of the job security that characterized the traditional relationship is gone. The key question is no longer "What have you done for me?" but "What can you do for me in the future?"

One of the first questions to arise in the current business environment is whether organizations have a formal statement of the employment relationship. Responses to our 1999 survey question on this issue showed that only 32 percent of the companies in the

Fortune 1000 actually have a formal statement of their social or employment contract. This is the same number we obtained in our 1996 survey, the first survey that asked about the employment contract. Concerns about making a commitment that could lead to legal liability may be partly responsible for this low rate. It may also be that organizations are unclear as to what kind of statement can be made in these turbulent times. When asked in our survey whether there is a clear contract, 70 percent said that at least to some extent it is changing so fast that it is not clear what the contract is. Finally, organizations may feel that any valid statement that they would make in this turbulent era is so unattractive that it is better left unsaid.

Interestingly enough, when asked about their formal contract statement, 49 percent of the companies that have one said that it was new in the last three years. Although this represents only a small portion of all firms (16 percent), it is an interesting finding. It is also a good indication that the old employment contract is no longer applicable and that some companies are actively establishing a new one.

Table 11.1 shows how companies describe their current employment contract. Overall, the results show little change from 1996 to 1999. It may be that after the downsizing era and the changes it produced, we are now in a time of stability with respect to the employment contract. The first four questions address the issue of employment stability and security. Not surprisingly, given the data reported earlier about the amount of change occurring, corporations see themselves as meritocracies in which performance and skills are the keys to maintaining employment, providing, of course, that business conditions justify employing someone. There is a slight indication that job security may have taken a turn upward since the 1996 data were collected. In 1999, there was less agreement with the statement that "no one has a secure job" than there was in 1996. There was also slightly more agreement that outstanding performers have a job for life.

The meritocracy theme comes through strongly in the four items concerning what is rewarded. Seniority is clearly not rewarded significantly, nor is loyalty. Instead, rewards are tied to individual and group or organizational performance. This result is consistent with the results reported in Section 5, which showed an increase in the use of pay-for-performance plans.

The questions on responsibility for career development and performance show a lack of support for a paternalistic model. The clear

Table 11.1

Nature of the Employment Contract.

Employment Contract	Study	Mean (7-point scale)	Little or No Extent	Some Extent	Moderate Extent	Great Extent	Very Great Extent
Continued Employment Is Based on Performance	1996	4.0	1	4	20	48	28
	1999	4.0	2	3	19	48	29
Continued Employment Is Based on Continuing to Develop Skills and Knowledge	1996	3.4	3	15	34	37	10
	1999	3.3	4	12	41	35	9
No One Has a Secure Job	1996	3.1	12	21	25	26	16
	1999	2.8	14	30	26	18	12
Outstanding Performers Have a Job for Life	1996	2.5	32	22	20	20	6
	1999	2.6	31	21	20	17	12
Rewards Are Tied to Individual Performance	1996	3.6	1	11	30	44	15
	1999	3.6	3	7	31	42	17
Rewards Are Tied to Group or Organization Performance	1996	3.5	3	13	33	38	13
	1999	3.5	1	11	39	36	12
Loyalty to the Company Is Rewarded	1996	2.6	12	37	34	16	1
	1999	2.6	13	34	38	14	2
Rewards Are Tied to Seniority	1996	1.8	47	32	14	6	1
	1999	1.8	47	33	15	5	0
Career Development Is the Responsibility of the Individual	1996	3.7	1	9	26	48	15
	1999	3.6	0	11	26	49	14
Employees Are Expected to Manage Their Own Performance with Minimum Supervision	1996	3.1	2	20	43	30	5
	1999	3.1	4	15	49	30	3
Contract Fits the Corporate Business Strategy	1996	3.5	1	15	30	41	13
	1999	3.4	2	11	43	36	9
Contract Is Understood by Most Employees	1996	3.0	4	26	41	26	3
	1999	3.1	4	17	47	32	1
Employees Are Satisfied with the Contract	1996	2.8	6	34	40	17	3
	1999	3.0	7	17	48	27	1

(Continued)

Table 11.1 Nature of the Employment Contract. (Continued)

Employment Contract	Study	Mean (7-point scale)	Little or No Extent	Some Extent	Moderate Extent	Great Extent	Very Great Extent
Different Contracts Accommodate Different Types of Employees[a]	1999	2.1	39	26	22	13	1
Different Contracts Exist for Temporary and Part-Time Employees[a]	1999	2.9	24	19	15	30	12
Contract Supports a Balance Between Work Demands and Personal Life[a]	1999	2.8	9	34	34	18	5

[a]Not asked in 1996.

response is that employees are expected to develop themselves and their careers and to a moderate extent manage their own performance. Career management is no longer the responsibility of either the organization or management.

The next three items address the issue of the appropriateness of the employment contracts that firms have. The attitudes are somewhat favorable toward them and were unchanged from 1996 to 1999. Respondents see them as fitting the business strategy fairly well. They are also, though to a lesser degree, seen as being understood by most employees. Finally, 76 percent of the respondents reported that most employees were at least moderately satisfied with their employment contracts. This is an increase from 1996 but may be an overstatement of the satisfaction level since all of the individuals filling out this questionnaire were senior managers, and their view of employee satisfaction may be somewhat biased.

Two questions regarding whether companies possess more than one contract were asked for the first time in 1999. The first asked if there were different contracts for different types of employees, the answers seem to indicate that this is not a very common practice. There was more agreement that there are different contracts for temporary and part-time employees of many companies. Sixty-seven percent of the companies said that this was true to at least a moderate extent.

Finally, companies were asked how much their employment contracts support a balance between the demands of work and personal life. Responses to this question fell in the middle of the range. That is, most companies said it was either true to some extent or to a moderate extent. Only 15 percent felt that it was very true or not true at all. Apparently, when it comes to work–personal life balance, most companies have taken a middle position.

Overall, companies appear to have an employment contract that either explicitly or implicitly stresses that the relationship between individuals and their organizations depends on the individual's performance and, to some degree, skills. Loyalty, paternalism, and job security are clearly less important than performance.

The question of how well this new employment contract fits with employee involvement, total quality management, reengineering, and knowledge management is an interesting one. The strong performance emphasis in the new contract seems to fit quite well with all of them. The lack of employment security appears to fit best with reengineering, given its association with downsizing. It may fit least well with employee involvement, since some EI practices, particularly the use of teams, require individuals to be willing to commit themselves to collective performance and collective goals. EI also requires individuals to get involved in the business at a relatively deep level. This may not be possible if people don't stay with the organization for a fairly long period of time. Individuals may also be hesitant to get involved deeply if they feel the organization is not very committed to them and their development. With respect to knowledge management, the emphasis on continued employment's being based on the development of skills and knowledge seems to be a good fit. Similarly, career development being the responsibility of the individual emphasizes the importance of the individuals' having to be concerned about the development of knowledge. These issues and others concerned with how the employment contract influences the effectiveness of EI, TQM, reengineering, and knowledge management will be examined further later in the book.

Improvement Strategies

Employee involvement, total quality management, reengineering, and knowledge management efforts are often key parts of comprehensive change strategies. To get a sense of the overall changes that are occurring in Fortune 1000 corporations, we asked a series of questions about improvement strategies that go beyond a focus on EI, TQM, reengineering, and knowledge management. Specifically, we asked about major corporate restructuring activities, the use of competencies as an important part of business strategy, the introduction of new information and measurement technologies, and talent development. All four of these activities are important in their own right and can have an impact on the success and implementation of EI, TQM, reengineering, and knowledge management programs.

Restructuring. The desirability of a corporation's focusing on a limited set of businesses has its roots in Peters and Waterman's book *In Search of Excellence* (1982), which strongly recommended that companies "stick to their knitting." As Table 12.1 shows, reducing the number of business units has not been the most popular approach for companies in the Fortune 1000, although it was slightly more popular in 1999 then it was in 1996. There are a number of visible examples of major corporations that have adopted it, including ITT, Teledyne, Rockwell, and Westinghouse. It is only in comparison to other kinds of changes that it is not happening frequently. Part of the explanation for this undoubtedly rests in the fact that some of the Fortune 1000 corporations have always been focused on one business, such as public utilities and banks; there is no need for them to change.

Significantly more popular than reducing the number of different business units is creating new units and eliminating old ones. This is occurring even though companies are not actually reducing the number of different businesses they are in. Both in 1996 and 1999, it was common for most businesses to adjust their portfolio of business units, presumably in an attempt to position themselves better relative to the market. Over 80 percent of the companies have, to at least some extent, eliminated old units and created new ones. This is hardly surprising, since for decades this type of restructuring has been part of corporate change efforts.

Only 11 percent of the companies studied are creating global business units to a very great extent. Forty-five percent reported that they are doing it to little or no extent, a number that is slightly lower than in 1996. Thus despite the attention given to the global economy, our results indicate that most U.S. companies are not increasing their efforts to create global business units. In some

Table 12.1 **Percentage of Companies Using Improvement Strategies.**

Improvement Strategy	Study	Mean (5-point scale)	Little or No Extent	Some Extent	Moderate Extent	Great Extent	Very Great Extent
Reduce Number of Businesses	1996	2.0	48	22	13	11	6
	1999	2.2	40	24	18	14	4
Restructure by Creating New Units and Eliminating Old Ones	1996	2.9	18	27	20	24	12
	1999	2.9	18	20	27	27	9
Create Global Business Units	1996	2.4	39	18	14	18	11
	1999	2.3	45	15	11	17	11
Reduce Size of Corporate Staff	1996	2.9	17	25	26	20	12
	1999	2.7	18	24	32	18	8
Build a Team-Based Organization	1996	2.9	12	24	30	25	9
	1999	2.5	19	37	19	21	4
Use Temporary Project Teams to Perform Core Work	1996	2.6	16	31	29	21	3
	1999	2.6	23	24	30	19	4
Focus on Core Competencies	1996	3.4	5	21	22	36	17
	1999	3.4	4	14	28	45	10
Outsource Work	1996	3.0	9	24	33	23	11
	1999	3.0	11	19	36	31	4
Emphasize Employee Competencies	1996	3.2	5	22	29	34	10
	1999	3.0	9	26	33	28	5
Adopt New Information Technology	1996	3.5	7	14	24	34	21
	1999	3.3	5	16	33	34	12
Introduce New Performance Measures	1996	3.3	4	22	26	34	13
	1999	3.1	7	18	36	31	7
Develop Initiatives to Attract and Retain Key Talent[a]	1999	3.2	6	18	33	30	13
Develop Leadership Capability Throughout the Organization[a]	1999	3.3	4	18	31	34	13

[a]Not asked in 1996.

respects, this is not surprising, quite a few of the companies in the Fortune 1000 are in service businesses and other businesses where it is difficult to create global business units. They may be either focusing primarily on the domestic market or doing a small amount of global marketing and selling; hence they do not need to develop global business units.

Over 80 percent of the companies have, to at least some extent, made reductions in their corporate staff. This is a high rate of change but perhaps not a surprising one, given today's demanding business conditions. It is also consistent with the widespread use of reengineering. The results are slightly lower for 1999, suggesting that it may be becoming a slightly less common approach. The reduction of corporate staff is particularly interesting since it is a change that can support greater employee involvement by pushing decisions downward. It also creates the possibility for many of an organization's support activities to reside closer to the individuals who are actually manufacturing products or delivering services. It therefore fits well with the declining use of hierarchy for control purposes and with the downsizing of corporations.

We asked two questions about the use of teams as an approach to restructuring corporations. Eighty percent reported that to at least some extent, they were building a team-based organization. A surprisingly high percentage (77 percent) reported that they were using temporary project teams to perform the core work of the organization. Here corporations seem to be responding to the need to adopt structures and put together teams that can respond quickly to the changing business environment.

The results for the question asking about building a team-based organization are lower in 1999 than they were in 1996. More organizations also reported that they make little or no use of project teams (23 versus 16 percent). This suggests that the growth in team-based organizations may be over, particularly when this finding is combined with the results concerning self-managing work teams, which were reported in Section 6. Taken together, they suggest a decrease in the growth of teams and team-based structures. Part of this may be due to some of the articles and books that have focused on the problems with teams. It may also be that teams have reached a saturation point.

Competencies. Since the seminal writings of C. K. Prahalad and Gary Hamel (see, for example, Prahalad and Hamel, 1990), business strategists have paid a great deal of attention to core competencies. Their writing has emphasized the importance of using and developing core competencies as a key part of a business strategy.

The strategy literature argues that there are four characteristics of core competencies (Hamel, 1994; Rumelt, 1994). First, competencies represent a complex "bundle" of skills and technologies that span multiple businesses and products (for example, precision manufacturing). Second, competencies are more stable and evolve more slowly than the products and markets that have been the traditional focus of strategy. Third, core competencies are difficult to imitate. Witness the unsuccessful attempts of automakers around the world to match the productivity and quality of the Toyota production system during the past two decades. Finally, core competencies, rather than markets or products, are the true battleground for competition among firms.

The strategy literature emphasizes the importance of gaining competitive advantage by producing products and services that are related to the core competencies of an organization. For example, Sony's core competencies in miniaturization and precision manufacturing provide competitive advantages across a large number of product lines and markets.

The results in Table 12.1 strongly suggest that competencies are an important part of most organizational improvement strategies. Ninety-six percent of the organizations responded that at least to some extent they are focusing on core competencies in their improvement efforts. Over 50 percent reported that they do this to a great or very great extent. The majority also reported that to at least a moderate extent they are outsourcing work that is not related to their core competencies. Finally, the majority of the companies reported that they are focusing to a moderate or greater extent on the competencies of their employees.

Outsourcing and emphasizing the competencies of employees are, of course, key implementation practices if an organization wishes to focus on core competencies. These practices follow directly from the efforts of companies to focus on their core competencies and are a good indication that companies are using the core competency approach to develop and implement strategy. A comparison between the 1996 results and the 1999 results shows little change; in both years, a focus on competencies was rated highly.

Information and Measurement. The survey asked about changes in performance measures and information systems. Forty-six percent of companies reported that to a great or very great extent, they are engaged in the significant adoption of new information technology. This is hardly surprising, given our earlier finding that reengineering programs are extremely popular. Together, these results suggest that most major U.S. corporations are going through an information revolution that is reshaping the way they gather and distribute information, manage their operations, and do business. The positive answers to the question on performance measures suggest that in many cases the changes in companies' information systems involve the use of new performance measures.

It is surprising that there was no increase in the adoption of new information technology from 1996 to 1999; indeed, the figures showed a slight decrease. One possible explanation for this is that in 1999 many companies were more concerned about possible Y2K problems than about adopting new systems.

The massive changes that appear to be taking place in the use of information technology and the creation of new measures make an interesting contrast to our finding in Section 3 that most employees are not getting the kind of business information that supports employee involvement. With the increased presence of information technology, it should be easy to give more and more employees the kind of business information that we considered in Section 3. Perhaps this will happen once companies develop their new information systems and begin to realize their full power.

Human Talent. Two questions concerning maintaining and developing talent were asked for the first time in 1999. The first question confirmed that initiatives to attract and retain key talent are critical components of many companies' strategies. This is hardly surprising given the low unemployment rate in the United States and the increasing growth in knowledge work and technology-based jobs. Talent, particularly key technological talent, has become an increasingly scarce commodity, and organizations are being forced to compete in a tighter and tighter labor market (Cappelli, 1999).

The movement toward employee involvement and knowledge management in organizations creates a need for greater leadership capability not just at the top of the organization but throughout. It is therefore not surprising that organizations report that they are attempting to develop leadership talent at all levels. In fact, along with an emphasis on competencies and information technology, the development of leadership capability is rated at the top of the list of improvement strategies being pursued.

Conclusion. The results reported in this section clearly show that the changes taking place in corporations involve more than just employee involvement, total quality management, reengineering, and knowledge management efforts. Most corporations are changing their structures, strategies, information systems, and talent management approaches in major ways. This is a crucial point, because it means that EI, TQM, reengineering, and knowledge management efforts may be just a minor part of the changes being implemented in some organizations. This raises the important question, which we will analyze in Section 21, of how the choice of an improvement strategy is related to the adoption of EI, TQM, reengineering, and knowledge management as well as the question of how these different efforts are being coordinated and managed.

SECTION 13

Change Strategies

Creating change in a large corporation is more art than science. However, a growing body of literature does argue that there are certain characteristics associated with successful change efforts (see, for example, Mohrman and Associates, 1989; Beer and Nohria, 2000). These writings highlight the fact that organizational change is, first of all, extremely difficult to create and maintain because established patterns of behavior and established practices tend to become institutionalized and resistant to change. Even after behaviors cease to contribute to organizational effectiveness, they often continue simply because individuals are comfortable with them and because they have served their purpose well.

Because change is difficult to initiate, the first issue that any change effort must address is "Why change?" The best answers usually involve two elements to differing degrees: dissatisfaction with the status quo because it is dysfunctional and the development of a vision that describes a new and more effective way to operate. In many cases, mobilizing a major change effort requires a combination of both dissatisfaction with the existing state and a clear vision with respect to what type of change is needed.

Table 13.1 presents the results from three questions that asked about the degree to which organizations have a clear vision with respect to their organizational change efforts. One asked about business strategy, a second asked about beliefs concerning organizational effectiveness, and a third asked about mission and values statements. In both 1996 and 1999, all three of these were at least moderately present in the change efforts of most of the corporations in our study. Apparently, the writing and research on organizational change has had an impact on corporations; most have made some effort to articulate their mission, strategy, and organizational effectiveness philosophy.

Table 13.1
Percentage of Companies Using Change Strategies.

Description of Change Strategy	Study	Mean (5-point scale)	Little or No Extent	Some Extent	Moderate Extent	Great Extent	Very Great Extent
Guided by a Clearly Stated Business Strategy	1996	3.4	4	19	22	40	15
	1999	3.4	9	12	26	40	14
Guided by Clearly Stated Beliefs About What Makes an Organization Effective	1996	3.2	8	21	23	37	11
	1999	3.2	9	16	33	31	12
Guided by Mission and Value Statements	1996	3.3	6	25	21	28	21
	1999	3.2	11	21	21	24	21
Driven by a Threat to the Organization's Survival	1996	2.4	28	27	28	12	5
	1999	2.4	28	31	18	20	4

The final question in Table 13.1 asked whether the change effort was driven by threats to the organization's survival. Although this was true to a moderate or greater extent for almost 50 percent of the companies, it is apparently not the most powerful reason for change in many of the companies. Presumably, they are simply changing in order to improve their performance.

Table 13.2 presents the results from questions that asked about how organizational change and improvement efforts are implemented. The first four questions looked at how much integration and consistency existed across initiatives in different parts of the corporation. In both 1996 and 1999, most respondents rejected the view that their change efforts are made up of a series of unrelated initiatives. However, a significant number, 24 percent, do say that their efforts, to a moderate or greater extent, could be characterized as having unrelated initiatives. In reality, this number may be quite a bit higher given the faddism that has surrounded organizational change and the response biases that may exist because senior managers filled out the survey. In many respects, it is somewhat surprising that as many as 24 percent of senior managers would admit that their change efforts have this characteristic, since it is not generally considered a desirable feature.

The next two questions asked about the degree to which change efforts are similar across business units and integrated on a companywide basis. The answers generally indicate that they are moderately integrated companywide; 66 percent of the respondents said that to a

Description of Change Implementation Strategy	Study	Mean (5-point scale)	Little or No Extent	Some Extent	Moderate Extent	Great Extent	Very Great Extent
Made Up of a Series of Unrelated Initiatives	1996	2.0	39	31	17	12	1
	1999	1.9	45	32	14	7	3
Integrated Companywide	1996	3.0	11	26	25	26	11
	1999	2.9	14	19	37	23	6
Occurring Differently in Different Business Units	1996	2.9	13	24	27	30	7
	1999	2.7	13	36	26	21	4
Same No Matter What Country Employees Work In	1996	2.0	51	19	11	13	6
	1999	2.1	45	23	16	11	6
Based on a Bottom-Up Implementation Strategy	1996	2.3	24	36	25	14	1
	1999	2.0	38	32	19	10	1
Led by Top Management	1996	3.9	1	11	18	43	28
	1999	4.0	1	6	22	40	32
Based on a Plan Covering Three or More Years	1996	3.0	20	15	25	26	15
	1999	2.7	29	19	19	19	14

Table 13.2 Percentage of Companies Using Change Implementation Strategies.

moderate or greater extent, the efforts were integrated companywide. But they also indicated that change can occur differently in different business units.

In response to the question concerning a bottom-up implementation strategy, only 30 percent say that such a strategy exists to a moderate or greater extent. These change efforts therefore seem closer to the thinking associated with total quality management and reengineering than to the thinking associated with employee involvement. That is, they are top-down, not bottom-up, participative efforts. It is also noticeable that strategies were less likely to be bottom-up in 1999 than in 1996.

There is a relatively strong trend for companies to say that their efforts are not the same from country to country. For example, 45 percent said that to little or no extent are their efforts the same from country to country. A number of companies also allow variation by business units. Hence many change efforts cannot be categorized as monolithic, top-down, by-the-numbers processes.

Instead, they allow for some variation in how they are implemented and developed throughout large corporations. The trend from 1996 to 1999, although not strong, seems to be in the direction of having more integrated top-down change approaches.

The results show that to a great extent, change efforts are led by top management. Although this doesn't necessarily mean that management has a clear vision of why change is necessary and can articulate this, it does suggest that organizational improvement efforts are getting considerable attention from the top of the organization.

The final question asked about the degree to which the change effort is based on a plan extending three years or more. As in 1996, the distribution of responses for 1999 is rather unusual. Twenty-nine percent said it was basically not true of their organization, while 14 percent said it was true to a very great extent. Perhaps the best way to summarize the responses is to say that companies vary tremendously in the degree to which they have long-range plans concerning their change efforts. Almost an equal number have and do not have them. Given the length of time that it may take to implement large-scale change efforts, we find it a bit surprising that more do not have a three-year or longer plan. Yet in light of the pace of change in the business environment, planning that far ahead can be a difficult and inexact exercise. That is probably why corporations were somewhat less likely to have long-range plans in 1999 than in 1996.

Overall, the change efforts in the Fortune 1000 are similar in some important respects. They tend to be based on a strategy and beliefs about organizational effectiveness. They are not necessarily driven by a threat to the organization's survival, and they are likely to be led by top management. There is variance, however, in how change strategies are implemented and structured within companies.

PART FOUR

Effectiveness

Employee Involvement Effectiveness

When asked, the overwhelming majority of companies responded that their employee involvement efforts are successful. As Table 14.1 indicates, 82 percent indicated that their experience has been positive or very positive, and no company reported a negative experience. This response pattern is virtually identical to the one obtained in 1993 and 1996. This is a very impressive result, particularly the lack of any negative experiences.

Table 14.2 gives information about perceived changes in performance that result from EI efforts. Based on a statistical analysis, we grouped the performance measures into three types of outcomes or factors: direct performance outcomes, profitability and competitiveness, and employee satisfaction and quality of worklife. As with the more global assessments of EI efforts, firms overwhelmingly reported a positive experience for every outcome measured. This is true for 1993, 1996, and 1999.

There is a small tendency for companies to perceive the strongest impact on quality of products and services, customer service, and productivity. It is noteworthy that a relatively large number of respondents (almost one-fifth of the sample) indicated that they were unable to judge the impact of employee involvement efforts on profitability and competitiveness, and a relatively large percentage perceived no impact on these outcomes. Of those reporting either a positive or negative experience, however, most rated it as positive.

Table 14.1	Experience with Employee Involvement Efforts (percentage).		
Experience	1993 (n = 279)	1996 (n = 212)	1999 (n = 143)
Very Negative	0	0	0
Negative	1	3	0
Neither Negative nor Positive	18	16	18
Positive	68	70	72
Very Positive	13	11	10

Table 14.2	Effects of EI on Performance (percentage).							
Effect	Study	Mean (5-point scale)	Very Negative	Negative	Neither Negative nor Positive	Positive	Very Positive	No Basis to Judge
DIRECT PERFORMANCE OUTCOMES								
Productivity	1993	4.1	0	0	5	63	16	17
	1996	4.1	0	1	4	67	18	10
	1999	4.0	0	1	12	58	15	13
Quality of Products or Services	1993	4.2	0	0	4	62	20	14
	1996	4.2	0	1	6	61	24	9
	1999	4.1	0	0	11	61	16	12
Customer Service	1993	4.2	0	0	6	56	22	15
	1996	4.3	0	1	7	51	32	10
	1999	4.2	0	0	9	54	27	11
Speed	1993	4.0	0	0	10	59	13	18
	1996	3.7	0	3	28	41	6	22
	1999	3.5	1	1	35	32	4	26
PROFITABILITY AND COMPETITIVENESS								
Profitability	1993	3.9	0	0	19	51	8	22
	1996	4.0	0	1	15	51	15	19
	1999	3.9	0	1	20	48	14	18
Competitiveness	1993	3.9	0	0	14	57	7	22
	1996	4.0	0	0	17	53	13	17
	1999	3.8	0	1	25	47	8	19
EMPLOYEE SATISFACTION AND QUALITY OF WORKLIFE								
Employee Satisfaction	1993	4.0	0	2	13	59	12	15
	1996	4.1	0	0	10	59	19	13
	1999	4.0	0	1	19	52	17	11
Employee Quality of Worklife	1993	3.9	0	1	15	58	7	19
	1996	4.0	0	1	14	58	12	15
	1999	3.8	1	3	19	48	10	19

Effect	Study	Mean (5-point scale)	Very Negative	Negative	Neither Negative nor Positive	Positive	Very Positive	No Basis to Judge
OTHERS								
Turnover	1996	3.4	0	1	44	21	4	30
	1999	3.4	1	3	46	26	6	19
Absenteeism	1996	3.5	0	0	40	23	4	32
	1999	3.4	1	1	44	24	4	27
Employee Loyalty	1996	3.6	0	2	34	37	6	21
	1999	3.6	0	1	39	35	6	19
Knowledge Development	1999	3.8	1	1	22	50	9	18

Note: Not all questions were asked in all studies.

Table 14.2 also presents data on the impact of EI in four additional areas. In general, it is not seen as having a major positive impact on employee turnover, absenteeism, or loyalty. Interestingly, the results are slightly more positive with respect to knowledge development. Most respondents feel it has a positive or very positive impact.

The results are very similar for 1993, 1996, and 1999. The only significant change is a decrease in the degree to which EI is perceived to have a favorable effect on speed. One possible reason for this is a growing realization in companies of what it takes to compete on the basis of speed and the realization that it may take more than EI practices to achieve world-class performance. It may also reflect the time it takes to make some decisions participatively. Particularly with respect to major decisions, involvement may slow down decision making to an unacceptable degree.

Table 14.3 provides information on how the extent of adoption of employee involvement practices is related to outcome measures, as well as to satisfaction with the overall EI effort. The results for 1993, 1996, and 1999 are quite similar. They show a strong relationship between the degree to which EI practices are adopted and the success of EI efforts. In 1993, 1996, and 1999, the correlations for information sharing, knowledge development, and power sharing are high, while the correlations for rewards are somewhat lower and in some cases not significant. Overall, when it comes to getting positive results from EI efforts, more is clearly better.

		EI OUTCOMES			
EI Practices	**Study**	**Direct Performance Outcomes**[a]	**Profitability and Competitiveness**	**Employee Satisfaction and Quality of Worklife**	**Experience with EI Overall**
Information Index	1993	.29***	.27***	.14*	.23***
	1996	.22**	.23**	.21**	.17*
	1999	.13	.12	.15	.07
Knowledge Index	1993	.31***	.31***	.21**	.31***
	1996	.44***	.38***	.20**	.26***
	1999	.29**	.33***	.27**	.17*
Rewards Index	1993	.17**	.13*	.12	.24***
	1996	.05	.16	.06	.12
	1999	.25*	.38***	.07	.14
Power Index	1993	.22***	.23***	.23***	.39***
	1996	.40***	.37***	.19*	.40***
	1999	.31**	.28**	.24*	.26**
EI Overall	1993	.33***	.28***	.22***	.38***
	1996	.39***	.38***	.26***	.31***
	1999	.31**	.34***	.22*	.22*

Table 14.3 Relationship Between Extent of Adoption of EI Practices and EI Outcomes.

[a]Productivity, customer satisfaction, quality, and speed.
Correlation coefficients: * = weak relationship ($p \leq .05$);
** = moderate relationship ($p \leq .01$);
*** = strong relationship ($p \leq .001$).

Although it is logical to assume that the adoption of more EI practices leads to more positive EI outcomes, it is important to recognize that the causal direction may be the reverse of this. That is, it may be that there is a relationship because when EI activities are successful, companies expand their use of EI practices. In many respects, the best way to think of the relationship between the effectiveness of an EI program and the degree that practices are used may be one of mutual causality. Success leads to more adoption, but more adoption also leads to more success because it creates an organization that has a commitment to employee involvement.

Total Quality Management. We pointed out in Section 1 that although both TQM and EI stress employee involvement as well as training and skills development, there are some key differences between them. The TQM literature attends more to work process and customer outcomes. The EI literature emphasizes the design of work and business units for fuller business involvement and employee motivation. In addition, employee involvement emphasizes making the employee a stakeholder in business performance. EI and TQM practices may contribute to organizational effectiveness in a complementary and reinforcing way so that the presence of one enhances the impact of the other.

Table 14.4 shows the correlations between the use of TQM practices in companies with TQM programs and the company's perceived outcomes from its EI activities. The use of the core TQM practices and of cost of quality is related to the performance and company outcomes of EI in 1993 and 1996 and to a lesser extent in 1999. It is much less strongly related to employee outcomes from EI. The use of the production-oriented TQM practices relates to three kinds of EI outcomes in 1993 and 1996, but it does not relate to employee outcomes in 1996 or 1999. A similar pattern exists for the use of cost-of-quality monitoring. Both the core and the production TQM practices are related to satisfaction with the impact of EI in 1993 and 1996 but not in 1999. Generally, the relationships are stronger in 1993 and 1996 than in 1999. This may reflect change in the use of TQM as it has become more targeted and specialized. Overall, the results suggest that the more organizations use TQM practices, the more positive results they get from EI efforts, particularly with respect to organizational performance outcomes. TQM appears to help EI programs have a more positive impact on organizational performance.

Reengineering. The outcomes of employee involvement programs are significantly correlated with the amount of reengineering practice use in companies with reengineering efforts. As shown in Table 14.5, the work structure and cost reduction practices relate to EI direct performance and profitability outcomes. Not surprisingly, employee satisfaction is unrelated to the use of reengineering practices. A possible explanation for these relationships is that reengineering brings to EI programs a stronger orientation toward performance and the bottom line, as well as practices that are particularly targeted at producing improvements in organizational performance. Thus reengineering serves to facilitate the organizational performance impact of EI programs.

There are no significant relationships between the e-commerce items and the EI outcomes. Apparently, these practices do not make EI efforts more successful despite the potential they have to improve

Table 14.4　Relationship Between Extent of Adoption of TQM Practices and EI Outcomes.

TQM Practices	Study	EI OUTCOMES			
		Direct Performance Outcomes[a]	Profitability and Competitiveness	Employee Satisfaction and Quality of Worklife	Experience with EI Overall
Core TQM Practices	1993	.28***	.27***	.15*	.33***
	1996	.36***	.27**	.07	.29***
	1999	.12	.33**	.11	.11
Production-Oriented Practices	1993	.39***	.26***	.29 ***	.21**
	1996	.40***	.29**	.16	.32***
	1999	.14	.24	−.08	.16
OTHER PRACTICES					
Cost-of-Quality Monitoring	1993	.24***	.26***	.13	.16*
	1996	.40***	.38***	.17	.30***
	1999	.01	.26*	−.05	.18
Collaboration with Suppliers in Quality Efforts	1993	.18*	.11	.10	.25***
	1996	.13	.19	−.08	.20*
	1999	.31*	.32**	.10	.15
Percentage Covered	1993	.30***	.29***	.17**	.40***
	1996	.28***	.30***	.25***	.14
	1999	.15	.13	.07	.24**

[a]Productivity, customer satisfaction, quality, and speed.
Correlation coefficients:　* = weak relationship ($p \leq .05$);
　　** = moderate relationship ($p \leq .01$);
　　*** = strong relationship ($p \leq .001$).

information flow and decision making in organizations. This result may reflect the fact that these e-commerce practices are not being used in a way that facilitates employees' making more decisions and receiving more information.

The relationships between company experience with EI and the adoption of reengineering practices are stronger in 1996 than in 1999. One possible explanation for this is that reengineering programs are increasingly being installed in a way that does not support EI. One clue that this may be occurring is the finding that reengineering practices do not improve employee satisfaction.

Table 14.5 Relationship of EI Outcomes to Reengineering Use.

Reengineering Practices	Study	EI OUTCOMES			
		Direct Performance Outcomes[a]	Profitability and Competitiveness	Employee Satisfaction and Quality of Worklife	Experience with EI Overall
Work Structure	1996	.37***	.31***	.09	.37***
	1999	.16	.24*	.03	−.04
Cost Reduction	1996	.35***	.34***	.03	.29***
	1999	.23*	.26*	−.07	−.02
E-Commerce[b]	1996	—	—	—	—
	1999	.05	.03	−.07	−.06
Percentage Covered	1996	.11	.07	−.10	.13
	1999	.25*	.20*	.06	.09

[a]Productivity, customer satisfaction, quality, and speed.
[b]These questions were not asked in 1996.
Correlation coefficients: * = weak relationship ($p \leq .05$);
** = moderate relationship ($p \leq .01$);
*** = strong relationship ($p \leq .001$).

Knowledge Management. There is an obvious relationship between knowledge management practices and the potential success of employee involvement efforts. Learning and knowledge development are critical elements in most employee involvement programs. Not only are they required so that individuals can do their work better, but they are crucial to the successful implementation and operation of EI activities and programs since they require learning and knowledge management. Hence a relationship should be expected between knowledge management practices and EI outcomes.

Table 14.6 presents the relationships between employee involvement outcomes and knowledge management practices. The correlations are generally positive, and a number of them are significant. The strongest relationships concern rewards for knowledge development and sharing. Apparently, these practices improve the performance outcomes and the profitability and competitiveness outcomes of EI programs. This may well be because they provide a direct reward for behaviors that are needed to make EI programs successful.

The use of communities of practice and rotational assignments also show significant relationships to performance outcomes and profitability and competitiveness outcomes. Again, these are specific

Table 14.6 **Relationship of EI Outcomes to Use of Knowledge Management.**

Knowledge Management Practices	EI OUTCOMES			
	Direct Performance Outcomes[a] 1999	Profitability and Competitveness 1999	Employee Satisfaction and Quality of Worklife 1999	Experience with EI Overall 1999
MANAGEMENT PRACTICES	.17	.26**	.12	.17*
Knowledge-Sharing Conferences	−.01	.07	.05	.08
IT-Enabled Knowledge Storing and Transfer	.07	.14	.04	.08
External and Internal Benchmarking	.12	.18	.12	.23**
Visits to Customers, Suppliers, and Others for Learning	.11	.07	−.01	.18*
Lessons Learned or Postmortem Reviews	.17	.23*	.05	.16
Communities of Practice or Networks	.21*	.22*	.18	.16
Internet Access for Obtaining Information and Knowledge	.15	.15	−.03	−.01
External Partnerships to Develop New Knowledge	.07	.28**	.09	.08
Rotational Assignments for Development	.23*	.29**	.30**	.14
REWARDS	.26**	.36***	.22*	.02
Rewards for Developing Knowledge Assets	.30**	.36***	.22*	−.02
Rewards for Sharing Knowledge	.19	.32***	.18	.06

[a]Productivity, customer satisfaction, quality, and speed.
Correlation coefficients: * = weak relationship ($p \leq .05$);
           ** = moderate relationship ($p \leq .01$);
          *** = strong relationship ($p \leq .001$).

activities that are directly related to the substance of EI programs, so it is not surprising that there is a positive relationship.

Two of the knowledge management practices are related to employee satisfaction. Rewards for developing knowledge and rotational assignments show positive relationships to employee satisfaction. Two knowledge management practices show significant relationships to company experience with EI. Benchmarking and visits are positively related to experience with EI. They obviously have a common element of providing individuals with an opportunity to learn more about how to manage and operate an organization and thus should be helpful in providing individuals with information about what it takes to have a successful EI program.

Overall, the relationship between knowledge management practices and employee involvement activity outcomes is best characterized as positive and in a few cases strong. Perhaps the greatest surprise in the results is that the correlations are not even stronger. Knowledge management practices such as the ones asked about generally seem to be very consistent with what is required to make EI activities successful.

Employment Contract. Table 14.7 shows the relationship between seventeen items concerning the employment contract and four measures of the impact of employee involvement programs. There are a number of statistically significant relationships between the features of the employment contract and the organization's overall experience with EI efforts, as well as with the direct performance and profitability outcomes. There are also some differences between the 1996 results and the 1999 results.

The two contract items concerning continued employment show quite strong relationships. Continued employment based on performance and based on developing skills and knowledge are both associated with the success of EI efforts.

Answers to questions having to do with a traditional loyalty-based employment relationship (tying rewards to seniority, rewarding loyalty, and having a job for life) tend to show little relationship to the success of employee involvement efforts. This finding once again makes the point that successful employee involvement activities do not necessarily require a corporate commitment to long-term or lifetime employment.

Interestingly, rewards tied to individual performance do not show a significant relationship to EI outcomes in either 1996 or 1999, but

Table 14.7 **Relationship of Employment Contract to EI Outcomes.**

Employment Contract	Study	EI OUTCOMES			
		Direct Performance Outcomes[a]	Profitability and Competitiveness	Employee Satisfaction and Quality of Worklife	Experience with EI Overall
Continued Employment Is Based on Performance	1996	.27***	.22**	.02	.09
	1999	.25*	.20*	.09	.18*
Continued Employment Is Based on Continuing to Develop Skills and Knowledge	1996	.46***	.29***	.15*	.34***
	1999	.14	.19	.13	.19*
No One Has a Secure Job	1996	.03	.09	−.12	−.08
	1999	−.11	.10	−.29**	.08
Outstanding Performers Have a Job for Life	1996	.07	.02	.11	.22***
	1999	.02	.02	.12	.12
Rewards Are Tied to Individual Performance	1996	.11	.11	.01	.10
	1999	−.02	.21*	−.05	−.13
Rewards Are Tied to Group or Organization Performance	1996	.22**	.25***	.06	.32***
	1999	.36***	.25**	.08	.24**
Loyalty to the Company Is Rewarded	1996	.13	.01	.11	.11
	1999	−.02	.15	.15	−.05
Rewards Are Tied to Seniority	1996	−.05	−.04	.05	−.03
	1999	−.15	−.16	−.10	−.04
Career Development Is the Responsibility of the Individual	1996	.00	.06	−.05	−.07
	1999	.11	.01	−.17	.13
Employees Are Expected to Manage Their Own Performance with Minimum Supervision	1996	.22**	.19*	.04	.10
	1999	.31**	.18	.17	.14
Contract Fits the Corporate Business Strategy	1996	.30***	.31***	.06	.20**
	1999	.14	.14	.09	.16
Contract Is Understood by Most Employees	1996	.21*	.16	.16*	.11
	1999	.31**	.33***	.27**	.25**
Employees Are Satisfied with the Contract	1996	.21*	.26***	.09	.06
	1999	.13	.21*	.33***	.22**

Table 14.7   (Continued)

| Employment Contract | Study | EI OUTCOMES | | | |
		Direct Performance Outcomes[a]	Profitability and Competitiveness	Employee Satisfaction and Quality of Worklife	Experience with EI Overall
Different Contracts Accommodate Different Types of Employees[b]	1996	—	—	—	—
	1999	−.10	−.16	−.12	−.05
Different Contracts Exist for Temporary and Part-Time Employees[b]	1996	—	—	—	—
	1999	−.05	−.19	−.10	−.15
Contract Supports a Balance Between Work Demands and Personal Life[b]	1996	—	—	—	—
	1999	.05	−.11	.32***	.10
Things Are Changing So Fast, It Is Unclear What the Contract Is	1996	−.05	−.08	−.12	−.17*
	1999	−.11	.03	−.22*	−.08

[a]Productivity, customer satisfaction, quality, and speed.
[b]Not asked in 1996.
Correlation coefficients: * = weak relationship ($p \leq .05$);
                                        ** = moderate relationship ($p \leq .01$);
                                        *** = strong relationship ($p \leq .001$).

when they are tied to group and organizational performance, they do, as would be expected from the EI literature, which stresses collective rewards. Having an employment contract that fits the business strategy (1996 only), satisfies employees, and is understood are also related to the effectiveness of the employee involvement effort. These results fit with the view that EI works when individuals have information about the business, have the power to influence it, and are given rewards based on its success.

A number of the employment contract items are related to employee satisfaction. Not surprisingly, having an employee contract that supports a balance between work and personal life is positively associated with employee satisfaction. Having a well-understood employment contract increases employee satisfaction, as might be expected, since employment contracts help define the relationship employees have with their organization. It also allows individuals to hold an organization accountable for delivering the rewards promised and helps them make intelligent choices about whether to work for a particular organization. Finally, establishing that no one has a secure job is negatively related to employee satisfaction. Again, this is not surprising, since job security is a reward positively valued by many individuals.

Change Strategy. Table 14.8 shows the relationships between the measures of change strategy and the outcomes of employee involvement efforts. Most of the items that are positively related to the performance outcomes can be characterized as direction or consistency items. They indicate that change efforts that are tied to a business strategy, are based on clear beliefs, have mission and values statements, are integrated, are similar across companies, are long-term, and are led by top management tend to have the most successful EI programs. The importance of theme, vision, and mission is further established by the negative correlation with the item asking about unrelated initiatives.

Interestingly, the item that asks about a bottom-up strategy reveals two significant relationships in 1999. It showed no significant relationship in the 1996 study, which led to the conclusion that programs are most successful when they are led from the top, not from the bottom up. The current data reinforce the importance of programs being led by the top but suggest that a bottom-up implementation strategy may also be helpful. Although this sounds contradictory, it is possible to combine leadership at the top, which sets a vision and a direction, with a bottom-up implementation strategy that turns over much of the detailed implementation to the people who are actually going to be affected by the EI practices.

The employee satisfaction and quality-of-worklife outcome is only weakly related to the change strategy measures. The relationship is slightly stronger in 1999 than in 1996. Two items, being guided by a mission statement and being led by top management, show significant relationships.

Conclusion. Overall, the data suggest that organizations are very satisfied with the results of their employee involvement efforts. Such efforts produce significant gains in a number of areas. This is particularly true with respect to such direct performance outcomes as productivity, quality of products, and customer service. These tend to make organizations more competitive and more profitable.

The data also suggest that there a number of factors associated with successful employee involvement efforts. Such efforts are most successful when a package of EI practices are adopted on a broad scale. It is clear that the more EI practices are adopted, the more successful EI efforts are. Employee involvement efforts are also aided by the adoption of other practices. A number of TQM, reengineering, and knowledge management practices were found to be positively associated with the success of employee involvement efforts. This

		EI OUTCOMES			
	Study	Direct Performance Outcomes[a]	Profitability and Competitiveness	Employee Satisfaction and Quality of Worklife	Experience with EI Overall
Characteristics of Change Strategy					
Guided by a Clearly Stated Business Strategy	1996	.24**	.26***	.08	.35***
	1999	.24*	.13	.22*	.14
Guided by Clearly Stated Beliefs About What Makes an Organization Effective	1996	.21**	.24**	.12	.38***
	1999	.19	.07	.15	.17
Guided by Mission and Value Statements	1996	.23**	.29***	.17*	.34***
	1999	.19	.19	.21*	.22**
Driven by a Threat to the Organization's Survival	1996	−.01	−.01	−.04	−.01
	1999	−.01	−.08	−.10	−.11
CHANGE IMPLEMENTATION STRATEGIES					
Made Up of a Series of Unrelated Initiatives	1996	−.07	−.07	−.06	.23***
	1999	.08	.06	.20*	−.08
Integrated Companywide	1996	.12	.24**	.12	.30***
	1999	.11	−.01	.12	.09
Occurring Differently in Different Business Units	1996	.08	.05	−.14	−.01
	1999	−.01	.07	−.05	−.07
Same No Matter What Country Employees Work In	1996	.07	.03	−.03	.03
	1999	.32***	.30**	−.01	.13
Based on a Bottom-Up Implementation Strategy	1996	−.04	.02	−.08	.09
	1999	.29**	.25*	.07	.12
Led by Top Management	1996	.16*	.19*	.11	.28***
	1999	.35***	.23*	.29**	.06
Based on a Plan Covering Three Years or More	1996	.12	.14	.12	.24***
	1999	.03	.04	.16	.12

[a]Productivity, customer satisfaction, quality, and speed.
Correlation coefficients: * = weak relationship ($p \le .05$);
         ** = moderate relationship ($p \le .01$);
         *** = strong relationship ($p \le .001$).

clearly suggests that EI efforts need to be viewed as part of but not necessarily all of an organization's change efforts.

Finally, the data suggest that the employment contract and change strategies that organizations adopt can influence the success of employee involvement efforts. Contracts that are consistent with the spirit of employee involvement tend to be ones that are associated with successful EI efforts. Furthermore, change strategies that are led by top management and have a clear vision statement tend to be associated with successful employee involvement programs. This leads to the obvious conclusion that employee involvement efforts need to be installed in a way that is consistent with the company's values and needs to be in an organization that has a compatible strategy and top management support.

Total Quality Management Effectiveness

In 1999, fully 87 percent of companies with TQM programs reported that their experience has been positive or very positive (see Table 15.1). This level is slightly higher than in 1993 and 1996. Although we should not overinterpret this relatively small increase in satisfaction, it seems to indicate a slight improvement in the perceived effectiveness of TQM programs. It also means that TQM programs now have a slightly higher rating than employee involvement programs (87 percent versus 82 percent, respectively). The use of TQM may be declining, but its impact is very positive among its users.

Table 15.2 shows the perception of the impact of TQM programs on a number of organizational effectiveness outcomes. For 1993,

Table 15.1	Experience with Total Quality Management (percentage).		
Experience	1993 (n = 279)	1996 (n = 212)	1999 (n = 143)
Very Negative	0	0	0
Negative	1	4	1
Neither Negative nor Positive	16	20	12
Positive	66	70	78
Very Positive	17	6	9

Table 15.2

Effects of TQM on Performance (percentage).

Effect	Study	Mean (5-point scale)	Very Negative	Negative	Neither Negative nor Positive	Positive	Very Positive	No Basis to Judge
DIRECT PERFORMANCE OUTCOMES								
Productivity	1993	4.0	0	1	11	66	14	9
	1996	4.0	0	0	14	60	17	9
	1999	4.0	0	0	16	66	13	5
Quality of Products or Services	1993	4.2	0	0	3	69	20	7
	1996	4.2	0	0	5	61	27	7
	1999	4.1	0	0	8	70	20	3
Customer Service	1993	4.2	0	0	3	70	20	8
	1996	4.2	0	0	6	61	28	5
	1999	4.1	0	0	7	70	18	5
Speed	1993	4.0	0	0	9	68	11	12
	1996	3.7	0	2	33	43	7	15
	1999	3.5	0	3	42	39	4	13
PROFITABILITY AND COMPETITIVENESS								
Profitability	1993	3.9	0	0	19	53	10	17
	1996	4.0	0	0	15	63	10	12
	1999	4.0	0	0	13	61	16	10
Competitiveness	1993	4.0	0	0	9	68	9	14
	1996	4.1	0	0	7	66	14	13
	1999	3.9	0	0	18	65	9	8
EMPLOYEE SATISFACTION AND QUALITY OF WORKLIFE								
Employee Satisfaction	1993	3.8	0	1	19	61	6	13
	1996	3.8	0	2	19	60	7	12
	1999	3.8	0	1	25	55	7	13
Employee Quality of Worklife	1993	3.8	0	1	21	56	7	16
	1996	3.7	1	2	23	54	3	18
	1999	3.6	0	1	35	46	5	13

(Continued)

| Table 15.2 | | Effects of TQM on Performance (percentage). (Continued) | | | | | | |

Effect	Study	Mean (5-point scale)	Very Negative	Negative	Neither Negative nor Positive	Positive	Very Positive	No Basis to Judge
OTHERS								
Turnover	1996	3.2	1	0	51	13	2	33
	1999	3.3	0	1	55	25	3	17
Absenteeism	1996	3.2	1	2	48	13	2	35
	1999	3.2	0	1	60	18	1	20
Employee Loyalty	1996	3.4	0	3	42	27	2	25
	1999	3.4	0	3	50	25	5	17
Knowledge Development	1999	3.8	0	0	27	60	5	8

Note: Not all questions were asked in all studies.

1996, and 1999, the results are quite positive and similar. On virtually all of the ratings, at least two-thirds of the respondents indicated that the impact of TQM has been positive, with almost no companies indicating negative effects. A significant number of respondents did report that they could not judge the outcomes. Another small group felt that the impact of TQM was neutral on particular outcomes. It is also worth noting that the results are slightly lower for the two employee outcome items.

The results in 1993, 1996, and 1999 show that corporations perceive TQM's impact to be slightly higher for the direct performance outcomes than for the other groupings. The one area where outcomes decreased in 1999 is speed. Interestingly enough, this is also the only area where ratings for employee involvement decreased significantly. This lends credence to the argument that the decline is due to raising the bar or standard about what constitutes helping with speed in a world where quick action is increasingly important.

Although clearly in the positive range, companies are experiencing slightly less impact on employee satisfaction and worklife quality than on the performance outcomes. This pattern resembles the one found for EI programs, though the results for employee satisfaction are slightly higher for EI. The results for turnover, absenteeism, loyalty, and knowledge development also resemble those for EI.

They are lower than those for other outcomes, and more companies reported that they have no basis to judge how they are affected by TQM efforts.

Table 15.3 shows how the use of specific TQM practices relates to the three kinds of outcomes and to overall satisfaction with TQM. For companies with TQM efforts, the use of core TQM practices is significantly related to direct performance outcomes, company performance, and satisfaction with TQM. It is less strongly related to employee outcomes. The use of production-oriented TQM practices is linked to direct and company performance and to satisfaction with TQM in the 1996 study. It is not significantly related to employee outcomes. The use of the two individual TQM practices, cost-of-quality monitoring and collaboration with suppliers, is related to company performance, direct performance, and satisfaction with TQM in 1996, but the relationship is weaker in 1999.

We also examined whether the percentage of employees covered by TQM efforts relates to the outcomes. The results in Table 15.3 show that the three outcomes and the company's overall satisfaction with TQM are all higher when a greater percentage of employees are covered (1996 only).

The general pattern of results for TQM efforts shows that it is successful and is contributing to company outcomes. This finding is supported by the favorable rating of TQM programs and by the finding that the amount of use of TQM practices is related to company performance. In addition, there is a strong relationship between the use of core and production-oriented practices and two measures of performance: direct performance outcomes and profitability. However, there are few significant relationships with employee outcomes, suggesting that widespread adoption of TQM does not necessarily mean a more satisfying work situation for employees. Also, these relationships are weaker in 1999 than they were in 1993 (not shown) and in 1996. There is no obvious reason why these relationships are lower in 1999.

Employee Involvement. Table 15.4 shows that most of the indices of employee involvement use are related to the TQM outcomes. Power sharing, an emphasis of both TQM and EI, is the EI index that is most strongly related to the employee outcomes of TQM. Rewards, in contrast, are not related to the outcomes of TQM. The relationships with the organizational outcomes are somewhat weaker in 1999 than in 1993 and 1996 but not those associated with employee satisfaction.

Table 15.3 **Relationship of TQM Outcomes to Extent of Adoption of TQM Practices.**

TQM Practices	Study	TQM OUTCOMES			
		Direct Performance Outcomes[a]	Profitability and Competitiveness	Employee Satisfaction and Quality of Worklife	Experience with TQM Overall
CORE PRACTICES OVERALL	1996	.47***	.38***	.22*	.34***
	1999	.28*	.39**	.25*	.20
Quality Improvement Teams	1996	.41***	.36***	.14	.42***
	1999	.41***	.43**	.19	.24*
Quality Councils	1996	.24*	.21*	.15	.14
	1999	.28*	.32**	.23	.28*
Cross-Functional Planning	1996	.35***	.33***	.18	.28**
	1999	.12	.17	.07	−.04
Work Simplification	1996	.37***	.30***	.07	.27**
	1999	.00	.14	.15	.10
Customer Satisfaction Monitoring	1996	.34***	.24**	.16	.21*
	1999	.26*	.31*	.22	.11
Direct Employee Exposure to Customers	1996	.23*	.06	.08	.01
	1999	.08	.10	.19	.04
PRODUCTION-ORIENTED PRACTICES OVERALL	1996	.38***	.40***	.13	.31***
	1999	.16	.17	.07	.09
Self-Inspection	1996	.34***	.36***	.11	.22*
	1999	−.03	.09	.03	.17
Statistical Control Method Used by Front-Line Employees	1996	.28**	.33***	.05	.39***
	1999	.11	.18	−.06	.04
Just-in-Time Deliveries	1996	.31**	.13	.10	.17
	1999	.23	.10	.00	.02
Work Cells or Manufacturing Cells	1996	.36**	.41***	.19	.28**
	1999	.10	.15	.15	.05
OTHER PRACTICES					
Cost-of-Quality Monitoring	1996	.29**	.39***	.12	.35***
	1999	.07	.11	.00	.05

		TQM OUTCOMES			
TQM Practices	Study	Direct Performance Outcomes[a]	Profitability and Competitiveness	Employee Satisfaction and Quality of Worklife	Experience with TQM Overall
Collaboration with Suppliers in Quality Efforts	1996	.34***	.28**	.06	.23**
	1999	.29*	.33**	.12	.11
PERCENTAGE COVERED	1996	.37***	.27**	.19*	.39***
	1999	.22	.16	.12	.17

[a]Productivity, customer satisfaction, quality, and speed.
Correlation coefficients: * = weak relationship ($p \le .05$);
 ** = moderate relationship ($p \le .01$);
 *** = strong relationship ($p \le .001$).

Table 15.3 (Continued)

Overall, the results suggest that the more organizations use EI practices, the more likely they are to have successful TQM programs. This finding is not unexpected: most TQM proponents advocate high levels of employee involvement as a part of their TQM efforts. However, the data do make an important point: the impact of TQM programs that do not include EI practices will be less positive both for employee outcomes and performance outcomes.

Reengineering. Table 15.5 shows the relationship between the TQM outcomes and the use of reengineering. These are consistently positive for three of the four possible outcome areas in 1996, but the relationships are much weaker for 1999. Not surprisingly, employee satisfaction is unrelated to the use of reengineering practices in both 1996 and 1999. The positive relationships are not unexpected, given the complementarity of the change activities that are involved in reengineering and total quality management. As noted in Section 1, both tend to emphasize taking a process orientation, and in many cases both often result in the ability to reduce the number of employees in an organization.

There is no significant relationship between the e-commerce reengineering items and TQM outcomes. The relationships are negative, but none of them reach statistical significance. There is no obvious explanation for why the use of e-commerce practices might have a negative impact on TQM. Since the relationships are generally insignificant, it is probably best to conclude only that e-commerce applications do not improve the effectiveness of total quality management programs. In some respects, this is not surprising, since

| Table 15.4 | Relationship of TQM Outcomes to EI Use. |

		TQM OUTCOMES			
EI Indices	Study	Direct Performance Outcomes[a]	Profitability and Competitiveness	Employee Satisfaction and Quality of Worklife	Experience with TQM Overall
EI Overall	1993	.21**	.29***	.19*	.25***
	1996	.45***	.38***	.24*	.15
	1999	.11	.26*	.33*	.01
Information	1993	.20**	.20**	.13	.14
	1996	.34***	.31***	.24*	.04
	1999	.08	.12	.16	−.07
Knowledge and Skills	1993	.17*	.31***	.20**	.27***
	1996	.40***	.42***	.17	.21*
	1999	.17	.27*	.33**	.12
Rewards	1993	.11	.10	−.01	.10
	1996	.19	.19	.01	−.03
	1999	.10	.17	.09	−.08
Power Sharing	1993	.22**	.33***	.25***	.23***
	1996	.37***	.37***	.26**	.37***
	1999	.02	.09	.33*	.14

[a]Productivity, customer satisfaction, quality, and speed.
Correlation coefficients: * = weak relationship ($p \leq .05$);
** = moderate relationship ($p \leq .01$);
*** = strong relationship ($p \leq .001$).

they are generally unrelated except for their focus on lateral process and moving information efficiently.

Knowledge Management. Table 15.6 shows relationships between the use of knowledge management practices and total quality management outcomes. All but three of the relationships are nonsignificant, and one of the significant relationships is negative. There is some support for knowledge management supporting TQM in the case of lessons learned and access to the Internet, which show significant relationships to TQM outcomes. However, the data do not show that most knowledge management practices are significantly related to the effectiveness of TQM programs. Hence it appears that adopting knowledge management practices does little to make total quality programs more effective. This is a

| Table 15.5 | Relationship of TQM Outcomes to Reengineering Use. |

| | | TQM OUTCOMES | | | |
Reengineering Indices	Study	Direct Performance Outcomes[a]	Profitability and Competitiveness	Employee Satisfaction and Quality of Worklife	Experience with TQM Overall
Work Structure	1996	.34***	.39***	−.01	.22*
	1999	.08	.08	−.11	.07
Cost Reduction	1996	.26*	.36***	.03	.29**
	1999	−.03	−.01	−.19	−.13
E-Commerce[b]	1996	—	—	—	—
	1999	−.12	−.07	−.21	−.05
Percentage Covered	1996	.15	.06	−.07	.10
	1999	.14	.26*	.13	.02

[a]Productivity, customer satisfaction, quality, and speed.
[b]These questions were not asked in 1996.
Correlation coefficients: * = weak relationship ($p \leq .05$);
** = moderate relationship ($p \leq .01$);
*** = strong relationship ($p \leq .001$).

somewhat surprising outcome, since total quality management programs emphasize the importance of knowledge development and sharing and organizations need to develop knowledge about how to run TQM practices.

Employment Contract. Table 15.7 presents the results for the relationship between the employment contract and total quality management outcomes. Particularly in 1996, positive relationships exist with employment contracts that emphasize performance and the development of skills and knowledge. Having employment contracts that fit the business strategy and satisfy employees is also a positive.

An employee contract that supports a balance between work and personal life demands has a positive relationship to performance outcomes and profitability. It also has a positive but not significant relationship to company experience with total quality management overall. The findings offer support for the argument that providing a balance between work and personal life can be good for both the employee and the organization, at least when they are engaged in a major change like installing a total quality program.

Two items have a negative relationship with satisfaction and quality of worklife: no one has a secure job, and it is not clear what the

Table 15.6 **Relationship of TQM Outcomes to Use of Knowledge Management.**

Knowledge Management Practices	TQM OUTCOMES			
	Direct Performance Outcomes[a] 1999	Profitability and Competitiveness 1999	Employee Satisfaction and Quality of Worklife 1999	Experience with TQM Overall 1999
MANAGEMENT PRACTICES	.12	.15	−.12	.02
Knowledge-Sharing Conferences	.08	−.04	−.20	.06
IT-Enabled Knowledge Storing and Transfer	−.03	.01	−.24	−.23*
External and Internal Benchmarking	.11	.17	−.23	.05
Visits to Customers, Suppliers, and Others for Learning	.03	.11	−.17	.04
Lessons Learned or Postmortem Reviews	.21	.25*	.01	.22
Communities of Practice or Networks	.12	.18	−.01	.09
Internet Access for Obtaining Information and Knowledge	.19	.28*	.08	.03
External Partnerships to Develop New Knowledge	.13	.05	−.09	.03
Rotational Assignments for Development	.04	.14	.03	.06
REWARDS	.12	.05	.08	−.04
Rewards for Developing Knowledge Assets	.15	.09	.10	−.04
Rewards for Sharing Knowledge	.06	.01	.04	−.04

[a]Productivity, customer satisfaction, quality, and speed.
Correlation coefficients: * = weak relationship ($p \leq .05$);
      ** = moderate relationship ($p \leq .01$);
    *** = strong relationship ($p \leq .001$).

Table 15.7 **Relationship of Employment Contract to TQM Outcomes.**

Employment Contract	Study	TQM OUTCOMES			
		Direct Performance Outcomes[a]	Profitability and Competitiveness	Employee Satisfaction and Quality of Worklife	Experience with TQM Overall
Continued Employment Is Based on Performance	1996	.23*	.24*	.04	.10
	1999	.14	.16	−.03	.01
Continued Employment Is Based on Continuing to Develop Skills and Knowledge	1996	.24*	.38***	.02	.16
	1999	.10	.13	−.07	.00
No One Has a Secure Job	1996	−.02	−.05	−.27**	−.31***
	1999	−.13	.09	−.01	−.14
Outstanding Performers Have a Job for Life	1996	.00	−.11	.27**	.23**
	1999	.19	.16	.11	.22
Rewards Are Tied to Individual Performance	1996	.11	.21*	.18	.08
	1999	.03	.16	−.09	−.04
Rewards Are Tied to Group or Organization Performance	1996	.02	.05	.02	.03
	1999	.08	.10	.21	.07
Loyalty to the Company Is Rewarded	1996	.12	.07	.17	.16
	1999	.16	.22	.29*	.12
Rewards Are Tied to Seniority	1996	−.10	−.08	.04	.05
	1999	.15	.00	.05	.11
Career Development Is the Responsibility of the Individual	1996	.19	.09	−.08	−.05
	1999	.03	.13	−.01	.04
Employees Are Expected to Manage Their Own Performance with Minimum Supervision	1996	.10	.08	−.15	-.03
	1999	−.04	−.02	.08	.01
Contract Fits the Corporate Business Strategy	1996	.33***	.27**	.10	.16
	1999	−.01	.18	.04	.03

(Continued)

Table 15.7 Relationship of Employment Contract to TQM Outcomes. (Continued).

Employment Contract	Study	TQM OUTCOMES			
		Direct Performance Outcomes[a]	Profitability and Competitiveness	Employee Satisfaction and Quality of Worklife	Experience with TQM Overall
Contract Is Understood by Most Employees	1996	.26**	.17	.07	.09
	1999	.06	.16	.10	.07
Employees Are Satisfied with the Contract	1996	.20*	.21*	.05	.08
	1999	−.01	.12	.09	.09
Different Contracts Accommodate Different Types of Employees[b]	1996	—	—	—	—
	1999	−.16	−.08	−.12	.03
Different Contracts Exist for Temporary and Part-Time Employees[b]	1996	—	—	—	—
	1999	.06	.06	−.12	.05
Contract Supports a Balance Between Work Demands and Personal Life[b]	1996	—	—	—	—
	1999	.31*	.28*	.25	.19
Things Are Changing So Fast, It Is Unclear What the Contract Is	1996	−.22*	−.16	−.24*	−.18*
	1999	−.18	−.09	−.13	−.13

[a]Productivity, customer satisfaction, quality, and speed.
[b]These questions were not asked in 1996.
Correlation coefficients: * = weak relationship ($p \leq .05$);
** = moderate relationship ($p \leq .01$);
*** = strong relationship ($p \leq .001$).

contract is. These two items are also negatively related to organizations having a positive experience with their TQM programs. Apparently, at least with respect to total quality management efforts, the lack of a clear employment contract and job security is a significant negative. This finding, of course, fits with the literature on TQM, which emphasizes not blaming individuals and making them feel secure.

Change Strategy. Table 15.8 shows the relationship between total quality management outcomes and change strategy. The strongest relationships are all in 1996 and are with the items concerning direction. TQM programs are regarded as successful when they have a clear sense of direction that is integrated companywide and is tied to the business strategy. There is also a significant relationship between two of the outcome measures and the item asking about having a plan covering three years or more.

| Table 15.8 | Relationship of Change Strategy to TQM Outcomes. |

		TQM OUTCOMES			
	Study	Direct Performance Outcomes[a]	Profitability and Competitiveness	Employee Satisfaction and Quality of Worklife	Experience with TQM Overall
CHARACTERISTICS OF CHANGE STRATEGY					
Guided by a Clearly Stated Business Strategy	1996	.31***	.35***	.18	.11
	1999	.14	.22	.11	.19
Guided by Clearly Stated Beliefs About What Makes an Organization Effective	1996	.26**	.29**	.27**	.25**
	1999	.15	.12	−.03	.13
Guided by Mission and Value Statements	1996	.32***	.25**	.25**	.27**
	1999	.17	.13	.19	.18
Driven by a Threat to the Organization's Survival	1996	.05	−.05	.17	.05
	1999	.03	−.12	.05	−.02
CHANGE IMPLEMENTATION STRATEGIES					
Made Up of a Series of Unrelated Initiatives	1996	−.16	−.15	−.18	−.13
	1999	−.03	.03	−.01	−.14
Integrated Company-wide	1996	.27**	.28**	.08	.22*
	1999	.10	.01	−.00	.01
Occurring Differently in Different Business Units	1996	−.11	−.04	−.15	−.05
	1999	−.07	.01	−.11	−.11
Same No Matter What Country Employees Work In	1996	.17	.11	.19	.15
	1999	.08	.01	−.01	−.07
Based on a Bottom-Up Implementation Strategy	1996	.02	.07	−.03	.06
	1999	−.01	.11	−.01	.17
Led by Top Management	1996	.17	.14	.11	.21*
	1999	.15	.14	.22	.06
Based on a Plan Covering Three Years or More	1996	.19	.20*	.18	.25**
	1999	.13	.14	.16	.06

[a]Productivity, customer satisfaction, quality, and speed.
Correlation coefficients: * = weak relationship ($p \leq .05$);
    ** = moderate relationship ($p \leq .01$);
  *** = strong relationship ($p \leq .001$).

Conclusion. Overall, the results with respect to total quality management are very positive. Companies are clearly are satisfied users of TQM programs. It is also clear that the more organizations adopt such practices, the better results they achieve. In the 1993 and 1996 data, it is also clear that adopting employee involvement practices and reengineering practices contributed significantly to the success of TQM. This is not clear in the 1999 data. The data also do not provide strong support for the contention that knowledge management practices are helpful in making total quality management programs successful. Finally, the results with respect to the employment contract and change strategy show that in 1999 there was little relationship between them and the outcomes of total quality management programs. This is a noticeable contrast to the data for 1996 and 1993.

In general, the 1999 data concerning factors related to the effectiveness of TQM gave results in the same general direction as the 1996 data, but fewer of the relationships achieved statistical significance. This is a surprising and difficult result to explain. It may have something to do with the maturity of total quality management programs, which by 1999 had often been in place for a number of years. It is possible that at the beginning of TQM efforts, non-TQM activities and practices are more important in influencing the success of TQM efforts than they are as TQM efforts mature. It is also important to note that by 1999, fewer companies had TQM efforts, so there is a change in the nature of the sample of companies that was studied.

SECTION 16

Process Reengineering Results

Reengineering became a widely used approach to improving organizational effectiveness during the 1990s, as the results presented in Section 8 clearly show. Perhaps because of its popularity, it is often accused of being faddish and potentially damaging to companies and individuals. Our data do not support this accusation.

The results in Table 16.1 show that reengineering efforts are in fact viewed positively. In 1996, only 7 percent of the companies said that their experience was negative, while 66 percent rated it positive or very positive. This is a high endorsement level but lower than the ratings obtained for TQM (76 percent) and employee involvement programs (81 percent) in the same year.

The results of the 1999 survey are even more positive; indeed, they are very similar to the results for TQM and employee involvement, with

Table 16.1	Experience with Process Reengineering Efforts (percentage).	
Experience	1996 (n = 212)	1999 (n = 143)
Very Negative	1	0
Negative	6	4
Neither Negative nor Positive	28	18
Positive	61	72
Very Positive	5	7

80 percent of the respondents saying that they have had a positive experience with reengineering. There is no testable explanation in our data for why the results were more positive in 1999 than in 1996. It may be due to the shift of reengineering away from reducing staff and restructuring work toward the installation of computer-based information systems and lateral processes that focus on e-commerce and the Web.

Table 16.2 helps establish the relative strengths and weaknesses of process reengineering efforts. The employee satisfaction and quality-of-worklife items tend to show neutral to slightly negative results. So unlike EI and TQM efforts, reengineering efforts often do not have a positive impact on employees and in about 20 percent of the cases have a negative impact on the human side of the enterprise. Consistent with this are the relatively negative results for turnover, absenteeism, and loyalty. The results for the direct performance outcomes and the profitability and competitiveness outcomes are strikingly different from those for the employee and other outcomes; they are overwhelmingly positive. For example, 91 percent of the respondents reported positive results in the area of productivity. The quality of products and services was seen as improved by 71 percent of the respondents. Improved profitability was reported by 76 percent of the respondents. Finally, 61 percent perceived increases in speed and 78 percent in competitiveness. Overall, the results show a mixed impact for process reengineering: a very positive impact on operational results, competitiveness and profitability and a much less positive impact on employees.

A comparison between the 1999 and 1996 data shows a great deal of similarity, with the 1999 results being slightly more positive. This fits with the earlier result of reengineering programs being rated

Table 16.2 **Effects of Reengineering on Performance (percentage).**

Effect	Study	Mean (5-point scale)	Very Negative	Nega-tive	Neither Negative Nor Positive	Positive	Very Positive	No Basis to Judge
DIRECT PERFORMANCE OUTCOMES								
Productivity	1996	4.0	0	2	11	68	11	9
	1999	4.1	0	2	4	75	16	4
Quality of Products or Services	1996	3.8	1	1	22	58	10	10
	1999	3.8	0	2	23	64	7	5
Customer Service	1996	3.9	0	2	19	56	15	8
	1999	4.0	0	2	9	67	17	5
Speed	1996	3.9	0	3	21	50	16	11
	1999	3.7	0	3	29	52	9	7
PROFITABILITY AND COMPETITIVENESS								
Profitability	1996	4.0	0	1	15	58	16	9
	1999	4.0	0	1	15	64	12	8
Competitiveness	1996	4.0	0	1	13	63	12	12
	1999	4.0	0	1	12	66	12	9
EMPLOYEE SATISFACTION AND QUALITY OF WORKLIFE								
Employee Satisfaction	1996	3.2	1	20	36	32	1	11
	1999	3.4	0	12	29	41	2	16
Employee Quality of Worklife	1996	3.1	1	17	39	23	3	18
	1999	3.3	1	8	49	22	4	17
OTHERS								
Turnover	1996	3.0	0	10	56	10	0	25
	1999	3.1	1	9	53	18	0	19
Absenteeism	1996	3.0	2	2	56	7	1	33
	1999	3.1	1	7	56	15	0	22
Employee Loyalty	1996	2.9	4	16	44	12	1	24
	1999	3.1	2	7	51	20	0	22
Knowledge Development	1999	3.7	0	3	29	52	4	12

Note: Not all questions were asked in all studies.

more positively overall in 1999. One area where the results are somewhat lower is speed. Like employee involvement and total quality management, this rating drop may reflect higher standards for speed in 1999.

Table 16.3 shows the relationship between the amount of adoption of reengineering practices and the outcomes from reengineering. The work restructuring practices generally show strong relationships to the direct performance outcomes and to profitability and competitiveness. They are also quite strongly related to satisfaction with the reengineering effort overall. Their relationships with employee satisfaction and quality of worklife are significant but slightly lower.

There is one interesting difference between the 1996 and 1999 data. Major information system redesign is positively related to outcomes in 1996 but not in 1999. This finding may reflect the fact the many of the large ERP and other information system redesign efforts that were begun in the mid-1990s ended up being problematic and failed to live up to expectations. Overall, the work-restructuring practices show a strong relationship to the outcomes of reengineering efforts. Greater use of them results in more positive employee outcomes and greater organizational effectiveness.

The cost reduction practices associated with reengineering show generally positive relationships to the direct performance outcomes and to profitability and competitiveness. They show a somewhat weaker relationship to satisfaction with the reengineering effort overall. The lower correlation of overall satisfaction with reengineering may well reflect the lack of a positive relationship between the adoption of these practices and employee satisfaction and quality of worklife. It is clear from the correlations involving employee satisfaction and worklife quality that doing more work (or even the same work) with fewer people or less supervision is not associated with positive outcomes for employees and in fact may lead to negative outcomes.

The results for e-commerce show a positive but often not significant relationship between the adoption of e-commerce practices and the outcomes of reengineering efforts. Electronic transactions with suppliers and customers are both positively related to profitability and competitiveness. Similarly, electronic transactions with customers are positively related to experience with reengineering overall. None of the other relationships in the table are significant. Thus the results do not make a strong case for e-commerce contributing to the effectiveness of reengineering efforts.

Table 16.3 — Relationship Between Extent of Adoption of Reengineering Practices and Reengineering Outcomes.

Reengineering Practices	Study	REENGINEERING OUTCOMES			
		Direct Performance Outcomes[a]	Profitability and Competitiveness	Employee Satisfaction and Quality of Worklife	Experience with Reengineering Overall
WORK STRUCTURE	1996	.58***	.52***	.34***	.48***
	1999	.37***	.35***	.26*	.35***
Process Simplification	1996	.58***	.42***	.27**	.49***
	1999	.36***	.34***	.21	.28**
Creation of Cross-Functional Units	1996	.43***	.42***	.29***	.38***
	1999	.25*	.29**	.12	.32***
Major Information System Redesign	1996	.38***	.30***	.19*	.24**
	1999	.03	.01	−.01	.06
Enriched Multi-skilled Individual Jobs	1996	.43***	.31***	.26**	.35***
	1999	.38***	.26*	.27*	.29**
Multiskilled Teams	1996	.45***	.40***	.32***	.38***
	1999	.32***	.34***	.26*	.31***
COST REDUCTION	1996	.31***	.43***	.05	.27***
	1999	.14	.23*	−.04	.18
Doing Same Work with Fewer People	1996	.29***	.34***	−.04	.16*
	1999	−.03	−.01	−.27*	−.04
Doing Same Work with Less Supervision	1996	.21*	.34***	.04	.22**
	1999	.09	.14	.01	.16
Lower Overall Cost Structure	1996	.33***	.45***	.13	.33***
	1999	.29**	.46***	.17	.34***
E-COMMERCE[b]	1996	—	—	—	—
	1999	.10	.18	.04	.20
Installation of an Enterprise Resource Planning (ERP) System[b]	1996	—	—	—	—
	1999	−.06	.01	.05	.11
Electronic Transactions with Suppliers[b]	1996	—	—	—	—
	1999	.12	.25*	.11	.15

Table 16.3 (Continued)

Reengineering Practices	Study	REENGINEERING OUTCOMES			
		Direct Performance Outcomes[a]	Profitability and Competitiveness	Employee Satisfaction and Quality of Worklife	Experience with Reengineering Overall
Electronic Transactions with Customers[b]	1996	—	—	—	—
	1999	.19	.20	−.05	.22*
PERCENTAGE COVERED	1996	.23**	.24**	.11	.19*
	1999	.25*	.22*	.02	.06

[a]Productivity, customer satisfaction, quality, and speed.
[b]These questions were not asked in 1996.
Correlation coefficients: * = weak relationship ($p \leq .05$);
** = moderate relationship ($p \leq .01$);
*** = strong relationship ($p \leq .001$).

The results showing the relationship between the percentage of employees covered and the outcomes of reengineering are similar to those found for cost reduction. Covering a greater percentage of the employees contributes positively to direct performance outcomes and profitability and competitiveness but not to employee satisfaction and quality of worklife. Overall, these results are consistent with the general impact of reengineering reported in Table 16.2. Reengineering has many benefits for the performance of organizations, but its impact on employees is not necessarily positive.

Given these results, we find it hardly surprising that reengineering is both popular and controversial. An organizational change effort that corporations view as producing very positive results for company performance but as having a negative or neutral impact on employees is bound to be controversial. Indeed, our results may understate the seriousness of reengineering's negative impact on employees, since we received our answers from senior managers in the corporations, and they may not be as aware of all the negative human resource impacts of reengineering as employees at lower levels in the organization may be. If we had talked to the rank-and-file employees in these companies, we might have gotten more negative ratings for reengineering. However, the data did frequently come from human resource executives, who ought to have at least some awareness of how the practices are affecting most of a firm's employees.

Employee Involvement. With the significant differences in orientation that exist between employee involvement and reengineering, it is an open question as to how the presence of employee involvement practices will affect the effectiveness of reengineering. Table 16.4 shows that the presence of EI practices is associated with more positive outcomes from reengineering efforts in 1996 but is not as strongly related in 1999. Power sharing is the employee involvement practice that is most strongly related to reengineering outcomes.

Although the relationships in Table 16.4 are not exceptionally strong, they do indicate that to some degree, EI practices can improve the effectiveness of reengineering programs. This may well come about because EI deals with some of the employee issues that many reengineering programs neglect. Thus the use of EI activities may help improve the impact of reengineering programs on employees and organizational effectiveness.

Total Quality Management. Table 16.5 looks at the relationship between reengineering outcomes and the use of TQM practices.

Table 16.4 Relationship of Reengineering Outcomes to Employee Involvement.

		REENGINEERING OUTCOMES			
EI Indices	Study	Direct Performance Outcomes[a]	Profitability and Competitiveness	Employee Satisfaction and Quality of Worklife	Experience with Reengineering Overall
EI Overall	1996	.27**	.26**	.21*	.13
	1999	.09	.10	.20	.16
Information	1996	.18*	.12	.02	.04
	1999	−.02	−.03	.06	.03
Knowledge and Skills	1996	.24**	.22**	.28***	.16*
	1999	.09	.00	.21	.11
Rewards	1996	.08	.11	.08	−.03
	1999	.10	.13	.13	.17
Power Sharing	1996	.25**	.29***	.26**	.22**
	1999	.09	.12	.23*	.18

[a]Productivity, customer satisfaction, quality, and speed.
Correlation coefficients: * = weak relationship ($p \leq .05$);
** = moderate relationship ($p \leq .01$);
*** = strong relationship ($p \leq .001$).

Table 16.5 **Relationship of Reengineering Outcomes to Use of TQM Practices.**

| TQM Practices | Study | REENGINEERING OUTCOMES | | | |
		Direct Performance Outcomes[a]	Profitability and Competitiveness	Employee Satisfaction and Quality of Worklife	Experience with Reengineering Overall
Core Practices Overall	1996	.33**	.41***	−.01	.17
	1999	.36**	.17	.33*	.32**
Production-Oriented Practices Overall	1996	.33**	.37***	.23*	.15
	1999	.42***	.10	.26	.25*
OTHER PRACTICES					
Cost-of-Quality Monitoring	1996	.16	.32**	.01	.22*
	1999	.27*	.01	.30*	.26*
Collaboration with Suppliers in Quality Efforts	1996	.26*	.36***	−.04	.18
	1999	.26*	.18	.18	.22
Percentage Covered	1996	.15	.05	.23**	.05
	1999	−.08	−.21*	−.04	−.19*

[a]Productivity, customer satisfaction, quality, and speed.
Correlation coefficients: * = weak relationship ($p \leq .05$);
                            ** = moderate relationship ($p \leq .01$);
                            *** = strong relationship ($p \leq .001$).

In both 1996 and 1999, there were generally positive relationships between the use of TQM practices and the effectiveness of reengineering programs. This is particularly true when the focus is on reengineering's direct performance outcomes and its profitability and competitiveness outcomes (1996 only). There is some relationship between the adoption of TQM practices and the impact of reengineering on employee satisfaction and quality of worklife. This suggests that at least to some degree, the use of quality management practices such as work simplification and self-inspection can make reengineering a positive experience for employees.

Knowledge Management. The relationship between knowledge management practices and reengineering outcomes was studied for the first time in 1999. The results presented in Table 16.6 show generally positive but weak relationships. Rewards for developing knowledge, rotational assignments for development, and reviews of

Table 16.6	Relationship of Reengineering Outcomes to Use of Knowledge Management.

	REENGINEERING OUTCOMES			
Knowledge Management Practices	Direct Performance Outcomes[a] 1999	Profitability and Competitiveness 1999	Employee Satisfaction and Quality of Worklife 1999	Experience with Reengineering Overall 1999
MANAGEMENT PRACTICES	.13	.11	.10	.17
Knowledge-Sharing Conferences	.07	.03	.03	.10
IT-Enabled Knowledge Storing and Transfer	.11	.06	.03	.02
External and Internal Benchmarking	−.04	−.01	−.00	−.03
Visits to Customers, Suppliers, and Others for Learning	.03	.00	−.11	.05
Lessons Learned or Postmortem Reviews	.06	.19	.18	.27**
Communities of Practice or Networks	.17	.07	.19	.19
Internet Access for Obtaining Information and Knowledge	.12	.05	−.07	.05
External Partnerships to Develop New Knowledge	.08	.12	.11	.16
Rotational Assignments for Development	.23*	.17	.23*	.24*
REWARDS	.18	.10	.16	.22*
Rewards for Developing Knowledge Assets	.22*	.13	.12	.25*
Rewards for Sharing Knowledge	.11	.05	.18	.16

[a]Productivity, customer satisfaction, quality, and speed.
Correlation coefficients: * = weak relationship ($p \leq .05$);
** = moderate relationship ($p \leq .01$);
*** = strong relationship ($p \leq .001$).

lessons learned all show a positive relationship to one or more of the outcomes of reengineering efforts. The relationships, however, are not strong, implying that knowledge management most likely does have a big impact on the outcomes produced by reengineering efforts.

Employment Contract. Table 16.7 looks at the relationship between the employment contract and reengineering outcomes. In 1996, there was little relationship between the success of reengineering and the nature of the employment contract. The relationships that do exist are relatively similar to those for EI and TQM. For example, tying rewards to group or organizational performance is significantly related to reengineering outcomes and is also related to the success of EI programs.

The results for 1999 are in the same general direction as those for 1996 but in some cases considerably stronger. The items concerned with the nature of the employment contract, such as whether it fits with business strategies, whether it is understood, and whether people are satisfied with it, show consistent relationships to the success of reengineering programs. Tying rewards to group or organization performance is also strongly related to three of the four outcomes of reengineering programs. It is related particularly strongly to an organization's experience with respect to reengineering efforts.

Overall, the data suggest that having an employment contract that supports a reengineering program can help the reengineering program succeed. Specifically, it suggests that an employment contract that rewards group performance is well understood and articulated, and relates to the business strategy is likely to have a favorable impact on the outcomes of reengineering efforts.

Change Strategy. The results for reengineering outcomes and change strategy are presented in Table 16.8. The 1996 data consistently support the view that reengineering is more successful when the change strategy has a sense of direction and top management leadership. The results from 1999 generally tend to be in the same direction, but many of relationships that were statistically significant in 1996 are not significant in 1999. One relationship that clearly holds up is leadership by top management, which shows an even stronger correlation in 1999 than it did in 1996. Thus we have consistent evidence that it is important to have a change effort that is led by top management. It also appears to be important that it be similar in different business units. Occurring differently in different business units has a significant negative correlation with experience with reengineering efforts.

Table 16.7 **Relationship of Employment Contract to Reengineering Outcomes.**

Employment Contract	Study	REENGINEERING OUTCOMES			
		Direct Performance Outcomes[a]	Profitability and Competitiveness	Employee Satisfaction and Quality of Worklife	Experience with Reengineering Overall
Continued Employment Is Based on Performance	1996	.18*	.17*	−.01	.07
	1999	.06	.06	.26*	.24*
Continued Employment Is Based on Continuing to Develop Skills and Knowledge	1996	.21*	.10	.11	.14
	1999	.03	−.03	.33**	.19*
No One Has a Secure Job	1996	.23**	.05	−.07	.05
	1999	.03	.05	−.12	.05
Outstanding Performers Have a Job for Life	1996	.04	.10	.08	.07
	1999	−.07	−.01	−.04	−.07
Rewards Are Tied to Individual Performance	1996	.08	.07	−.04	−.09
	1999	.03	.12	.08	.09
Rewards Are Tied to Group or Organization Performance	1996	.19*	.16*	.18*	.19*
	1999	.16	.21*	.29**	.41***
Loyalty to the Company Is Rewarded	1996	−.03	−.06	.18*	.04
	1999	.00	.12	−.02	−.01
Rewards Are Tied to Seniority	1996	−.05	−.03	.01	.01
	1999	−.06	−.16	−.17	−.09
Career Development Is the Responsibility of the Individual	1996	.11	.02	−.06	−.11
	1999	−.02	−.03	−.03	.06
Employees Are Expected to Manage Their Own Performance with Minimum Supervision	1996	−.03	−.03	−.02	.03
	1999	.10	.06	−.01	.22*
Contract Fits the Corporate Business Strategy	1996	.15	.17*	.09	.11
	1999	.17	.24*	.21	.32***
Contract Is Understood by Most Employees	1996	.13	.17*	.02	.04
	1999	.24*	.23*	.14	.32***
Employees Are Satisfied with the Contract	1996	.14	.11	.18*	.03
	1999	.29**	.28**	.25*	.28**

		REENGINEERING OUTCOMES			
Employment Contract	Study	Direct Performance Outcomes[a]	Profitability and Competitiveness	Employee Satisfaction and Quality of Worklife	Experience with Reengineering Overall
Different Contracts Accommodate Different Types of Employees[b]	1996	—	—	—	—
	1999	−.06	−.02	−.08	−.06
Different Contracts Exist for Temporary and Part-Time Employees[b]	1996	—	—	—	—
	1999	−.08	.02	−.27*	−.06
Contract Supports a Balance Between Work Demands and Personal Life[b]	1996	—	—	—	—
	1999	.08	.08	.19	.16
Things Are Changing So Fast, It Is Unclear What the Contract Is	1996	−.10	−.11	−.10	−.03
	1999	−.06	−.02	−.14	−.18

[a]Productivity, customer satisfaction, quality, and speed.
[b]Not asked in 1996.
Correlation coefficients: * = weak relationship ($p \leq .05$);
** = moderate relationship ($p \leq .01$);
*** = strong relationship ($p \leq .001$).

Conclusion. The results support the conclusion that reengineering efforts are generally successful. Indeed, the assessment of them is more positive in 1999 than it was in 1996. Reengineering has a particularly favorable impact on productivity, competitiveness, and profitability. The results are more mixed with respect to cost reduction. The 1996 data argue strongly that the use of more cost reduction practices leads to better outcomes from reengineering programs, but the results for 1999 are not as strong. The results also strongly argue that more is better with respect to the use of work structure practices.

The 1999 data show little relationship between the adoption of EI practices and the success of reengineering efforts except with respect to employee outcomes. The results are more positive for TQM practices. The adoption of some TQM practices is positively related to the success of reengineering efforts. The same conclusion applies to the use of knowledge management, in some cases, it too helps make reengineering more successful.

Having an employment contract that is understood by employees, fits the business strategy, and satisfies the employees is associated

| Table 16.8 | Relationship of Change Strategy to Reengineering Outcomes. |

		REENGINEERING OUTCOMES			
	Study	Direct Performance Outcomes[a]	Profitability and Competitiveness	Employee Satisfaction and Quality of Worklife	Experience with Reengineering Overall
CHARACTERISTICS OF CHANGE STRATEGY					
Guided by a Clearly Stated Business Strategy	1996	.28***	.33***	.01	.30***
	1999	.15	.10	.10	.05
Guided by Clearly Stated Beliefs About What Makes an Organization Effective	1996	.26**	.35***	.13	.30***
	1999	.19	.05	.21	.07
Guided by Mission and Value Statements	1996	.21*	.17*	.13	.23**
	1999	.13	.13	.23*	.14
Driven by a Threat to the Organization's Survival	1996	.07	.12	−.07	.13
	1999	.00	−.12	.04	−.11
CHANGE IMPLEMENTATION STRATEGIES					
Made Up of a Series of Unrelated Initiatives	1996	−.19*	−.30***	−.03	−.20**
	1999	.11	.03	−.06	−.04
Integrated Companywide	1996	.24**	.27***	.09	.24***
	1999	.24*	.12	.19	.07
Occurring Differently in Different Business Units	1996	.03	−.06	−.06	−.02
	1999	−.19	−.20	−.12	−.28**
Same No Matter What Country Employees Work In	1996	−.00	−.03	−.11	.05
	1999	.28**	.21*	.09	.28**
Based on a Bottom-Up Implementation Strategy	1996	.17*	.10	.20*	.29***
	1999	.03	.15	.13	.17
Led by Top Management	1996	.35***	.33***	.08	.22**
	1999	.37***	.34***	.31**	.27**
Based on a Plan Covering Three Year Plans or More	1996	.13	.15	−.02	.16*
	1999	−.05	−.07	−.07	−.02

[a]Productivity, customer satisfaction, quality, and speed.
Correlation coefficients: * = weak relationship ($p \leq .05$);
** = moderate relationship ($p \leq .01$);
*** = strong relationship ($p \leq .001$).

with the success of reengineering efforts. Finally, certain change strategies also tend to be associated with the success of reengineering. The strongest relationship here involves the degree to which the change effort is led by top management. Having top management leadership is strongly associated with the success of reengineering efforts.

SECTION 17

Knowledge Management Effectiveness

The knowledge management efforts of most corporations are relatively new and still evolving. Little research has been done on their effectiveness, their impact on organizational performance, or even the perceived effectiveness of knowledge management efforts.

Table 17.1 presents the overall assessment of knowledge management activities in our 1999 sample of Fortune 1000 companies. It shows a very large number of companies taking a neutral position with respect to their knowledge management activities. Virtually no companies gave a negative rating, and almost half gave positive ratings. These results are in clear contrast with the results for employee involvement, total quality management, and reengineering, which are consistently more positive and do not have such a high percentage of neutral responses. Why is evaluation of knowledge management so neutral? It may reflect the fact that organizations are still trying to learn about and assess the effectiveness of their knowledge management efforts as well as the fact that many organizations do not have formal knowledge management activities. It may also stem from the fact that the outcomes from these programs are not always highly visible or directly tied to key performance areas.

Table 17.1	Experience with Knowledge Management Efforts (percentage).
Experience	1999 (n = 143)
Very Negative	0
Negative	1
Neither Negative nor Positive	50
Positive	45
Very Positive	5

The results in Table 17.2, which show the impact of knowledge management efforts on a variety of outcomes, are very much in line with the overall rating of knowledge management efforts but are slightly more positive. They show a high level of neutrality and indecision, with about a quarter or more of the respondents reporting that they have no basis for judging the impact of the effort. With respect to direct performance, profitability, and employee satisfaction, the scores are virtually identical and are positive. With respect to the other outcomes, such as turnover, absenteeism, and employee loyalty, the programs are rated as neutral. Finally, they are rated as more likely to contribute to knowledge development than to be neutral, but even here, the ratings are not overwhelmingly

Table 17.2   **Effects of Knowledge Management on Performance (percentage).**

Effect	Study	Mean (5-point scale)	Very Negative	Nega-tive	Neither Negative nor Positive	Positive	Very Positive	No Basis to Judge
DIRECT PERFORMANCE OUTCOMES								
Productivity	1999	3.6	1	0	29	43	3	24
Quality of Products or Services	1999	3.6	1	0	28	46	2	24
Customer Service	1999	3.7	1	0	24	44	7	25
Speed	1999	3.5	1	2	32	36	2	28
PROFITABILITY AND COMPETITIVENESS								
Profitability	1999	3.6	1	1	27	46	3	24
Competitiveness	1999	3.7	1	1	24	42	5	28
EXPLOYEE SATISFACTION AND QUALITY OF WORKLIFE								
Employee Satisfaction	1999	3.5	1	2	35	32	5	26
Employee Quality of Worklife	1999	3.4	2	1	37	31	2	28
OTHERS								
Turnover	1999	3.2	2	1	48	15	0	34
Absenteeism	1999	3.1	2	0	49	12	0	38
Employee Loyalty	1999	3.3	2	2	42	21	2	32
Knowledge Development	1999	3.7	2	2	22	45	6	24

Note: Not all questions were asked in all studies.

positive. Surprisingly, the ratings for knowledge development are no higher than the ratings EI, TQM, and reengineering received with respect to knowledge development. Overall, the ratings suggest that companies are not yet seeing important payoffs from their knowledge management efforts.

The results showing the relationship between the amount of use of knowledge management practices and the outcomes of knowledge management programs are presented in Table 17.3. The relationships between the amount of adoption and the outcomes of the program are generally positive and significant. Clearly, greater use of knowledge management practices leads to higher ratings for the knowledge management activities of a company. This is particularly true with respect to performance outcomes, profitability, and overall experience with knowledge management efforts. It is also generally true for employee satisfaction, but this result is not as strong.

Employee Involvement. The relationship between EI efforts and knowledge management efforts is potentially quite positive. Employee involvement emphasizes knowledge, skills, and learning, and hence there is good reason to believe that adopting EI practices may be quite compatible with having an effective knowledge management effort. The actual relationship between knowledge management outcomes and employee involvement practices is shown in Table 17.4. It shows generally positive and in a number of cases significant relationships between the adoption of employee involvement practices and the effectiveness of knowledge management activities. As might be expected, the results are particularly strong for the adoption of power sharing and for knowledge and skill development practices.

Total Quality Management. Like employee involvement, TQM places a strong emphasis on learning. It focuses particularly on learning about quality problems and educating employees to make work process improvements. Thus there are good reasons to believe that the adoption of TQM practices may be associated with the success of knowledge management efforts.

The results in Table 17.5 show a generally positive but weak relationship between the amount of adoption of TQM practices in companies with TQM efforts and knowledge management outcomes. The relationships are lower than might be expected given the problem-solving and learning orientation aspects of TQM programs. Only one item, cost-of-quality monitoring, shows a strong positive relationship, perhaps because it leads to a problem-solving activities that help with the knowledge management of an organization.

| Table 17.3 | Relationship Between Extent of Adoption of Knowledge Management Practices and Knowledge Management Outcomes. |

Knowledge Management Practices	KNOWLEDGE MANAGEMENT OUTCOMES			
	Direct Performance Outcomes[a] 1999	Profitability and Competitiveness 1999	Employee Satisfaction and Quality of Worklife 1999	Experience with Knowledge Management Overall 1999
MANAGEMENT PRACTICES	.46***	.41***	.28**	.47***
Knowledge-Sharing Conferences	.26*	.19	.11	.45***
IT-Enabled Knowledge Storing and Transfer	.36***	.30**	.24*	.36***
External and Internal Benchmarking	.31**	.30**	.18	.30***
Visits to Customers, Suppliers, and Others for Learning	.27**	.24*	.08	.32***
Lessons Learned or Postmortem Reviews	.44***	.43***	.28**	.39***
Communities of Practice or Networks	.49***	.42***	.31**	.40***
Internet Access for Obtaining Information and Knowledge	.19	.23*	.06	.20*
External Partnerships to Develop New Knowledge	.35***	.34***	.27**	.31***
Rotational Assignments for Development	.40***	.36***	.38***	.26**
REWARDS	.38***	.37***	.23*	.32***
Rewards for Developing Knowledge Assets	.37***	.36***	.21*	.32***
Rewards for Sharing Knowledge	.35***	.34***	.22*	.28***

[a]Productivity, customer satisfaction, quality, and speed.
Correlation coefficients: * = weak relationship ($p \leq .05$);
** = moderate relationship ($p \leq .01$);
*** = strong relationship ($p \leq .001$).

Table 17.4	Relationship of Knowledge Management Outcomes to Employee Involvement.

| | KNOWLEDGE MANAGEMENT OUTCOMES | | | |
EI Indices	Direct Performance Outcomes[a] 1999	Profitability and Competitiveness 1999	Employee Satisfaction and Quality of Worklife 1999	Experience with Knowledge Management Overall 1999
EI Overall	.27*	.29**	.28*	.26**
Information	.21*	.20*	.20	.18*
Knowledge and Skills	.26*	.23*	.31**	.15
Rewards	.15	.22*	.15	.22*
Power Sharing	.27**	.29**	.28**	.29***

[a]Productivity, customer satisfaction, quality, and speed.
Correlation coefficients: * = weak relationship ($p \leq .05$);
  ** = moderate relationship ($p \leq .01$);
  *** = strong relationship ($p \leq .001$).

Table 17.5	Relationship of Knowledge Management Outcomes to Use of TQM Practices.

| | KNOWLEDGE MANAGEMENT OUTCOMES | | | |
TQM Practices	Direct Performance Outcomes[a] 1999	Profitability and Competitiveness 1999	Employee Satisfaction and Quality of Worklife 1999	Experience with Knowledge Management Overall 1999
Core TQM Practices Overall	.26	.25	.22	.16
Production-Oriented Practices Overall	.11	.16	.14	.24*
OTHER PRACTICES				
Cost-of-Quality Monitoring	.33*	.40**	.35**	.22
Collaboration with Suppliers in Quality Efforts	.26	.21	.16	.16
PERCENTAGE COVERED	−.04	.00	.07	.13

[a]Productivity, customer satisfaction, quality, and speed.
Correlation coefficients: * = weak relationship ($p \leq .05$);
  ** = moderate relationship ($p \leq .01$);
  *** = strong relationship ($p \leq .001$).

Reengineering. The relationship between knowledge management outcomes and reengineering is potentially positive for at least some of the practices that are part of reengineering. This is particularly true with respect to the improvements that reengineering efforts can bring in the information systems of companies with respect to their ability to transfer learning from one part of an organization to another. Reengineering can also lead to experimentation that can develop new knowledge and ultimately improve the effectiveness of any knowledge management effort.

The results of the relationship between the knowledge management outcomes and the use of reengineering practices are shown in Table 17.6. They show significant correlations for the work structure and e-commerce reengineering practices. Work structure practices are strongly related to the effectiveness of knowledge management efforts on all four outcomes. E-commerce is related to direct performance and profitability outcomes. This finding is not surprising, since information systems can be a major way to disseminate new learning when they are appropriately structured and designed. Overall, the results suggest that information system redesign can be an important enabler of knowledge management systems. The data show that organizations that install new work structures tend to have more effective knowledge management efforts.

Employment Contract. As is true with other major organizational improvement efforts, the employment contract can potentially affect knowledge management efforts. Indeed, there is reason to

| Table 17.6 | Relationship of Knowledge Management Outcomes to Use of Reengineering Practices. |

| | **KNOWLEDGE MANAGEMENT OUTCOMES** | | | |
Reengineering Indices	Direct Performance Outcomes[a] 1999	Profitability and Competitiveness 1999	Employee Satisfaction and Quality of Worklife 1999	Experience with Knowledge Management Overall 1999
Work Structure	.41***	.36***	.31**	.24*
Cost Reduction	.22	.19	.09	.14
E-Commerce	.31**	.33**	.18	.14
Percentage Covered	.01	.05	.05	.11

[a]Productivity, customer satisfaction, quality, and speed.
Correlation coefficients: * = weak relationship ($p \leq .05$);
** = moderate relationship ($p \leq .01$);
*** = strong relationship ($p \leq .001$).

argue that it might very strongly influence knowledge management practices since key features of the employment contract concern learning, development, and knowledge sharing.

Table 17.7 shows the relationship between the employment contract and knowledge management outcomes. As with employee involvement, TQM, and reengineering, some elements of the employment contract are strongly related to the effectiveness of the knowledge management program. Particularly strongly related is the fit with the business strategy, the understanding of the employment contract, and employee satisfaction with the contract.

There is a relationship between the continued employment of individuals being based on performance and the knowledge management outcomes. This result, when combined with the significant relationship that exists between tying rewards to the organization's performance, strongly suggests that the reward system features of the employment contract influence knowledge management outcomes. It seems particularly desirable to stress performance as a key feature of the employment contract in order to facilitate knowledge management. Although this relationship is somewhat indirect, it is not surprising, since effective knowledge management, as well as knowledge transfer and development, requires individuals to be motivated to improve their performance and to be focused on improving organizational performance.

Change Strategy. Change strategy is likely to be a key driver of the effectiveness of knowledge management. As with EI, TQM, and reengineering, why and how a knowledge program is instituted are critical determinants of its effectiveness. So it is not surprising to see in Table 17.8 that there are a number of significant relationships between the characteristics of the change strategy and the effectiveness of the knowledge management outcomes. Particularly crucial in making knowledge management successful is the clarity of the business strategy and beliefs about how it relates to organizational effectiveness.

As far as change implementation strategies are concerned, there is a clear relationship between the degree of change that is implemented on a companywide basis and the effectiveness of knowledge management efforts. This is not surprising, since effective knowledge management often does require a systematic companywide effort, and of course this outcome fits with the use of a companywide e-commerce system, which is also related to the effectiveness of knowledge management efforts. Not surprisingly, there is a relationship between the degree to which efforts are similar across countries

Table 17.7 **Relationship of Employment Contract to Knowledge Management Outcomes.**

Employment Contract	KNOWLEDGE MANAGEMENT OUTCOMES			
	Direct Performance Outcomes[a] 1999	Profitability and Competitiveness 1999	Employee Satisfaction and Quality of Worklife 1999	Experience with Knowledge Management Overall 1999
Continued Employment Is Based on Performance	.22*	.24*	.27**	.19*
Continued Employment Is Based on Continuing to Develop Skills and Knowledge	.15	.16	.20	.19*
No One Has a Secure Job	−.08	.04	−.09	−.03
Outstanding Performers Have a Job for Life	.25*	.21*	.13	.01
Rewards Are Tied to Individual Performance	.06	.17	−.06	.01
Rewards Are Tied to Group or Organization Performance	.26*	.28**	.24*	.22*
Loyalty to the Company Is Rewarded	−.01	.03	.04	.00
Rewards Are Tied to Seniority	−.06	−.02	−.03	.01
Career Development Responsibility Is the Individual	−.03	.09	−.08	−.04
Employees Are Expected to Manage Their Own Performance with Minimum Supervision	.06	.10	−.01	.09
Contract Fits the Corporate Business Strategy	.28**	.34***	.13	.15
Contract Is Understood by Most Employees	.32**	.34***	.25*	.18*
Employees Are Satisfied with the Contract	.34***	.37***	.25*	.26**
Different Contracts Accommodate Different Types of Employees	−.02	.08	−.05	−.01
Different Contracts Exist for Temporary and Part-Time Employees	−.05	−.12	−.11	−.04

Table 17.7 (Continued)

| | KNOWLEDGE MANAGEMENT OUTCOMES | | | |
Employment Contract	Direct Performance Outcomes[a] 1999	Profitability and Competitiveness 1999	Employee Satisfaction and Quality of Worklife 1999	Experience with Knowledge Management Overall 1999
Contract Supports a Balance Between Work Demands and Personal Life	.18	.17	.26*	.08
Things Are Changing So Fast, It Is Unclear What the Contract Is	−.09	−.12	−.15	−.04

[a]Productivity, customer satisfaction, quality, and speed.
Correlation coefficients: * = weak relationship ($p \leq .05$);
** = moderate relationship ($p \leq .01$);
*** = strong relationship ($p \leq .001$).

and the effectiveness of the knowledge management program. This fits the general finding that a consistent change effort on a corporatewide basis leads to effective change, and it should help organizations learn from and share learning with all their parts. Finally, there is a small but significant relationship between change efforts being led by top management and the effectiveness of the knowledge management effort. This is not surprising, since it tends to be true of all of the improvement efforts that have been reviewed so far.

Conclusion. Overall, the results with respect to the effectiveness of knowledge management practices show that these efforts have promise but have not yet demonstrated success. It is clear that the more knowledge management practices are adopted, the greater the payoff. This finding suggests that the use of knowledge management practices is likely to increase. The results also generally show that adopting EI, TQM, and particularly certain reengineering practices can lead to more effective knowledge management efforts. In the case of reengineering, the key seems to be adopting information technology as part of the reengineering program. Generally, the items having to do with information technology and e-commerce were related to the effectiveness of the knowledge management activities.

Knowledge management practices show some of the same relationships to the employment contract and the change strategy as were seen with EI, TQM, and reengineering. Knowledge management efforts are more successful when the employment contract is supportive of the business strategy, the contract is understood by

| Table 17.8 | Relationship of Change Strategy to Knowledge Management Outcomes. |

	KNOWLEDGE MANAGEMENT OUTCOMES			
Characteristics of Change Strategy	Direct Performance Outcomes[a] 1999	Profitability and Competitiveness 1999	Employee Satisfaction and Quality of Worklife 1999	Experience with Knowledge Management Overall 1999
Guided by a Clearly Stated Business Strategy	.24*	.29**	.24*	.20*
Guided by Clearly Stated Beliefs about What Makes an Organization Effective	.28**	.22*	.24*	.28***
Guided by Mission and Value Statements	.18	.20*	.21*	.18*
Driven by a Threat to the Organization's Survival	−.05	−.05	−.10	−.04
CHANGE IMPLEMENTATION STRATEGIES				
Made Up of a Series of Unrelated Initiatives	−.19	−.21*	−.14	−.17
Integrated Companywide	.31**	.28**	.26*	.28***
Occurring Differently in Different Business Units	−.17	−.22*	−.07	−.14
Same No Matter What Country Employees Work In	.26*	.27**	.09	.30***
Based on a Bottom-Up Implementation Strategy	.16	.18	.10	.15
Led by Top Management	.26**	.23*	.19	.17
Based on a Plan Covering Three Years or More	.12	.19	.00	.06

[a]Productivity, customer satisfaction, quality, and speed.
Correlation coefficients: * = weak relationship ($p \leq .05$);
                          ** = moderate relationship ($p \leq .01$);
                         *** = strong relationship ($p \leq .001$).

employees, and employees are satisfied with it. Also, tying rewards to group and organizational performance is related to the effectiveness of the knowledge management programs. Finally, with respect to change strategy, knowledge management efforts are most effective when there is an integrated change strategy that is driven by business strategy and when the change strategy is consistently applied throughout the organization and is led by top management.

Financial Effects

What is the effect of employee involvement, total quality management, reengineering, and knowledge management practices on the financial performance of companies that adopt them? The answer is of critical importance for the future of these improvement efforts. Ultimately, if they are to survive, they must show that they improve corporate performance.

Studies looking at the performance impact of a range of organizational and management practices are rare. Moreover, most studies do not address the question of whether the performance effects are strong enough to influence company financial performance or which practices have the strongest impacts. A number of studies have examined the effects of specific EI and TQM practices on work groups, plants, offices, and production lines (see, for example, Cotton and others, 1988; Easton and Jarrell, 1998; Golembiewski and Sun, 1990; Ichniowski and others, 1996; Staw and Epstein, 2000). In general, these studies report positive effects in areas ranging from financial performance to company reputation. The results are consistent with the positive ratings of EI and TQM that we have reported in earlier sections.

Some studies have examined the effects of EI and related practices on performance in specific industries, such as the steel, auto, and apparel industries. For example, MacDuffie and Krafcik (1992) found that an index of ten involvement-oriented practices predicted productivity and quality in a study of auto assembly plants worldwide. These studies use many different measures of involvement, often making it difficult to know how well the findings apply to different combinations of EI practices. The focus on single industries is an advantage in that it automatically controls for many industry-specific differences in financial performance, technology, and a host of other factors that otherwise make it difficult to establish a direct relationship between management practices and financial performance. At the same time, findings from studies in one industry may not be generalizable to other industries.

Studies have examined the effects of organizational culture on performance at the firm level. For example, Denison (1990) looked at thirty-four firms that had done employee attitude surveys in at least part of their organization. He found that firms with culture scores showing more participation had a higher return on investment and return on sales over a period of five years after the survey. Similarly, Hansen and Wernerfelt (1989) found that a participative culture, as measured by employee surveys, was related to return on assets in sixty firms. Kotter and Heskett (1992) found a relationship between company cultures and company financial performance. Their measures of culture overlap somewhat with practices that are part of EI and TQM. Finally, Collins and Porras (1994) compared eighteen visionary companies to their competitors and found that the visionary companies created many times more shareholder value. These studies used employee attitudes as measures of culture, but they did not measure the use of EI and TQM practices.

Several studies have shown a link between human resource management practices and firm performance. Huselid (1995) used a broad index of human resource practices that overlaps in part with our measures of EI and TQM practices. He found a significant relationship between these practices and return on assets. Huselid and Becker (1996) showed a relationship between these same human resource management practices and the market value of corporations. Becker and Huselid (1998), in an analysis of 1996 survey data, focused on high performance work system practices and found a relationship between them and measures of market value, return on assets, and sales per employee.

A very well done study by Easton and Jarrell (1998) found a significant relationship between the adoption of TQM practices and both stock returns and financial results. Little academic research has been done on the impact of reengineering efforts on corporate performance. Consequently, our research on this is particularly important. There also is little research on the impact of knowledge management practices, due almost certainly to the recency of most company efforts in this area.

We should not underestimate the difficulty of demonstrating a relationship between management practices and firm performance. Our studies have shown that the typical company uses most EI, TQM, reengineering, and knowledge management practices with only a small part of its workforce, and there are virtually no firms that use them on an organizationwide basis. Thus it is impossible to compare truly high-user companies with low users or nonusers to see how much effect these practices have when they are universally adopted. This means that the impacts must be strong in order for them to be detected in statistical analyses due to the limited variability in the degree to which firms use these approaches. In addition, since some EI, TQM, reengineering, and knowledge management efforts may be only a few years old, firms may still be learning how to implement and manage them appropriately. Further, their effects may only now be starting to appear in the firms' financial results because it takes time for management practices to change behaviors and for behavioral changes to lead to changes in financial results.

Unfortunately, at this point, we have no data that indicate the lag time between installing management practices and changes in company financial performance. It seems almost certain that this lag time varies from one practice to another. For example, cost-cutting practices such as those associated with reengineering programs may have a more rapid impact than the creation of teams. In any case, lack of knowledge about lag times makes it hard to find strong relationships. Finally, how a firm is organized and managed is just one of many influences on its financial performance; the relationship of this factor to performance at any point in time may therefore be relatively weak.

Performance Results. To examine the effects of EI, TQM, reengineering practices, and knowledge management on firm financial performance measures, we obtained 1992 through 1999 data on company performance for the 361 firms that responded to one or more of the surveys done in 1993, 1996, and 1999. Data were obtained from Compustat, a database of publicly traded companies. We also drew on the industry identification data and the data on company employment levels reported in *Fortune* magazine.

We used one measure of firm economic productivity: sales per employee, a simple but relatively common productivity indicator. We used four measures of financial return: return on sales, return on assets, return on investment, and return on equity. We used two measures of market performance: total return to investors and market-to-book ratio. Some researchers believe that return on sales and return on assets are most closely related to corporate efficiency, while return on investment, return on equity, total return to investors, and market-to-book ratio are indicators of overall corporate effectiveness.

For each of our performance measures, we calculated a 1993, a 1996, and a 1999 result. To get the 1993 result, we averaged the 1992, 1993, and 1994 results. To get the 1996 result, we averaged the 1995 and 1996 results (1997 was not available when we did these analyses for our 1998 report). To get the 1999 result, we averaged the 1998 and 1999 results (2000 results were not available when we did these analyses). We used averages because of the instability of financial performance results; various accounting decisions and environmental events can change the results for a given year in ways that may not reflect the actual performance of the companies. Averaging results across years is one way to reduce the effect of unusual conditions.

Our analysis is unique among the available studies of firm performance. The predictors are our indices of EI, TQM, reengineering, and knowledge management practices. Thus we are studying the use of specific practices, not employee attitudes that may be influenced by financial performance. We are also studying a variety of management practices; as a result, we can compare the effectiveness of different management approaches. We use a number of different company performance measures as outcomes, not just one or two measures. Finally, we look at the relationship of practices and performance over a multiple-year span of time.

Our statistical analyses used a number of control variables. There are strong industry effects for return measures and firm productivity. For example, sales per employee and return on investment tend to be systematically different for the steel and banking industries. Accordingly, we controlled for industry in our analyses by using SIC codes. We also used performance data for all available firms, not just those that completed surveys in 1993, 1996, and 1999. We constructed a control variable for firms that did not provide a survey so that we could use their performance data for comparison purposes. We also controlled for capital intensity (property, plant, and equipment per employee). This can vary systematically both across and also within industries and can greatly influence performance on financial outcome measures. Finally, we controlled for level of union membership.

We conducted separate multiple regression analyses of the effects of EI, TQM, reengineering, and knowledge management on each performance outcome. We first trimmed the sample by eliminating the top and bottom 1 to 1.5 percent of firms on each measure. This is a common procedure in the analysis of firm performance; it recognizes that extremely good or extremely poor performance is more likely due to temporary market conditions or other factors than the result of top management practices. We next entered all the control variables in a block and treated them as a group for additional power. Finally, we entered the EI, TQM, reengineering, and knowledge management indices in a block.

The control variables were strongly related to the measures of performance. They accounted for a large portion of the variance in performance, confirming the importance of controlling for them when analyses are done to determine the effects of management practices on firm performance.

The regression results reported in Table 18.1 show the relationship between EI use and performance in 1993, 1996, and 1999. The

Table 18.1	Regression Results for Financial Performance and EI Usage.

	EI USE		
Financial Measure	1993	1996	1999
Sales per Employee	***	***	
Return on Sales	***		
Return on Assets	**	***	
Return on Investment		***	
Return on Equity	***		
Total Return to Investors			

Correlation coefficients: * = weak relationship ($p \leq .05$);
** = moderate relationship ($p \leq .01$);
*** = strong relationship ($p \leq .001$).

results indicate that the overall use of EI practices is significantly related to five measures of corporate performance in at least one of the studies. The strength and consistency of the relationship varies. Sales per employee was strongly related to the use of EI practices in both 1993 and 1996. The same pattern exists for return on assets. The results for return on sales, return on investment, and return on equity show a mixed pattern, significant in one year but not significant in the others. Total return to investors is the one measure that was not significantly related to EI usage in 1993, 1996, or 1999, but the results are in the direction of high EI use being associated with a higher total return.

Table 18.2 presents the results for the relationship between financial results and TQM usage. There are no significant relationships for 1993 or 1999 data, but there are three statistically significant relationships for 1996. Return on sales, return on assets, and return on equity all show statistically significant relationships between the use of TQM and the financial performance of the companies. There is no obvious explanation for why the 1996 results are significant but the 1993 and 1999 results are not.

Comparing these results to the employee involvement results reveals two interesting trends. Neither shows a significant relationship to total return to investors. Both show significant results for return on sales, return on assets, and return on equity. Sales per employee shows a strong relationship to employee involvement practices but not to TQM. Sales per employee, generally speaking, is a measure

Table 18.2	Regression Results for Financial Performance and TQM Usage.		
		TQM USE	
Financial Measure	1993	1996	1999
Sales per Employee			
Return on Sales		*	
Return on Assets		**	
Return on Investment			
Return on Equity		***	
Total Return to Investors			

Correlation coefficients: * = weak relationship ($p \le .05$);
** = moderate relationship ($p \le .01$);
*** = strong relationship ($p \le .001$).

of productivity, and in some respects it is surprising that it is related to EI but not to TQM practices.

Table 18.3 presents the results for the relationship between financial performance and reengineering usage in 1996 and 1999 (no reengineering data were collected in 1993). In the 1996 study, four financial measures show strong relationships to the use of reengineering: return on sales, return on assets, return on investment, and return on equity. These results clearly suggest that reengineering does have an impact on financial performance.

It is important to point out here that the two kinds of reengineering practices had somewhat different impacts on performance. The work-restructuring items were positively related to financial performance—more use of them clearly led to higher financial performance. Just the opposite was true with respect to the cost reduction items. More use of them tended to be associated with poorer financial performance.

There are several obvious explanations for the negative impact of cost reduction practices. It is possible that some of the downsizing and cost reduction activities damaged the firm's ability to perform. The second explanation is that companies, when they downsize and reduce costs, take large financial write-offs that cause their publicly reported accounting data to drop significantly, and this could result in the negative relationships. Of course, any initial drop in financial performance because of the cost reduction activities may be more

	REENGINEERING USE	
Table 18.3 **Regression Results for Financial Performance and Reengineering Usage.**		
Financial Measure	1996	1999
Sales per Employee		
Return on Sales	***	
Return on Assets	***	
Return on Investment	***	
Return on Equity	***	
Total Return to Investors		

Correlation coefficients: * = weak relationship ($p \leq .05$);
** = moderate relationship ($p \leq .01$);
*** = strong relationship ($p \leq .001$).

than offset in the future as the cost reduction activities pay off in better financial results.

The regressions for the relationship of knowledge management practices to financial performance were not significant. There are a number of possible reasons for this, but two are most likely. First, since many of these practices are new, it is possible that they simply have not had time to affect the financial measures that were used. Second, it may be that the knowledge management practices studied simply do not have a strong impact on the financial measures studied. Both of these explanations probably contributed to the lack of a relationship. Knowledge management is not focused on the kinds of behaviors that are likely to have a strong or immediate effect on company financial performance or the price of a company's stock. It is simply one part of a management approach that over the years may lead to better products and sales.

Overall, the results show that management practices involving EI, TQM, and reengineering are related to most of the measures of financial performance. Sales per employee is the one measure that was related only to the adoption of employee involvement practices. This is the most productivity-oriented measure used; it is therefore not surprising that it has slightly different relationships to the management practices than the other measures, which are more focused on profitability. It is not entirely clear why it relates more strongly to employee involvement. It does raise the question as to whether EI drives productivity more than the other practices. We do not yet have an answer.

We should also note that none of the measures are significantly related to total return to investors. There is an obvious explanation for this. Unlike the other financial measures, which primarily measure the organization's internal operating effectiveness, the results concerning total return to investors depend very much on stock market conditions and other external conditions and events beyond the direct control of most companies. Probably because of this and the volatility of the stock market, our statistical analysis showed that this measure had a higher level of variance than the other measures. It is therefore not surprising that this measure did not reach statistical significance.

Finally, it is important to note that none of the relationships are significant for the 1999 study. They are in the same direction as the significant results found in 1993 and 1996 but did not reach statistical significance. One contribution to this result is the smaller sample size for the 1999 study. With a smaller sample, a larger relationship is required to obtain a significant result. Another explanation is that the economic prosperity of 1999 produced some atypical financial results that were not always tied to how well companies were managed.

Size of Impact. How large is the effect of EI, TQM, and reengineering on corporate performance? The percentage of the performance variance that is accounted for by these practices is relatively small in all the analyses. However, this does not mean that an increase in usage cannot have a significant impact on performance.

One way to estimate how much a change in one measure will cause another to change is to look at the effect of a one-standard-deviation change. Increasing the use of EI and TQM practices by one standard deviation means covering approximately an additional 30 percent of employees. Such an increase represents at least a doubling of many companies' EI and TQM efforts, but it is achievable. In fact, a significant number of companies are already at this level.

Our 1993 study found that an increase of one standard deviation has quite noticeable effects on the performance measures (Lawler, Mohrman, and Ledford, 1995). Such an increase in coverage is associated with increases in total factor productivity of 1.0 percent, in return on assets of 1.1 percent, in return on sales of 2.0 percent, in return on investment of 2.8 percent, and in return on equity of 3.1 percent.

Table 18.4, which is taken from our 1993 study report, compares the financial performance of high, medium, and low adopters of EI and

Table 18.4	Financial Effects of EI and TQM Usage in 1993 (percentage).		

| Financial Measure | EI AND TQM USE | | |
	Low	Medium	High
Return on Sales	6.3	8.3	10.3
Return on Assets	4.7	5.8	6.9
Return on Investment	9.0	11.8	14.6
Return on Equity	16.6	19.7	22.8

TQM practices (Lawler, Mohrman, and Ledford, 1995). It presents the results for firms within one standard deviation of the mean (medium use), those one standard deviation or more above the mean (high use), and those one standard deviation or more below the mean (low use) in the use of EI and TQM practices. In comparison to low users, high users enjoy a 63 percent higher return on sales, a 47 percent higher return on assets, a 62 percent higher return on investment, and a 37 percent higher return on equity. (Percentages are calculated by taking the difference between high and low users and comparing it to low-use performance. For example, in the case of return on sales, 10.3 minus 6.3 equals 4.0, which is 63 percent of 6.3.) These results should capture the attention of anyone concerned with firm performance, since they suggest that companies that are above average in the adoption of EI and TQM practices perform significantly better on these key financial measures.

Table 18.5 compares the financial performance of high, medium, and low users of EI in 1996 and 1999. Companies more than one standard deviation above and below the mean are separated from medium users. The results are consistent in showing that high-use corporations perform significantly better than low-use corporations. In 1996, high users show a 25 percent higher return on sales, a 34 percent higher return on assets, a 26 percent higher return on investment, and a 40 percent higher rate of return on equity. The results for 1999 are very similar to the 1996 results for these measures. These large and very impressive differences between high and low users suggest that high-use companies perform much better financially.

Table 18.5 contains two measures that were not reported in 1993: return to investors and market-to-book ratio. In 1996 and again in 1999, high users had a greater return to investors than low users did (21.5 versus 44.8 in 1996 and −.7 versus 11.9 in 1999). In 1999, the market-to-book ratio for high users is more than twice what it is for

Table 18.5	Financial Effects of EI Usage (percentage).

| Financial Measure | Study | EI USE | | |
		Low	Medium	High
Return on Sales	1996	8.3	10.1	10.4
	1999	6.9	9.7	11.5
Return on Assets	1996	9.2	10.6	12.3
	1999	9.3	9.7	11.2
Return on Investment	1996	15.2	16.3	19.1
	1999	14.2	15.7	17.1
Return on Equity	1996	19.8	22.7	27.8
	1999	23.4	20.7	26.6
Return to Investors	1996	21.5	27.2	44.8
	1999	−.7	2.8	11.9
Market to Book (Ratio)	1999	.7	1.3	1.8

low users. These are extremely large differences, particularly given the earlier regression results that showed that return to investors is not as strongly related to EI as the other financial measures are. One difference between these analyses is that we used control factors in the regression analysis but not in the comparison between high and low users. So one possible explanation for this result is that companies that are high adopters of EI are also well managed and designed and positioned in a number of ways that contribute to good performance. In other words, high users may be different from low users in several ways that contribute to financial performance. Still, even if the findings do somewhat overstate the impact of EI on financial performance and stock prices, they strongly suggest that management practices can influence stock performance.

The financial effects of TQM for 1996 and 1999 are shown in Table 18.6. They show a general tendency for high users to outperform low users. The largest differences are on return on equity and return to investors. The differences for TQM are generally smaller and less consistent than those for EI, suggesting that EI has more influence on financial performance.

Table 18.7 shows the results for reengineering. High users outperform low users on all measures in 1996 but not in 1999. As with EI

Table 18.6 Financial Effects of TQM Usage (percentage).

Financial Measures	Study	TQM USE		
		Low	Medium	High
Return on Sales	1996	9.8	9.7	8.7
	1999	9.4	10.5	9.0
Return on Assets	1996	10.1	10.7	10.3
	1999	9.8	8.1	11.9
Return on Investment	1996	15.6	16.6	15.3
	1999	15.1	14.0	18.5
Return on Equity	1996	18.3	23.5	25.3
	1999	18.8	22.5	25.4
Return to Investors	1996	23.9	33.5	27.5
	1999	−.7	2.9	1.2
Market to Book (Ratio)	1999	1.3	1.5	1.2

Table 18.7 Financial Effect of Reengineering Usage (percentage).

Financial Measures	Study	REENGINEERING USE		
		Low	Medium	High
Return on Sales	1996	9.9	9.4	11.7
	1999	10.0	9.5	9.8
Return on Assets	1996	9.1	10.6	10.2
	1999	10.8	9.4	9.7
Return on Investment	1996	13.4	16.4	15.4
	1999	15.3	16.0	14.7
Return on Equity	1996	19.3	20.5	29.0
	1999	21.3	21.9	21.0
Return to Investors	1996	28.5	26.7	33.7
	1999	−4.9	3.1	−.7
Market to Book (Ratio)	1999	1.4	1.3	1.3

and TQM, the differences are particularly large with respect to return on equity (50 percent higher in 1996). Overall, the 1996 results in particular clearly support the argument that the extensive use of reengineering practices is associated with good financial performance.

Taken together, the results from 1993, 1996, and 1999 suggest that high usage of employee involvement, total quality management, and reengineering is often associated with high performance. Companies who are high users of EI, TQM, and reengineering tend to perform significantly better. The results are particularly strong for EI.

What Accounts for the Financial Effects? Whenever a relationship exists, we must question whether it is a causal one. In this case, it is very important to determine whether the adoption of management practices involving EI, TQM, and reengineering causes firm performance. If it does, a strong case can be made for the widespread adoption of these practices. If it doesn't, there is little reason for companies to adopt them.

There are a variety of alternative explanations for the relationships we have reported here. For example, it is possible that firms with higher rates of return adopt EI, TQM, and reengineering practices because they can afford to do so.

Our study cannot prove causality because it is correlational rather than experimental. But there is one way to rule out some alternative explanations for the relationship between EI, TQM, and reengineering practices and financial performance. Through the analysis of changes in practices and performance over time, we can reach some conclusion about causation. Because of shifts in the makeup of our sample and the changing composition of the Fortune 1000, our sample of repeated firms is too small to enable us to do an adequate longitudinal matched-sample analysis from 1987 to 1999. We can, however, examine the time-lagged relationships between employee involvement and financial performance in 1993 and 1996.

Particularly revealing with respect to causality is the comparison of the time-lagged effects of EI, TQM, and reengineering usage on financial performance to the time-lagged effects of financial performance on EI, TQM, and reengineering usage. The interpretation of these relationships is relatively straightforward. If the stronger relationships occur when practices are used to predict later financial performance, then the causal relationship is from the practice to financial performance, not the reverse. This conclusion is based on the assumption that the financial performance effects of the implementation of EI and TQM will not be observable for several years, which seems likely because of the time it takes people to learn how to perform effectively in these new ways and to introduce improvements in processes and methods.

To determine for our sample of companies the most likely direction of causality, we did time-lagged analyses from the 1993 practice data to the 1996 financial performance data and from the 1993 financial data to the 1996 practice data. The strongest relationships were clearly those for the 1993 practice data to the 1996 financial data. This provides relatively strong evidence that practices cause financial performance rather than the reverse. We should note here, however, that the lagged results were not as strong as the results reported earlier relating the 1993 and 1996 practice data to the financial performance data for the same years. This suggests that the time lag used (three years) might be too long and that the financial impact of these practices shows up more quickly. In any case, the evidence strongly argues for the interpretation that practices cause financial performance rather than the reverse.

We believe that the relationships among employee involvement, total quality management, reengineering, and firm performance are intriguing and significant. They strongly suggest that firms can improve their financial performance by adopting an appropriate mix of EI, TQM, and reengineering practices. Our analyses of the financial impact of these practices support the favorable ratings we received when firms were asked to evaluate the success of their EI, TQM, and reengineering programs and practices. Overall, our study suggests that EI, TQM, and reengineering work and that by adopting them on a widespread basis, firms can gain a significant competitive advantage.

PART FIVE

Predictors of Practice Adoption

Organizational Size, Downsizing, and Delayering

There are a number of reasons to believe that the adoption of EI, TQM, reengineering, and knowledge management may be related to organizational size and structure. Studies of organizations have found organizational size to be associated with the adoption of a variety of management practices. Large size in particular seems to be associated with the existence of formal programs and change efforts. As far as structures are concerned, downsizing and delayering are both possible results of installing EI, TQM, and reengineering. They may also be actions that create the need for EI, TQM, reengineering, and knowledge management efforts.

Organizational Size. Researchers have found organizational size, as measured by number of employees, to be one of the best predictors of innovation adoption in general (Rogers, 1983). Larger firms tend to have greater resources for innovation, including corporate staff groups that can champion change and provide change-oriented support. They may also have a greater need for formal programs to improve their performance, since they tend to have formalized practices and procedures that make change difficult. In addition, larger organizations are more complex and diverse, providing many more places where innovation can be initiated.

Larger firms are in many respects prime candidates for EI, TQM, reengineering, and knowledge management efforts. They often experience motivational, communication, and coordination problems because it is hard for employees and managers to see the impact of their work on customers and on company performance. Large size can also lead employees to feel that they are part of an impersonal, bureaucratic system. Moreover, work in large firms is more likely to be highly segmented, with many different groups being involved in complex processes and many places where work process problems can result from handoffs and conflicting priorities. Employees in large firms are therefore prime targets for the kinds of process improvement changes that are part of TQM, reengineering, and knowledge management efforts.

Several factors work against innovation in large organizations. First, segmentation, bureaucratic structures, and the resulting rigidity can all interfere with an organization's ability to develop an effective approach to change and to disseminate successful innovations throughout. In addition, size makes it hard for change initiatives to have a quick impact on company performance. As a result, managers may become discouraged with the pace of change, and employees may have difficulty believing that change initiatives are serious or will make a difference. Furthermore, most large companies have a history of "flavor of the month" change initiatives that are briefly championed by different parts of the organization and are not coordinated with each other. As a result, employees may ignore or resist most change efforts (Lawler, 1996; Beer and Nohria, 2000).

Table 19.1 shows the relationship between organizational size and the adoption of employee involvement practices in our five surveys. It indicates that larger firms have slightly higher adoption rates than smaller firms. In 1999, larger firms tended to make more use of employee involvement overall and of power-sharing practices in particular. The relationship between EI and size is relatively constant over the five surveys.

Table 19.2 shows the relationships between size and the amount of use of TQM practices by companies with TQM efforts. The results vary from study to study. The results generally show positive but weak relationships between size and the adoption of TQM practices. In 1990, percentage covered was significantly related to organizational size. In 1993, no practice was related to size. In 1996, almost all practices were related to organization size. The 1999 results show positive but weak relationships.

Table 19.3 shows that there are no statistically significant relationships between organizational size and the adoption of reengineering

Table 19.1	Relationship Between Firm Size and Adoption of EI Practices.				
EI Indices	1987	1990	1993	1996	1999
EI Overall	.15*	.22***	.16*	.22**	.20*
Information	.07	.11	.09	.04	.12
Knowledge and Skills	.09	.09	−.01	.16*	.17
Rewards	.06	.14*	.18**	.08	.07
Power Sharing	.25***	.28***	.13*	.29***	.20*

Correlation coefficients: * = weak relationship ($p \le .05$);
** = moderate relationship ($p \le .01$);
*** = strong relationship ($p \le .001$).

Table 19.2   Relationship Between Firm Size and Adoption of TQM Practices.

TQM Practices	1990	1993	1996	1999
Core Practices Overall[a]	—	.07	.27**	.20
Production-Oriented Practices Overall[a]	—	.09	.25**	.07
OTHER PRACTICES				
Cost-of-Quality Monitoring	.10	−.06	.26**	.04
Collaboration with Suppliers in Quality Efforts	.07	.05	.29***	.04
PERCENTAGE COVERED	.20***	.02	.12	.17*

[a]Not asked in 1990.
Correlation coefficients: * = weak relationship ($p \le .05$);
    ** = moderate relationship ($p \le .01$);
    *** = strong relationship ($p \le .001$).

Table 19.3   Relationship Between Firm Size and Adoption of Reengineering Practices.

Reengineering Indices	1996	1999
Work Structure	.10	.11
Cost Reduction	.10	−.01
E-Commerce[a]	—	.15
Percentage Covered	.10	.19*

[a]Not asked in 1996.
Correlation coefficients: * = weak relationship ($p \le .05$);
    ** = moderate relationship ($p \le .01$);
    *** = strong relationship ($p \le .001$).

practices in companies with reengineering efforts. The correlations are generally positive, but none of them is statistically significant with the exception of percentage covered in 1999. There is no obvious explanation for the weakness of these relationships.

The relationships between firm size and the adoption of knowledge management practices are shown in Table 19.4. As a general rule, larger firms do more knowledge management. The major significant relationships all involve management practices, particularly benchmarking, visits, communities of practice, and rotational assignments.

Table 19.4	Relationship Between Firm Size and Adoption of Knowledge Management Practices.

Knowledge Management	1999
MANAGEMENT PRACTICES	.26**
Knowledge-Sharing Conferences	.14
IT-Enabled Knowledge Storing and Transfer	.16
External and Internal Benchmarking	.28***
Visits to Customers, Suppliers, and Others for Learning	.23**
Lessons Learned or Postmortem Reviews	.09
Communities of Practices or Networks	.30***
Internet Access for Obtaining Information and Knowledge	.03
External Partnerships to Develop New Knowledge	.12
Rotational Assignments for Development	.32***
REWARDS	.05
Rewards for Developing Knowledge Assets	.04
Rewards for Sharing Knowledge	.06

Correlation coefficients: * = weak relationship ($p \leq .05$);
** = moderate relationship ($p \leq .01$);
*** = strong relationship ($p \leq .001$).

The fact that these relationship are significant is hardly surprising since they are things that are particularly likely to pay dividends for large companies and in some cases (especially visits and benchmarking), things that can be readily funded in large companies. Communities of practices and networks make particular sense for large organizations because large companies often have a great degree of diversity among employees and therefore opportunities for learning from one another. The same is true of rotational assignments, which offer particularly good learning experiences for individuals in large organizations.

Downsizing and Delayering. During the 1990s, companies took many measures to strengthen their competitive position and adapt to an increasingly competitive business environment. Downsizing and delayering were two of the most prominent actions taken. In some cases, they were the first step in large-scale change programs: companies cut levels and headcounts and then expected the remaining organizational members to find new ways to do things with fewer people. This approach has sometimes led to changes in processes and to increased employee involvement and empowerment. In other cases, downsizing and delayering were the result of a planned reconfiguration of work processes. Employee involvement was encouraged by moving managerial responsibilities and decision making closer to the level at which products were developed and manufactured and services were delivered.

In 1993, nearly half—47 percent—of the firms studied reported that they decreased in size during the past ten years (see Table 19.5); the figure climbed to 51 percent in 1996, clearly indicating that the trend toward downsizing had lost none of its steam. But the results for 1999 differ significantly from those for 1993 and 1996: only 38.5 percent of the firms reported decreasing in size in 1999, and 59.8 percent said they grew larger. This is strong evidence that the

Table 19.5	Changes in Workforce Size During the Past Ten Years.		
	PERCENTAGE OF COMPANIES		
	1993	1996	1999
Decreased by More Than 50 Percent	5.1	4.3	4.2
Decreased 41 to 50 Percent	6.3	3.8	5.6
Decreased 31 to 40 Percent	7.4	4.8	2.1
Decreased 21 to 30 Percent	9.2	15.2	4.9
Decreased 10 to 20 Percent	10.7	16.7	12.0
Decreased Less Than 10 Percent	8.8	6.2	7.0
No Change	4.8	4.3	4.2
Increased Less Than 20 Percent	10.7	17.6	7.7
Increased 21 to 40 Percent	10.3	7.6	12.7
Increased 41 to 60 Percent	3.7	3.3	5.6
Increased 61 to 80 Percent	2.6	1.4	6.3
Increased 81 to 100 Percent	3.7	2.9	2.1
Increased More Than 100 Percent	16.9	11.9	25.4

economic boom in the United States during the latter part of 1990s led to less downsizing and the significant addition of employees in Fortune 1000 companies. This is perhaps most noticeable in the finding that one-fourth of the companies in the sample increased their employee population by more than 100 percent. This figure probably reflects both internal growth and the wave of mergers and acquisitions that characterized the 1990s. And of course, the average firm may not have grown quite so dramatically during this period; our reports are from the large enterprises that make up the Fortune 1000.

As shown in Table 19.6, fully 63 percent of firms eliminated at least one layer of management in the past ten years, with more than two-thirds of those having reduced two or more levels. Apparently, firms continue to eliminate layers of management even though they are growing. The 1999 results do show a slight decrease in the tendency to reduce levels, which is hardly surprising given the growth in workforce size demonstrated in Table 19.5.

The literature on organizational effectiveness is filled with discussions of whether a move toward employee involvement is possible in an environment characterized by downsizing. Downsizing can result in greater job insecurity and perhaps less commitment as employees lose the sense that the company will provide a job for them as long as they carry out their responsibilities. In addition, downsizing may cause increased stress as a result of work overload and insecurity.

Table 19.6	Number of Layers of Management Removed During the Past Ten Years.		
	PERCENTAGE OF COMPANIES		
Number of Layers Removed	1993	1996	1999
None	28.9	21.7	37.1
One	28.6	33.3	20.0
Two	32.3	31.4	33.6
Three	6.4	10.6	7.1
Four	2.6	2.4	2.1
Five	0.8	0.5	0.0
Six or More	0.4	0.0	0.0

Reductions in layers of management can facilitate employee involvement. It can result in more autonomy and responsibility for employees and fewer required approvals. Delayering can also result in swifter decision making and a greater sense of control over decisions. In fact, in many organizations, it is difficult to imagine having meaningful employee involvement unless the size and shape of the hierarchy of control are changed.

Table 19.7 shows the relationship of changes in size and removing layers to the use of employee involvement practices in 1993, 1996, and 1999. Organizations that change in size are neither more nor less likely to have adopted employee involvement. However, a reduction in layers is associated with the adoption of EI.

A somewhat different pattern of EI adoption distinguishes firms that have reduced management layers from those that have not. Those

Table 19.7	Relationship of Downsizing and Removing Layers to EI Indices.		
EI Indices	Study	Downsizing	Layers
EI Overall	1993	.01	.20**
	1996	.03	.12
	1999	−.05	.25**
Information Sharing	1993	.01	.13*
	1996	−.08	.11
	1999	.04	.24**
Knowledge and Skills Development	1993	.03	.10
	1996	.07	.19**
	1999	−.10	.13
Rewards	1993	−.10	.04
	1996	.11	−.08
	1999	−.02	.11
Power Sharing	1993	.05	.24***
	1996	.06	.17*
	1999	−.04	.13

Correlation coefficients: * = weak relationship ($p \leq .05$);
** = moderate relationship ($p \leq .01$);
*** = strong relationship ($p \leq .001$).

that have delayered make significantly greater use of information-sharing, power-sharing, and knowledge development practices. The only area where there has not been greater adoption of EI by delayered firms is rewards. Thus it appears that flattening an organization drives or accompanies the introduction of EI practices, whereas changes in size do not. This underscores the idea that creating a highly involving organization is aided by a redesign of an organization's structure.

Table 19.8 shows that the use of TQM practices is not related to size change or delayering for companies with TQM programs. The finding that delayering does not seem to be associated with a greater use of TQM is a clear difference from the pattern for the use of EI and probably reflects EI's greater emphasis on restructuring and pushing decision making down the hierarchy.

Table 19.8	Relationship of Downsizing and Removing Layers to Use of TQM Practices.		
TQM Practices	Study	Downsizing	Layers
Core Practices Overall	1993	.07	.06
	1996	−.00	.04
	1999	−.07	.11
Production-Oriented Practices Overall	1993	.04	.11
	1996	−.12	.05
	1999	.00	.17
OTHER PRACTICES			
Cost-of-Quality Monitoring	1993	−.04	.01
	1996	−.10	.06
	1999	−.04	.10
Collaboration with Suppliers in Quality Efforts	1993	.02	.08
	1996	−.01	.11
	1999	−.06	.02
PERCENTAGE COVERED	1993	.24***	.13*
	1996	.10	.10
	1999	.03	.11

Correlation coefficients: * = weak relationship ($p \leq .05$);
** = moderate relationship ($p \leq .01$);
*** = strong relationship ($p \leq .001$).

Much of the discussion of reengineering has centered on its close relationship to downsizing and creating lateral processes that make management layers unnecessary. We therefore have every reason to expect that the adoption of reengineering practices will be associated with both downsizing and removing layers; indeed, in some cases, these two activities are assumed to be what reengineering is all about.

Table 19.9 shows the relationship for companies with reengineering efforts between the use of reengineering practices and the occurrence of downsizing and delayering. Interestingly, in the case of downsizing, there is a weak relationship in 1996 between the cost reduction practices and downsizing. The work restructuring practices, however, are not associated with downsizing in either 1996 or 1999. A significant relationship with percentage covered was found in both 1996 and 1999. The most obvious interpretation is that companies that adopt downsizing are generally in a cost reduction mode, and as they downsize, they focus primarily on operating with fewer people and less supervision.

The results for removing layers show that work restructuring, cost reduction practices, and percentage covered are related to removing layers in 1996 and, somewhat less strongly, in 1999. Often the reengineering of an organization's processes is a precondition to successful delayering, so it is not surprising to see a relationship

Table 19.9	Relationship of Downsizing and Removing Layers to Use of Reengineering Practices.		
Reengineering Indices	Study	Downsizing	Layers
Work Structure	1996	.01	.16*
	1999	−.01	.12
Cost Reduction	1996	.19*	.31***
	1999	.10	.18
E-Commerce[a]	1996	—	—
	1999	−.09	.13
Percentage Covered	1996	.18**	.14*
	1999	.28***	.27***

[a]Not asked in 1996.
Correlation coefficients: * = weak relationship ($p \leq .05$);
** = moderate relationship ($p \leq .01$);
*** = strong relationship ($p \leq .001$).

between work structuring and delayering. The cost reduction activities of reengineering are also closely associated with removing layers, as might be expected, since removing layers, like downsizing, is an effective way to remove costs from the organization.

The results for knowledge management practices are presented in Table 19.10. Changes in organization size are essentially unrelated to the adoption of knowledge management practices. The same, however, is not true for changes in the number of organizational levels. Organizations that have reduced levels tend to have a higher level of adoption of the management practices associated with knowledge management. They are, for example, more likely to use information technology, to benchmark, to visit others, to create

Table 19.10	Relationship of Downsizing and Removing Layers to Use of Knowledge Management Practices.		

	DOWNSIZING	LAYERS
Knowledge Management	1999	1999
MANAGEMENT PRACTICES	−.02	.23**
Knowledge-Sharing Conferences	.00	.14
IT-Enabled Knowledge Storing and Transfer	−.09	.18*
External and Internal Benchmarking	.01	.23**
Visits to Customers, Suppliers, and Others for Learning	.01	.24**
Lessons Learned or Postmortem Reviews	−.08	.16
Communities of Practices or Networks	−.05	.24**
Internet Access for Obtaining Information and Knowledge	.02	.10
External Partnerships to Develop New Knowledge	−.01	.04
Rotational Assignments for Development	.05	.21*
REWARDS	−.09	.10
Rewards for Developing Knowledge Assets	−.05	.07
Rewards for Sharing Knowledge	−.11	.11

Correlation coefficients: * = weak relationship ($p \leq .05$);
** = moderate relationship ($p \leq .01$);
*** = strong relationship ($p \leq .001$).

communities of practice, and to use rotational assignments. Most of these management practices are ways to learn about how to make an organization operate more effectively, and so it is not surprising that they might be used when a major organizational change such as delayering is taking place. The same management practices tend to be associated with the adoption of other change efforts such as employee involvement and total quality management. What the overall pattern suggests, therefore, is that as organizations go through major organizational change efforts, they are particularly likely to use management practices that allow them to learn about organizational change and to develop and transfer knowledge.

Conclusion. Table 19.11 summarizes the relationships found in this section. There is a general tendency for large size to be associated with EI, TQM, and knowledge management use. The relationship is strongest for employee involvement and knowledge management. This makes sense: large organizations often have more need to get individuals involved and have the opportunity to gain more from knowledge management.

Changes in organizational size are not strongly related to the adoption of EI, TQM, or knowledge management. They do bear some relationship to the adoption of reengineering with respect to the percentage of employees covered. The more the organization has reduced in size, the higher the percentage of employees that are covered.

Reduction in layers is related to the adoption of employee involvement, reengineering, and knowledge management. All of them are more likely to be practiced when layers are removed. This is consistent with the need to substitute systems for layers of management (Lawler, 1996). All three of these sets of practices have some capability to substitute or make unnecessary levels of management.

Table 19.11 Relationship of Structure to Change Efforts.

	Number of Employees	Downsizing	Delayering
Employee Involvement	Yes	No	Yes
Total Quality Management	Weak	No	No
Reengineering	No	Yes	Yes
Knowledge Management	Yes	No	Yes

Impact of Competitive Environment and Business Strategy

The tough competition that large U.S. companies face has spurred them to look for ways to make improvements in technology, work processes, and organization practices. Some business sectors have felt the impact of this competition for several decades; hence there is good reason to believe that it may have had a significant effect on how organizations are managed. One response to competitive pressures is to adopt employee involvement, total quality management, reengineering, and knowledge management practices in order to gain the performance advantages they offer. In this section, we investigate the relationship between competitive market conditions and the adoption of EI, TQM, reengineering, and knowledge management practices to determine what specific environments lead to the adoption of these practices. We also look at the relationship of business strategy to the adoption of these practices to determine if different strategies lead to the adoption of different practices.

Competitive Environment. Table 20.1 presents data on the competitive market conditions that companies report they face. The results are generally similar throughout the 1990s. Two-thirds or more of the companies reported experiencing the following market conditions to at least some extent: foreign competition, shorter product life cycles, declining markets, rapid growth, quality competition, intense cost competition, rapid change, and speed-to-market competition. Intense cost competition stands out as the most commonly experienced condition. There were some important changes from 1990 to 1999; the 1999 results show more companies facing rapidly growing markets and shorter product life cycles. There was also a slight decrease in the amount of quality competition.

Table 20.2 shows that three of the four market conditions that were measured are related to the adoption of employee involvement practices: foreign competition, rapidly growing markets, and extreme performance pressures. The measure of extreme performance pressure was created by combining the responses to five statistically related questions (regarding rapid environmental change, intense cost competition, and intense speed-to-market competition).

When companies face extreme performance pressures, employee involvement seems to be an attractive strategy, probably because it promises significant improvements in organizational performance rather than just the incremental change that might come about as a result of perfecting an existing management approach. The relationship between rapidly growing markets and the adoption of EI practices suggests that many organizations see employee involvement as a way to help them take advantage of the opportunities that growth creates.

Table 20.1

Percentage of Companies Reporting Various Characteristics of the Competitive Business Environment.

Business Environment	Study	Mean (5-point scale)	Little or No Extent	Some Extent	Moderate Extent	Great Extent	Very Great Extent
Heavy Foreign Competition	1990	2.5	37	21	14	17	11
	1993	2.4	32	27	15	18	9
	1996	2.5	32	27	10	20	10
	1999	2.5	39	15	18	17	12
Rapidly Growing Market	1990	2.2	33	32	23	9	4
	1993	2.2	35	32	19	12	3
	1996	2.7	20	28	27	11	14
	1999	2.6	22	27	26	16	8
Shorter Product Life Cycles	1990	2.4	33	22	26	14	6
	1993	2.5	29	24	22	20	6
	1996	2.8	24	21	23	20	13
	1999	2.7	20	27	22	22	8
Declining Markets	1990	2.2	30	38	19	10	4
	1993	2.4	22	35	27	12	5
	1996	2.2	32	32	21	10	4
	1999	2.2	31	31	28	7	4
Intense Quality Competition	1993	3.6	3	14	27	36	21
	1996	3.4	5	11	35	34	14
	1999	3.3	4	18	34	30	15
Intense Speed-to-Market Competition	1993	3.4	10	13	24	33	20
	1996	3.4	9	15	24	31	22
	1999	3.3	9	19	25	27	20
Intense Cost Competition	1993	4.4	0	2	10	32	56
	1996	4.3	1	1	13	33	52
	1999	4.2	1	4	13	39	42
Rapid Change	1993	3.9	1	10	24	32	32
	1996	4.0	1	8	17	36	38
	1999	4.0	1	4	28	30	36

Note: Not all questions were asked in all studies.

Table 20.2 — Relationship of Market Conditions to Adoption of EI Practices.

EI Indices	Study	Foreign Competition	Extreme Performance Pressures[a]	Declining Markets	Rapidly Growing Markets
EI Overall	1993	.17*	.26***	.00	.23***
	1996	.08	.17*	−.08	.18*
	1999	.25**	.18*	−.03	.26**
Information Overall	1993	.10	.11	.02	.15*
	1996	.04	.16*	−.10	.19**
	1999	.20*	.15	−.06	.19*
Knowledge Overall	1993	.15*	.20***	.02	.21***
	1996	.07	.17*	.03	.14*
	1999	.20*	.22*	−.08	.27**
Rewards Overall	1993	.06	.20***	−.07	.23***
	1996	.08	.00	−.15*	.12
	1999	.18*	.06	−.05	.12
Power Sharing Overall	1993	.27***	.24***	.07	.11
	1996	.15*	.18**	.06	.14*
	1999	.17	.11	.16	.13

[a]Rapid change, intense cost competition, intense speed-to-market competition, shorter product life cycles, and intense quality competition.
Correlation coefficients: * = weak relationship ($p \leq .05$); ** = moderate relationship ($p \leq .01$); *** = strong relationship ($p \leq .001$).

The amount of foreign competition is also related to the adoption of some EI practices, particularly in the 1999 results. This result follows logically from the consistent relationship between performance pressures and the adoption of employee involvement. Foreign competition is usually particularly intense.

Declining markets appear to make little difference in the adoption of employee involvement, perhaps because a declining market makes it difficult to justify the transition costs involved in moving to EI. Moreover, managers may not view EI as a means of making the cost reductions that are often needed in a declining market.

Table 20.3 presents the results regarding the adoption of total quality management practices by companies with TQM efforts. Rapidly

Table 20.3	Relationship of Market Conditions to Adoption of TQM Practices.				
TQM Indices	Study	Foreign Competition	Extreme Performance Pressures[a]	Declining Markets	Rapidly Growing Markets
Core Practices Overall	1993	.17*	.17*	.04	.08
	1996	.01	.06	−.04	.03
	1999	.16	.13	.09	−.09
Production-Oriented Practices Overall	1993	.30***	.25***	−.04	.15*
	1996	.35***	.32***	−.05	.13
	1999	.34**	.10	.18	−.06
OTHER PRACTICES					
Cost-of-Quality Monitoring	1993	.15*	.15*	−.02	.15*
	1996	.22*	.18*	.02	−.01
	1999	.11	−.03	.18	.02
Collaboration with Suppliers in Quality Efforts	1993	.17*	.15*	−.05	.07
	1996	.11	.13	−.03	.07
	1999	.18	.12	.13	.14
Percentage Covered	1993	.25***	.10	.11	−.04
	1996	.29***	.12	.02	−.01
	1999	.20*	.18*	−.07	.13

[a]Rapid change, intense cost competition, intense speed-to-market competition, shorter product life cycles, and intense quality competition.
Correlation coefficients: * = weak relationship ($p \leq .05$);
** = moderate relationship ($p \leq .01$);
*** = strong relationship ($p \leq .001$).

growing markets does not have a relationship to the adoption of TQM practices in the 1999 data. However, foreign competition is clearly related to their implementation in 1993, 1996, and 1999. Foreign competition is probably related because of the global emphasis on quality processes and certification programs that exists. Performance pressures also shows a relationship to the adoption of TQM practices, particularly production-oriented ones.

Table 20.4 shows the relationship between market conditions and the adoption of reengineering practices by companies with reengineering efforts. Although the relationships are not as strong as they are for employee involvement and total quality management, there

Table 20.4		Relationship of Market Conditions to Adoption of Reengineering Practices.			
Reengineering Indices	Study	Foreign Competition	Extreme Performance Pressures[a]	Declining Markets	Rapidly Growing Markets
Work Structure	1996	.06	.22**	−.06	.13
	1999	.03	.03	−.05	.03
Cost Reduction	1996	.05	.04	−.01	−.03
	1999	.18	.16	−.01	.05
E-Commerce[b]	1996	—	—	—	—
	1999	.06	.17	−.01	.25*
Percentage Covered	1996	.03	.01	−.02	.00
	1999	.27***	.23**	.03	−.10

[a]Rapid change, intense cost competition, intense speed-to-market competition, shorter product life cycles, and intense quality competition.
[b]Not asked in 1996.
Correlation coefficients: * = weak relationship ($p \leq .05$);
                           ** = moderate relationship ($p \leq .01$);
                           *** = strong relationship ($p \leq .001$).

are some significant relationships with the adoption of reengineering practices.

One market condition relates to the adoption of e-commerce practices. Rapidly growing markets is related to the overall use of e-commerce and to electronic transactions with customers. This relationship probably reflects the potential usefulness of e-commerce as a method to facilitate growth and, of course, potentially as a way to respond to growth that controls costs and allows for a quick increase in performance. Also positively related to electronic transactions with customers is extreme performance pressures.

The relationship of market conditions to knowledge management practices is shown in Table 20.5. There are a number of significant relationships here. Foreign competition, extreme performance pressure, and rapidly growing markets are generally related to the use of knowledge management practices. Only declining markets is not related to the use of knowledge management practices.

A number of knowledge management items are significantly related to the three market conditions. Visits, communities of practice, and access to the Internet are all significantly related to foreign competition, extreme performance pressures, and rapidly growing markets. One highly likely explanation for this is that these are all ways

| Table 20.5 | Relationship of Market Conditions to Adoption of Knowledge Management Practices. | | | |

Knowledge Management Practices	Foreign Competition	Extreme Performance Pressures[a]	Declining Markets	Rapidly Growing Markets
MANAGEMENT PRACTICES	.29***	.29***	.08	.23**
Knowledge-Sharing Conferences	.17*	.15	.13	.08
IT-Enabled Knowledge Storing and Transfer	.17*	.20*	.03	.08
External and Internal Benchmarking	.18*	.20*	.09	.08
Visits to Customers, Suppliers, and Others for Learning	.29***	.27***	.02	.17*
Lessons Learned or Postmortem Reviews	.10	.12	.06	.13
Communities of Practices or Networks	.26***	.25**	−.01	.21*
Internet Access for Obtaining Information and Knowledge	.27***	.33***	.06	.26**
External Partnerships to Develop New Knowledge	.15	.13	.07	.27***
Rotational Assignments for Development	.16	.09	−.02	.15
REWARDS	.21*	.09	−.07	.18*
Rewards for Developing Knowledge Assets	.23**	.06	−.05	.18*
Rewards for Sharing Knowledge	.16*	.11	−.08	.15

[a]Rapid change, intense cost competition, intense speed-to-market competition, shorter product life cycles, and intense quality competition.
Correlation coefficients: * = weak relationship ($p \leq .05$);
    ** = moderate relationship ($p \leq .01$);
   *** = strong relationship ($p \leq .001$).

to gather information about how to improve performance in situations where the environment is changing and demanding. One other interesting result concerns external partnerships, which are particularly likely in situations where markets are growing rapidly. The most logical explanation for this finding is the potential usefulness of external partnerships for quickly developing and obtaining new knowledge, a critical competitive issue in a rapidly growing market.

Overall, the results suggest that employee involvement, total quality management, reengineering, and knowledge management are most likely to be adopted when an organization faces tough competitive pressure. This finding supports the arguments that they are effective in improving performance and that they can often be complementary to each other. It also suggests that they are not just "nice to do" activities; they are improvement approaches adopted by companies facing difficult competitive conditions.

Business Strategy. The literature in the area of business strategy increasingly emphasizes the importance of organizations developing organizational competencies and capabilities that allow them to perform in particular ways (Prahalad and Hamel, 1990; Mohrman, Galbraith, and Lawler, 1998). Organizations can take a number of approaches to distinguish their products and services in competitive markets. Table 20.6 lists some of the major strategies that organizations can use to gain competitive advantage. The table shows that all of these, with the exception of being global and entering a new business, are part of most companies' strategy to some extent. About a quarter of the sample reports that being global is not an important part of their business strategy—hardly a surprising finding in a sample that includes some companies engaged in domestic businesses that have traditionally not been global (for example, insurance and utilities).

There was relatively little change in the use of business strategies from 1996 to 1999. The aspect that shows the largest change is being a low-cost competitor. It decreased, possibly because it is a competitive advantage that is difficult to achieve and one that is not always powerful in an era when customers are looking for products of high quality.

The most popular strategy in both 1996 and 1999 was developing a strong customer focus. Again, this is hardly surprising; regardless of a company's product or service, customer focus is a highly desirable and has received a great deal of attention in the management literature. Other highly rated strategies include lowering costs, improving quality, and improving speed.

A relatively large number of companies reported that they are developing an electronic commerce capability, and only 7 percent said that it is not a part of their business strategy. This question was not asked in 1996, but a good guess is that if it had been, many fewer companies would have cited e-commerce development as a characteristic of their business strategy.

Implementation is a significant challenge for any strategy. It is one thing to make "being close to customers" a strategy and quite another to put in place the practices and policies that will create a customer-focused organization. Employee involvement, total

Business Strategy	Study	Mean (5-point scale)	Little or No Extent	Some Extent	Moderate Extent	Great Extent	Very Great Extent
Increase Percentage of Revenue from New Products and Services	1996	3.5	5	15	23	37	20
	1999	3.4	8	16	23	40	13
Being a Global Company	1996	3.1	24	14	14	21	27
	1999	3.0	27	12	18	25	18
Develop a Strong Customer Focus	1996	4.5	1	1	7	30	62
	1999	4.5	1	2	6	31	60
Bring Products to Market More Quickly	1996	3.5	9	13	22	29	27
	1999	3.4	9	10	30	35	16
Build Knowledge and Intellectual Capital	1996	3.4	3	16	31	35	15
	1999	3.5	5	11	31	35	18
Become a Low-Cost Competitor	1996	4.0	4	9	16	30	41
	1999	3.7	7	10	27	23	34
Ensure High Levels of Quality	1996	4.2	0	5	11	42	41
	1999	4.2	0	4	12	49	35
Respond Quickly to Changes in the Market	1996	4.1	1	3	19	43	34
	1999	3.9	1	4	24	47	24
Be a Technology Leader	1996	3.7	4	11	27	28	30
	1999	3.5	6	15	24	30	25
Enter New Businesses[a]	1999	2.9	14	29	22	27	8
Develop E-Commerce Capability[a]	1999	3.4	7	18	23	31	21

[a]Not asked in 1996.

management, reengineering, and knowledge management all offer practices that can contribute to the development of strategically important organizational capabilities. However, it is unlikely that EI, TQM, reengineering, and knowledge management are equally effective in aiding the implementation of all business strategies. A key question, therefore, concerns the degree to which different strategies lead firms to use EI, TQM, reengineering, and knowledge management practices.

Table 20.7 shows the relationships between business strategy and the adoption of employee involvement practices. It clearly shows that in both 1996 and 1999, employee involvement was strongly associated with most of the nine strategies that were studied in 1996. It is also related to the two strategies that were studied for the first time in 1999. It is associated particularly strongly with being a technology leader, speeding products to market, and building knowledge and intellectual capital. It is least strongly related to becoming a low-cost competitor. In general, the results fit what might be expected for employee involvement. The literature on EI does not link it clearly to reducing costs. What is surprising is that EI is not more strongly related to increasing the percentage of revenue from new products and services, since there is evidence that a certain amount of involvement can help encourage innovation in the product development process (Mohrman, Cohen, and Mohrman, 1995).

The EI practices involving rewards clearly behave differently than those involving information, knowledge, and power. The reward items were not related to the adoption of any of the strategy approaches in 1996 but did show some significant relationships in 1999. It is unclear why this change occurred. It is interesting that the significant relationships involve items having to do with learning and change; perhaps this is because organizations find that to create a more knowledge-focused work environment, they have to change their reward systems.

Table 20.8 shows the relationship between business strategy and the adoption of TQM practices by companies with TQM efforts. The results show a pattern of significant relationships between a number of the strategy approaches and the adoption of TQM practices. Being a global company is particularly strongly related to the adoption of TQM. This is consistent with the result found earlier concerning the competitive environment; both results suggest that a focus on quality is an important part of operating a global company.

Not surprisingly, ensuring high quality is significantly related to the adoption of quality practices. Finally, developing a strong customer focus shows a consistent pattern of being positively related to the adoption of TQM practices. The overall pattern is one of generally positive relationships between the adoption of TQM and strategies having to do with global and customer focuses. This is not surprising, since quality is an important global issue and TQM places such a strong emphasis on customer focus.

As shown in Table 20.9, the adoption of reengineering practices by companies with reengineering efforts is related to most of the

Table 20.7 **Relationship of Business Strategy to Adoption of EI Practices.**

Business Strategy	Study	EI Overall	Information Sharing	Knowledge and Skills Development	Rewards	Power Sharing
				EI INDICES		
Increase Percentage of Revenue from New Products and Services	1996	.09	.10	.09	.05	.08
	1999	.23**	.19*	.08	.16	.24**
Being a Global Company	1996	.17*	.15*	.12	.11	.14
	1999	.21*	.17*	.25**	.16	.17*
Develop a Strong Customer Focus	1996	.33***	.26***	.23***	.14	.31***
	1999	.08	.06	.10	−.02	.17*
Bring Products to Market More Quickly	1996	.25***	.28***	.25***	.05	.18**
	1999	.31***	.23**	.32***	.22*	.23**
Build Knowledge and Intellectual Capital	1996	.32***	.28***	.31***	.05	.25***
	1999	.33***	.22**	.30***	.25**	.27***
Become a Low-Cost Competitor	1996	−.01	.06	.04	−.06	−.03
	1999	.01	−.02	.07	−.01	.05
Ensure High Levels of Quality	1996	.23**	.18**	.29***	.05	.27***
	1999	.15	.09	.15	.07	.19*
Respond Quickly to Changes in the Market	1996	.19*	.23***	.19**	.05	.12
	1999	.21*	.22**	.22*	.11	.10
Be a Technology Leader	1996	.29***	.28***	.20**	.13	.17*
	1999	.40***	.40***	.25**	.27**	.27**
Enter New Businesses[a]	1996	—	—	—	—	—
	1999	.26**	.23**	.18*	.14	.23**
Develop E-Commerce Capability[a]	1996	—	—	—	—	—
	1999	.25**	.24**	.11	.18*	.18*

[a]Not asked in 1996.
Correlation coefficients: * = weak relationship ($p \leq .05$);
                ** = moderate relationship ($p \leq .01$);
              *** = strong relationship ($p \leq .001$).

Table 20.8 **Relationship of Business Strategy to Adoption of TQM Practices.**

| Business Strategy | Study | TQM PRACTICES | | | | |
		Core TQM Practices[a]	Production-Oriented Practices[b]	Cost-of-Quality Monitoring	Collaboration with Suppliers in Quality Efforts	Percentage Covered
Increase Percentage of Revenue from New Products and Services	1996	.00	.13	.17*	.05	.06
	1999	.06	.31**	.06	.23*	.16
Being a Global Company	1996	.13	.42***	.27**	.23**	.27***
	1999	.14	.39***	.15	.21	.25**
Develop a Strong Customer Focus	1996	.30***	.32***	.19*	.23**	.16*
	1999	.14	.23	.28*	.14	.07
Bring Products to Market More Quickly	1996	.16	.43***	.30***	.25**	.07
	1999	.08	.08	.01	.14	.18*
Build Knowledge and Intellectual Capital	1996	.15	.26**	.10	.20*	−.01
	1999	.23	.25*	.23*	.19	.11
Become a Low-Cost Competitor	1996	.00	.06	.06	.08	.05
	1999	.24*	.27*	.27*	.16	.08
Ensure High Levels of Quality	1996	.41***	.36***	.33***	.36***	.19**
	1999	.18	.23*	.22	.16	.21*
Respond Quickly to Changes in the Market	1996	.01	.12	.08	.16	−.07
	1999	.05	.07	.04	.03	−.05
Be a Technology Leader	1996	.13	.33***	.23**	.26**	.08
	1999	.15	.23	.09	.11	.25**
Enter New Businesses[c]	1996	—	—	—	—	—
	1999	−.03	.18	.00	.25*	.09
Develop E-Commerce Capability[c]	1996	—	—	—	—	—
	1999	.31**	.16	.15	.29**	.03

[a]Quality improvement teams, quality councils, cross-functional planning, work simplification, customer satisfaction monitoring, and direct exposure to customers.
[b]Self-inspection, statistical control method, just-in-time deliveries, and work cells or manufacturing.
[c]Not asked in 1996.
Correlation coefficients: * = weak relationship ($p \leq .05$);
** = moderate relationship ($p \leq .01$);
*** = strong relationship ($p \leq .001$).

Table 20.9	Relationship of Business Strategy to Adoption of Reengineering Practices.

Business Strategy	Study	REENGINEERING PRACTICES			
		Work Structure	Cost Reduction	E-Commerce[a]	Percentage Covered
Increase Percentage of Revenue from New Products and Services	1996	.09	.02	—	−.09
	1999	.11	.16	.29**	.15
Being a Global Company	1996	.04	.16*	—	.07
	1999	.05	.18	.15	.18*
Develop a Strong Customer Focus	1996	.14	.08	—	.03
	1999	.13	.09	.09	.05
Bring Products to Market More Quickly	1996	.31***	.11	—	.06
	1999	.04	.16	.23*	.16
Build Knowledge and Intellectual Capital	1996	.34***	.22**	—	.10
	1999	.27**	.32***	.24*	.16
Become a Low-Cost Competitor	1996	.09	.31***	—	.07
	1999	.21*	.04	.13	.02
Ensure High Levels of Quality	1996	.30***	.28***	—	.10
	1999	.16	.26**	.13	.05
Respond Quickly to Changes in the Market	1996	.31***	.21**	—	.10
	1999	.30**	.27**	.34***	.04
Be a Technology Leader	1996	.23**	.09	—	.01
	1999	.19	.26**	.29**	.14
Enter New Businesses[a]	1996	—	—	—	—
	1999	.19*	.28**	.36***	.15
Develop E-Commerce Capability[a]	1996	—	—	—	—
	1999	.25*	.17	.29**	.16

[a]These questions were not asked in 1996.
Correlation coefficients: * = weak relationship ($p \le .05$);
** = moderate relationship ($p \le .01$);
*** = strong relationship ($p \le .001$).

strategy items. It is most frequently adopted when organizations are striving to build knowledge, improve quality, respond quickly to the market, enter a new business, and develop electronic commerce.

The results concerning the adoption of e-commerce practices are particularly interesting. The strongest relationships here involve new products, technology leadership, new businesses, and fast responses to the market. This presents a rather clear picture of the kinds of strategies that lead to e-commerce—ones that are driven by speed, innovation, and technology leadership. This, of course, fits with the argument that e-commerce can speed up organizations as well as increase their innovation and knowledge development.

The results for the adoption of knowledge management practices and business strategy are presented in Table 20.10. They generally show a positive relationship. Perhaps the most interesting result concerns the two strategy items that do not show a positive relationship to the management practices: developing a strong customer focus and being a low-cost competitor. Apparently, knowledge management is not seen as a way to reduce costs or focus on the customer. The reason for the lack of relationship with costs is perhaps more understandable than the one involving customer focus. It seems, on the surface, at least, that knowledge management, particularly if it is focused on learning about customers, could in fact help develop a customer focus. The relationships between strategy and the knowledge management reward practices are also significant in a number of cases. This finding supports the argument that making a company more knowledge-based requires reward system practices that reinforce knowledge development and communication.

As can be seen in Table 20.11, which is a summary of the relationships reported in Tables 20.7 through 20.10, all of the strategies are associated with the adoption of one or more of EI, TQM, reengineering, and knowledge management in 1996 and 1999. For example, being a global company is associated with the adoption of TQM practices and knowledge management. This is understandable, since quality is such a pervasive issue internationally. But employee involvement, in many cases, has been shown to improve the quality performance of organizations as well. It is therefore a bit surprising that being a global company is not more strongly associated with the adoption of EI practices.

Increasing speed to market is associated with all four kinds of practices. This is not surprising, since all of these practices can affect speed. Building knowledge and intellectual capital is strongly associated with employee involvement and, of course, knowledge

Table 20.10	Relationship of Business Strategy to Adoption of Knowledge Management Practices.	

| | KNOWLEDGE MANAGEMENT | |
Business Strategy	Management Practices	Rewards
Increase Percentage of Revenue from New Products and Services	.28***	.14
Be a Global Company	.30***	.21*
Develop a Strong Customer Focus	.08	.14
Bring Products to Market More Quickly	.39***	.24**
Build Knowledge and Intellectual Capital	.48***	.31***
Become a Low-Cost Competitor	−.10	−.06
Ensure High Levels of Quality	.24**	.20*
Respond Quickly to Changes in the Market	.31***	.17*
Be a Technology Leader	.34***	.24**
Enter New Businesses	.24**	.04
Develop E-Commerce Capability	.28***	.13

Correlation coefficients: * = weak relationship ($p \leq .05$);
** = moderate relationship ($p \leq .01$);
*** = strong relationship ($p \leq .001$).

management. There are a number of possible reasons for its relationship to knowledge management, but perhaps the main one is that knowledge workers are most often attracted to situations where they get large amounts of information, knowledge, power, and rewards.

Becoming a low-cost competitor is clearly linked to only one set of practices—the cost reduction aspects of reengineering. Ensuring quality, by contrast, is strongly related to reengineering and knowledge management. The relationship with employee involvement is somewhat weaker.

Responding quickly to the market is related to knowledge management and reengineering practices. This fits well with the emphasis

| Table 20.11 | | | Relationship of Business Strategy to Adoption of Practices. | | |

Business Strategy	Study	Employee Involvement	Total Quality Management	Reengineering	Knowledge Management[a]
Increase Percentage of Revenue from New Products and Services	1996				
	1999	Yes			Yes
Be a Global Company	1996		Yes		
	1999		Yes		Yes
Develop a Strong Customer Focus	1996	Yes	Yes		
	1999				
Bring Products to Market More Quickly	1996	Yes	Yes	Yes	
	1999	Yes		Yes	Yes
Build Knowledge and Intellectual Capital	1996	Yes		Yes	
	1999	Yes			Yes
Become a Low-Cost Competitor	1996			Yes	
	1999			Yes	
Ensure High Levels of Quality	1996	Yes	Yes	Yes	
	1999			Yes	Yes
Respond Quickly to Changes in the Market	1996			Yes	
	1999			Yes	Yes
Be a Technology Leader	1996	Yes	Yes		
	1999	Yes			Yes
Enter New Businesses[a]	1996	—	—	—	
	1999	Yes		Yes	Yes
Develop E-Commerce Capability[a]	1996	—	—	—	
	1999	Yes		Yes	Yes

[a]Not asked in 1996.

in reengineering on simplifying processes and creating vertical alignments.

Being a technology leader shows a significant relationship with employee involvement and knowledge management. This is not surprising, since being a technology leader usually requires effective management of knowledge as well as the effective management and use of knowledge workers. The latter typically requires developing employees' knowledge and giving them decision-making power.

Entering new businesses and adopting e-commerce show a significant relationship to employee involvement, reengineering, and knowledge management. It is not surprising that entering new businesses and developing electronic commerce are related to both employee involvement and knowledge management. They often require moving decision making into the hands of knowledge workers and the development of intellectual capital. Not surprisingly, the strongest relationship to reengineering practices is the e-commerce item.

Perhaps the best conclusion that can be reached concerning the relationships between strategy and the practices associated with EI, TQM, reengineering, and knowledge management is that the relationships are understandable and largely to be expected. Different strategies do seem to be associated with the adoption of different practices. This fits well with the arguments in the organizational effectiveness literature that strategy should determine the structure and practices of an organization. Our data suggest that this is exactly what happens when companies consider adopting employee involvement, total quality management, reengineering, and knowledge management. They look at the kinds of performance capabilities they need to implement their strategy, and they choose practices that produce these capabilities.

SECTION 21

Performance Improvement and Change Strategies

Decisions about whether to adopt employee involvement, total quality management, reengineering, and knowledge management are often part of a larger organizational change program that involves key changes in the organization's structure and strategy. They also are not simple to implement and, as noted in Section 13, raise a number of issues with respect to change strategy. This section focuses on whether there is a relationship between the kinds of practices that are adopted by corporations and their improvement and change strategies.

Performance Improvement. Table 21.1 shows the relationships for the various performance improvement strategies that we analyzed in Section 12 and the adoption of employee involvement practices. There is a consistent pattern of positive correlations between the thirteen performance improvement strategies and the indices of employee involvement. The one exception to the general pattern once again is the area of rewards, as the reward system practices are only weakly related to most of the performance improvement strategies. The rest of the EI indices are all strongly related to most of the performance improvement approaches. The weakest relationships are with the reduction in number of business units, which is not surprising since this has no obvious tie to employee involvement.

Among the items that enjoy the strongest relationships are building team-based organizations, emphasizing the competencies of employees, focusing on core competencies, attracting key talent, and developing leadership capability. Not surprisingly, knowledge development is strongly related to the degree to which the improvement strategy emphasizes the competencies of employees. Power-sharing practices are strongly related to the degree to which the strategy focuses core competencies and the competencies of employees. Power sharing is also strongly related to building a team-based organization and to developing a leadership capability.

Table 21.2 presents the relationship between the use of total quality management practices in companies with TQM efforts and the performance improvement strategy items. There are a number of relationships that are positive, and some of these are quite strong, particularly in the 1996 study. There is a strong relationship between building a team-based organization and the adoption of all kinds of TQM practices. The adoption of TQM practices is also strongly associated with the use of project teams, a focus on the core competencies of the organization, and outsourcing.

Table 21.1 **Relationship of Improvement Strategies to EI Practices.**

Improvement Strategies	Study	EI Overall	Information Sharing	Knowledge and Skills Development	Rewards	Power Sharing
				EI PRACTICES		
Reduce Number of Businesses	1996	.16*	.10	.11	.13	.15*
	1999	.11	.11	.10	.03	.05
Restructure by Creating New Units and Eliminating Old Ones	1996	.24***	.13	.19**	.12	.25***
	1999	.34***	.31***	.32***	.16	.28***
Create Global Business Units	1996	.15*	.08	.08	.17*	.13
	1999	.31***	.18*	.26**	.28***	.36***
Reduce Size of Corporate Staff	1996	.24***	.10	.23***	.16*	.23***
	1999	.21*	.19*	.19*	.04	.21*
Build a Team-Based Organization	1996	.36***	.26***	.35***	.13	.40***
	1999	.35***	.19*	.29***	.20*	.48***
Use Temporary Project Teams to Perform Core Work	1996	.24***	.26***	.21**	.03	.23***
	1999	.38***	.33***	.26**	.16	.43***
Focus on Core Competencies	1996	.36***	.27***	.32***	.13	.36***
	1999	.31***	.29***	.25**	.10	.34***
Outsource Work	1996	.27***	.18**	.20**	.14	.25***
	1999	.33***	.29***	.34***	.10	.29***
Emphasize Employee Competencies	1996	.36***	.29***	.33***	.15*	.34***
	1999	.36***	.33***	.34***	.08	.37***
Adopt New Information Technology	1996	.21**	.13	.18**	.09	.23***
	1999	.30***	.31***	.31***	.11	.18*
Introduce New Performance Measures	1996	.29***	.21**	.23***	.14	.31***
	1999	.39***	.39***	.27***	.15	.37***
Develop Initiatives to Attract and Retain Key Talent[a]	1996	—	—	—	—	—
	1999	.39***	.34***	.27**	.26**	.25**
Develop Leadership Capability Throughout the Organization[a]	1996	—	—	—	—	—
	1999	.37***	.30***	.30***	.20*	.35***

[a]Not asked in 1996.
Correlation coefficients: * = weak relationship ($p \leq .05$);
                            ** = moderate relationship ($p \leq .01$);
                          *** = strong relationship ($p \leq .001$).

Table 21.2 **Relationship of Improvement Strategies to TQM Practices.**

Improvement Strategies	Study	TQM PRACTICES				
		Core TQM Practices[a]	Production-Oriented Practices[b]	Cost-of-Quality Monitoring	Collaboration with Suppliers in Efforts	Percentage Covered
Reduce Number of Businesses	1996	.14	.10	.07	.16	.16*
	1999	.12	.24*	.28*	.19	−.02
Restructure by Creating New Units and Eliminating Old Ones	1996	.13	.19*	.10	.16	.01
	1999	−.01	.08	−.02	.08	.20*
Create Global Business Units	1996	.11	.33***	.18*	.16	.19**
	1999	.18	.32**	.09	.17	.30***
Reduce Size of Corporate Staff	1996	.24**	.21*	.08	.31***	.10
	1999	.13	.18	.15	.14	.10
Build a Team-Based Organization	1996	.35***	.63***	.35***	.40***	.21**
	1999	.34**	.14	.19	.07	.15
Use Temporary Project Teams to Perform Core Work	1996	.24**	.38***	.19*	.30***	.04
	1999	.25*	.25*	.22	.20	.10
Focus on Core Competencies	1996	.32***	.47***	.27**	.36***	.11
	1999	.20	.17	.17	.04	.04
Outsource Work	1996	.32***	.32***	.18*	.32***	.07
	1999	.21	.26*	.15	.21	.08
Emphasize Employee Competencies	1996	.29***	.26**	.13	.24**	.11
	1999	.14	.16	.17	.08	.15
Adopt New Information Technology	1996	.20*	.11	.03	.10	−.01
	1999	.12	−.06	.16	.08	.07
Introduce New Performance Measures	1996	.19*	.24**	.16	.19*	−.02
	1999	.08	.00	.06	.07	.16
Develop Initiatives to Attract and Retain Key Talent[c]	1996	—	—	—	—	—
	1999	.10	.17	.15	.21	−.01
Develop Leadership Capability Throughout the Organization[c]	1996	—	—	—	—	—
	1999	.23	.29*	.20	.22	.08

[a]Quality improvement teams, quality councils, cross-functional planning, work simplification, customer satisfaction monitoring, and direct exposure to customers.
[b]Self-inspection, statistical control method, just-in-time deliveries, and work cells or manufacturing.
[c]Not asked in 1996.
Correlation coefficients: * = weak relationship ($p \leq .05$);
** = moderate relationship ($p \leq .01$);
*** = strong relationship ($p \leq .001$).

Overall, the relationships in 1999 are not as strong as they were in 1996, nor are they as strong as they were for employee involvement. There is no obvious reason for the relationships in Table 21.2 to be weaker in 1999 than they were in 1996. Perhaps the adoption of TQM is increasingly influenced by things that are not captured by these improvement strategies. For example, the business strategies considered in Section 20 may be more important drivers, as evidenced by the fact that they do show significant relationships to the adoption of TQM practices.

Table 21.3 presents the results for the reengineering and performance improvement strategy items. The results for both 1996 and 1999 show strong positive correlations with the measures of reengineering activity in companies that have reengineering efforts. Only two performance improvement approaches, reducing the number of different business units and creating global business units, fail to show consistently strong positive correlations with the reengineering practices. Apparently, reengineering is being used to support a number of improvement strategies.

The relationships between the improvement strategies and the use of knowledge management are presented in Table 21.4. Overall, these relationships are quite strong. Only reducing the number of businesses fails to show a significant relationship to at least one of the two knowledge management areas. The link between the adoption of knowledge management practices and a number of the improvement strategies is particularly strong. The reward system items are significantly related to eleven of the thirteen improvement strategies, but the correlations are not as strong. Apparently, organizations that have aggressive improvement strategies adopt knowledge management practices that move and develop information but also reward system practices that reward knowledge management behaviors.

Overall, there are strong relationships between a company's performance improvement approaches and the adoption of employee involvement, total quality management (1996 only), reengineering, and knowledge management practices. This suggests that organizations do not randomly choose one of these four approaches and proceed with it. Instead, they adopt a pattern of practices that supports the development of the kind of organization that they need to become in order to be effective. This point is particularly clear in the contrast between building a team-based organization and reducing the number of business units. Organizations that say building a team-based organization is a major strategy are very likely to adopt employee involvement, reengineering, and knowledge management practices. By contrast, reducing the number of businesses shows

		REENGINEERING PRACTICES			
Improvement Strategies	Study	Work Structure	Cost Reduction	E-Commerce[a]	Percentage Covered
Reduce Number of Businesses	1996	.08	.13	—	.03
	1999	.22*	.16	.26**	.01
Restructure by Creating New Units and Eliminating Old Ones	1996	.22**	.29***	—	.17*
	1999	.26**	.28**	.17	.23**
Create Global Business Units	1996	.15*	.15	—	.10
	1999	.09	.14	.21*	.07
Reduce Size of Corporate Staff	1996	.18*	.48***	—	.27***
	1999	.30**	.41***	.28**	.19*
Build a Team-Based Organization	1996	.42***	.30***	—	.22***
	1999	.26**	.08	−.02	.10
Use Temporary Project Teams to Perform Core Work	1996	.36***	.30***	—	.31***
	1999	.33***	.23*	.38***	.13
Focus on Core Competencies	1996	.45***	.33***	—	.24***
	1999	.37***	.23*	.24*	.17*
Outsource Work	1996	.35***	.32***	—	.28***
	1999	.29**	.42***	.40***	.19*
Emphasize Employee Competencies	1996	.45***	.31***	—	.23***
	1999	.37***	.26**	.35***	.17*
Adopt New Information Technology	1996	.47***	.20**	—	.21**
	1999	.42***	.27**	.46***	.16
Introduce New Performance Measures	1996	.35***	.28***	—	.21**
	1999	.39***	.39***	.27**	.26**
Develop Initiatives to Attract and Retain Key Talent[a]	1996	—	—	—	—
	1999	.35***	.42***	.28**	.11
Develop Leadership Capability Throughout the Organization[a]	1996	—	—	—	—
	1999	.41***	.44***	.26**	.09

Table 21.3 Relationship of Improvement Strategies to Reengineering Activities.

[a]These questions were not asked in 1996.

	KNOWLEDGE MANAGEMENT PRACTICES	
Improvement Strategies	Management Practices	Rewards
Reduce Number of Businesses	.05	.09
Restructure by Creating New Units and Eliminating Old Ones	.28***	.22**
Create Global Business Units	.38***	.27***
Reduce Size of Corporate Staff	.32***	.09
Build a Team-Based Organization	.33***	.28***
Use Temporary Project Teams to Perform Core Work	.50***	.32***
Focus on Core Competencies	.42***	.40***
Outsource Work	.49***	.27***
Emphasize Employee Competencies	.47***	.38***
Adopt New Information Technology	.48***	.25**
Introduce New Performance Measures	.46***	.24**
Develop Initiatives to Attract and Retain Key Talent	.53***	.31***
Develop Leadership Capability Throughout the Organization	.59***	.30***

Table 21.4 Relationship of Improvement Strategies to Knowledge Management Practices.

Correlation coefficients: * = weak relationship ($p \le .05$);
** = moderate relationship ($p \le .01$);
*** = strong relationship ($p \le .001$).

little relationship to the adoption of employee involvement, TQM, reengineering, or knowledge management.

Knowledge management seems to be the improvement effort that is most strongly related to the thirteen improvement strategies considered here. This may reflect the fact that organizations realize that improving organizational effectiveness requires learning how to make employee involvement, total quality management, and reengineering efforts effective. They therefore adopt knowledge management practices regardless of the type of improvements they are striving for and the practices that they put in place in order to obtain the improvement.

Change Strategy. Table 21.5 shows the relationships between the adoption of EI practices and different change strategies that were

Table 21.5 **Relationship of Change Strategies to EI Practices.**

		EI PRACTICES				
Change Strategies	Study	EI Overall	Information Sharing	Knowledge and Skills Development	Rewards	Power Sharing
Guided by a Clearly Stated Business Strategy	1996	.44***	.41***	.39***	.14	.34***
	1999	.46***	.47***	.30***	.29***	.33***
Guided by Clearly Stated Beliefs about What Makes an Organization Effective	1996	.39***	.31***	.40***	.11	.38***
	1999	.44***	.32***	.27***	.27**	.42***
Guided by Mission and Value Statements	1996	.39***	.35***	.38***	.08	.37***
	1999	.39***	.30***	.26**	.20*	.43***
Driven by a Threat to the Organization's Survival	1996	.02	.04	.04	−.03	.12
	1999	.16	.14	.18*	−.06	.18*
Made Up of a Series of Unrelated Initiatives	1996	−.10	−.10	−.14*	.13	−.10
	1999	−.11	−.17*	−.06	−.14	.01
Integrated Companywide	1996	.37***	.29***	.36***	.13	.35***
	1999	.41***	.38***	.24**	.26**	.36***
Occurring Differently in Different Business Units	1996	.07	−.00	.04	.01	.12
	1999	.03	.05	.02	−.09	.10
Same No Matter What Country Employees Work In	1996	.07	.12	.09	.08	.08
	1999	.31***	.22**	.25**	.22**	.23**
Based on a Bottom-Up Implementation Strategy	1996	.10	.06	.06	.03	.19**
	1999	.28**	.20*	.27**	.06	.31***
Led by Top Management	1996	.28***	.24***	.24***	.14	.26***
	1999	.39***	.30***	.30***	.21*	.38***
Based on a Plan Covering Three or More Years	1996	.26***	.26***	.22***	.09	.28***
	1999	.39***	.35***	.20*	.22**	.34***

Correlation coefficients: * = weak relationship ($p \leq .05$);
** = moderate relationship ($p \leq .01$);
*** = strong relationship ($p \leq .001$).

considered in Section 13. In 1999, there was a positive relationship between eight of the change strategy items and the employee involvement practices. The use of employee involvement practices shows a clear relationship to many of the same change strategy items that are related to the effectiveness of employee involvement—specifically, items concerned with clear guidance of the change process, integration on a companywide basis, and leadership by senior management. Finally, the long-term orientation item also shows a significant positive correlation.

Adoption of reward system practices was not well predicted by any of the change strategy items in 1996, but the situation is somewhat different in the 1999 results; clarity of strategy, leadership by top management, integration, and long-term orientation all show positive correlations to the adoption of reward system practices. This pattern makes considerable sense, since reward system changes can be adopted and implemented effectively only when there is a clear strategy that these practices support, and they tend to require a relatively long implementation time as well as strong support by top management.

The change strategy item concerned with bottoms-up implementation has shown a mixed pattern. In 1996, it was not strongly related to EI practices, but the results are different in 1999, when, with the exception of the adoption of reward practices, the relationship between bottom-up strategy and the adoption of EI practices is significant. This makes more sense than the previous result of no relationship because of the philosophical fit between a bottom-up implementation strategy and employee involvement.

Noticeably not related to the adoption of EI practices is the question concerning organizational survival. Apparently, organizations that are changing in order to survive are not particularly likely to adopt employee involvement practices, probably because these practices may not produce fast bottom-line results.

Table 21.6 presents the results for total quality management; they are similar to those for employee involvement, although not as consistent between 1996 and 1999. A strong relationship exists among a significant number of the change strategy items and the adoption of both core and production-oriented TQM practices by companies with TQM efforts. Again, the items concerned with strategy, mission, and leadership show the strongest relationships. One additional item is related to the adoption of TQM in 1996 but not in 1999: changes are the same in all countries. Apparently, in the case of total quality management, change strategies that are associated

| Table 21.6 | Relationship of Change Strategies to TQM Practices. |

Change Strategies	Study	TQM PRACTICES				
		Core TQM Pracitices[a]	Production-Oriented Pracitices[b]	Cost-of-Quality Monitoring	Collaboration with Suppliers in Quality Efforts	Percentage Covered
Guided by a Clearly Stated Business Strategy	1996	.49***	.43***	.26**	.44***	.08
	1999	.33**	.19	.18	.17	.26**
Guided by Clearly Stated Beliefs about What Makes an Organization Effective	1996	.37***	.34***	.22*	.34***	.10
	1999	.34**	.30*	.32**	.16	.19*
Guided by Mission and Value Statements	1996	.39***	.35***	.27**	.28***	.19**
	1999	.27*	.15	.08	.01	.19*
Driven by a Threat to the Organiza-tion's Survival	1996	.14	.06	−.02	.06	.16*
	1999	.11	.09	−.01	.03	.07
Made Up of a Series of Unrelated Initiatives	1996	−.27**	−.13	−.17	−.14	.06
	1999	−.04	−.06	−.12	−.06	.06
Integrated Companywide	1996	.43***	.35***	.24**	.41***	.06
	1999	.44***	.32**	.35**	.17	.18*
Occurring Differ-ently in Different Business Units	1996	−.09	.00	−.01	−.03	−.01
	1999	−.03	.09	−.06	−.03	.09
Same No Matter What Country Employees Work In	1996	.41***	.36***	.27**	.35***	.10
	1999	.09	.20	.06	.10	.08
Based on a Bottom-Up Implementation Strategy	1996	.05	.10	−.05	.08	−.03
	1999	.15	.05	.14	.20	.06
Led by Top Management	1996	.40***	.43***	.18*	.34***	.11
	1999	.36**	.24*	.20	.28*	.19*
Based on a Plan Covering Three or More Years	1996	.40***	.26**	.12	.18*	.14*
	1999	.27*	−.01	.04	.03	.23**

[a]Quality improvement teams, quality councils, cross-functional planning, work simplification, customer satisfaction monitoring, and direct exposure to customers.
[b]Self-inspection, statistical control method, just-in-time deliveries, and work cells or manufacturing.
Correlation coefficients: * = weak relationship ($p \leq .05$);
       ** = moderate relationship ($p \leq .01$);
       *** = strong relationship ($p \leq .001$).

with high levels of adoption typically are integrated companywide, strategy driven, led by a strong vision and senior management, and oriented toward the long term.

Table 21.7 presents the results for reengineering, which are similar to those for EI and TQM. Reengineering practices tend to be adopted by companies with reengineering efforts when a clear strategy, mission, and beliefs drive programs; top management provides support; and practices are integrated companywide. This is particularly true for the work structure practices. Not surprisingly, the e-commerce practices are associated with integrated companywide efforts.

The results for the adoption of knowledge management practices are shown in Table 21.8. They are very similar to the results for EI, TQM, and reengineering. Knowledge management practices are implemented with change strategies that involve clearly stated business strategies, mission and value statements, beliefs about organizational effectiveness, company wide integration, and top management leadership.

As with EI, there is a significant correlation between the adoption of knowledge management and a bottom-up implementation strategy. This is not surprising, since knowledge management requires that people throughout an organization develop and share knowledge. Overall, however, the strong message is that knowledge management practices tend to be installed when there is a top-management-led companywide integrated change strategy. This makes sense because it typically takes a companywide effort to develop new knowledge and to facilitate its movement to the parts of the organization that can use it.

Our results suggest that EI, TQM, reengineering, and knowledge management programs tend to be implemented when change programs are organizationwide, guided by a business strategy and mission, and led from the top. In many ways, the reengineering, TQM, and knowledge management results are not surprising. These programs are typically sold as something that needs to be implemented in a consistent top-down way and led by senior management. The literature on employee involvement talks more about bottom-up strategies and does not emphasize as much the need for organizationwide efforts. Our results, however, suggest that EI practices are most frequently installed by efforts that are companywide and led from the top.

In the large organizations that we are studying, top-led change may be the only way to produce the kind of change that is required in

Table 21.7 **Relationship of Change Strategies to Reengineering Activities.**

		REENGINEERING PRACTICES			
Change Strategies	Study	Work Structure	Cost Reduction	E-Commerce[a]	Percentage Covered
Guided by a Clearly Stated Business Strategy	1996	.42***	.26***	—	.18**
	1999	.27**	.10	.23*	.18*
Guided by Clearly Stated Beliefs about What Makes an Organization Effective	1996	.41***	.25***	—	.18**
	1999	.37***	.21*	.31**	.04
Guided by Mission and Value Statements	1996	.31***	.23**	—	.08
	1999	.21*	−.02	.16	.02
Driven by a Threat to the Organization's Survival	1996	.06	.17*	—	.14*
	1999	.15	.17	.18	.28***
Made Up of a Series of Unrelated Initiatives	1996	−.26***	−.20**	—	−.16*
	1999	−.10	−.07	−.15	.04
Integrated Companywide	1996	.42***	.23**	—	.16*
	1999	.37***	.22*	.32***	.12
Occurring Differently in Different Business Units	1996	.02	.07	—	.07
	1999	−.02	.01	−.02	.13
Same No Matter What Country Employees Work In	1996	.08	.08	—	.11
	1999	.37***	.27**	.38***	.14
Based on a Bottom-Up Implementation Strategy	1996	.21**	.05	—	.12
	1999	.32***	.16	.34***	.18*
Led by Top Management	1996	.33***	.22**	—	.15*
	1999	.25**	.09	.22*	.20*
Based on a Plan Covering Three or More Years	1996	.28***	.21**	—	.18**
	1999	.04	.03	.12	.07

[a]These questions were not asked in 1996.
Correlation coefficients: * = weak relationship ($p \leq .05$);
** = moderate relationship ($p \leq .01$);
*** = strong relationship ($p \leq .001$).

	Table 21.8	Relationship of Change Strategies to Knowledge Management Practices.

| | KNOWLEDGE MANAGEMENT PRACTICES | |
Change Strategies	Management Practices	Rewards
Guided by a Clearly Stated Business Strategy	.33***	.30***
Guided by Clearly Stated Beliefs about What Makes an Organization Effective	.42***	.23**
Guided by Mission and Value Statements	.30***	.24**
Driven by a Threat to the Organization's Survival	.17*	.03
Made Up of a Series of Unrelated Initiatives	−.12	−.11
Integrated Companywide	.39***	.39***
Occurring Differently in Different Business Units	.07	−.11
Same No Matter What Country Employees Work In	.40***	.39***
Based on a Bottom-Up Implementation Strategy	.23**	.21*
Led by Top Management	.36***	.26**
Based on a Plan Covering Three or More Years	.21*	.13

Correlation coefficients: * = weak relationship ($p \leq .05$);
** = moderate relationship ($p \leq .01$);
*** = strong relationship ($p \leq .001$).

order for employee involvement, total quality management, reengineering, and knowledge management to be successfully implemented. Putting the practices associated with these programs into place is a complex effort that requires changing multiple systems within an organization; it may be unrealistic to argue that they should be installed in anything other than a top-led change effort. This is particularly likely to be true given the history of hierarchical management that exists in most of our sample companies. It also fits with the earlier finding that programs are more successful when their implementation takes a top-down approach. In essence, the data indicate that the most likely and effective way to change a traditional hierarchical organization is by having the hierarchy lead a change process that is integrated throughout the company.

Conclusion. Even though employee involvement, total quality management, reengineering, and knowledge management are quite different approaches to improving organizational performance, their adoption seems to be associated with many of the same conditions. They are particularly likely to be adopted when an organization is focusing on teams, core competencies, and the development of individual competencies.

It is also interesting to note that these change efforts are typically not driven by a threat to the organization's survival. This is a bit of a surprise because the so-called burning platform is often a reason given for instituting major organizational changes. Apparently, when organizations are facing threats to their survival, they do not introduce the kinds of programs we have studied, probably because they prefer activities that have a quicker, shorter-term effect on organizational cost and performance.

EI, TQM, reengineering, and knowledge management also all tend to be associated with the same general type of change process—one that is led by senior management and is guided by a sense of overall direction, mission, and consistency. Thus, in some respects, employee involvement, total quality management, reengineering, and knowledge management are more similar than different. They are adopted by organizations that are looking to organizational effectiveness and senior-management-led organizational processes as a key to improving their performance.

SECTION 22

Toward High Performance Organizations

A burgeoning global economy, the revolution in information technology, rapid advances in scientific knowledge, many new developments in the practice of management, and a host of other important changes have all converged to create a very different business environment than the one that existed in 1987 when we did our first study of Fortune 1000 companies. Our studies in 1990, 1993, 1996, and 1999 document that change has occurred in the way corporations are managed. The changes we have found suggest that companies are increasingly looking to organizational practices, structures, and designs as a powerful and sustainable source of competitive advantage.

One challenge in obtaining competitive advantage through a corporation's ability to organize itself is that there are many seemingly attractive approaches among which to choose. However, this should not obscure the fundamental point that learning how to organize and how to change an organization in response to a dynamic environment is a critical—perhaps the most critical—capability that an organization can develop. Basic to this capability is knowledge about what makes organizations effective.

Our studies were designed to show how and why organizations are changing their management practices with respect to the adoption of employee involvement, total quality management, reengineering, and knowledge management. They identify the effectiveness of these changes and as a result can provide a great deal of information about what makes organizations effective. This section highlights the most important findings and implications of our five studies.

Employee Involvement. The use and effectiveness of employee involvement management practices has been a major focus of our research on Fortune 1000 companies since 1987. Thus we have a considerable history of information on the evolution and development of employee involvement in corporations. A great deal has changed since the 1987 study. Adoption of employee involvement practices has increased, and we know a considerable amount about the effectiveness of EI and what causes companies to adopt it.

Amount of Use. The results of our studies from 1987 to 1996 showed continuous growth in the use of most EI practices in Fortune 1000 companies, but our 1999 results seem to indicate that its growth has reached a plateau. The 1999 results do show an increase in certain practices, but there is no strong continuation of the general upward use trend for EI practices. Although some practices in the areas concerned with knowledge, rewards, and power increased, the overall trend was, for the first time in our studies, not dramatically toward the greater use of EI practices.

Looking first at the data on information sharing, the 1999 data showed no significant increases from the 1996 data, which had attained the highest levels ever with respect to sharing all types of financial information with employees. Thus there is a still a tremendous opportunity for the greater sharing of business information with employees, particularly information about business operating results, competitors' performance, business plans and goals, and new technologies. Particularly with the extensive use of the Internet and information technology by Fortune 1000 companies, there is no reason why employees cannot have a great deal more information about the results and plans of their business. Some companies are already providing individuals with personal portals that allow them to access business information on a regular basis from either home or office, but most are not.

Knowledge development also showed no significant change from the level of training and development in which corporations engaged in 1996, which was only slightly higher than the level reached in 1993. Given the growing complexity of business and the emphasis on knowledge work, we expected stronger growth in the efforts of companies to develop the knowledge and skills of their employees. One optimistic sign in the results was the prevalence of training in information technology skills. This, along with job skills, was the area in which the most training occurred. Because we did not ask about IT skills prior to 1999, it is impossible to say how much increase there has been in IT skill training, but a good guess is that it has been appreciable. In fact, thanks to IT training, employees may actually have received more training in 1999 than in any previous year.

The reward system practices of companies continue to change. The changes from 1996 to 1999 were primarily in areas concerned with rewarding performance. Companies were using more performance reward practices in 1999 than they were before. The most popular approach was nonmonetary rewards for performance, but stock option plans grew, and so did gainsharing plans, group incentives, and individual incentives. In short, pay for performance has become increasingly popular. It is questionable whether the increased focus on pay for performance is clearly related to a desire to get employees more involved in the business. Some of the growth is in types of pay for performance practices that are not supportive of employee involvement—for example, the use of individual incentives. However, much of the growth is in practices that are consistent with employee involvement.

Until the 1999 survey, the biggest change in EI-oriented management practices was in the area of power sharing. Particularly noticeable was the growth in employee participation groups, quality circles, and survey feedback. There was also tremendous growth in the use of self-managing work teams and minibusiness units. Both minibusiness units and self-managing teams are focused on giving employees greater decision-making power. The 1999 data do not show a general growth in the area of power sharing; indeed, a few practices, such as quality circles and participation groups, were being used somewhat less frequently. There was some continued growth in survey feedback, which is the most widely used of the practices studied.

There is no clear explanation why growth in power sharing has slowed. We noted in our 1996 analysis that despite the rapid growth of these practices, they still affect only a small percentage of the total workforce in organizations and have by no means reached a saturation point. Some other factor must account for the slowdown in their adoption rate. It is possible that the slowdown reflects a conclusion by companies that EI is suitable only in certain areas and that these areas have been covered well. It does not appear that the slowing of the growth of adoption of EI practices is due to dissatisfaction with their effectiveness.

Adoption Patterns. Our analysis of who adopts EI practices strongly suggests that they are adopted by organizations who see EI as a useful competitive strategy. This conclusion is reinforced by the finding that companies that face extreme performance pressure and foreign competition are particularly likely to adopt employee involvement. Business strategy is also related to EI adoption. Organizations that are focused on building intellectual capital and on being technology leaders are more likely to adopt it.

There is also a relationship between the overall business improvement strategies of companies and their adoption of EI practices. For example, organizations that are focusing on their core competencies and emphasizing the competencies of employees are likely to adopt employee involvement. Finally, it is used in conjunction with certain change strategies. Organizations that have clear, unified change strategies are particularly likely to adopt EI practices.

Overall, our results suggest that employee involvement is frequently part of a reasonably complete and well-though-out change strategy. They also suggest that the adoption of employee involvement is usually associated with a business imperative. This argues that organizations will continue to use EI practices because they address important business issues.

Total Quality Management. Growth in total quality management programs had stopped by the time of our 1996 survey. The question at that point in time was whether TQM would decline in use or remain stable. The factors pointing to the likely continuation of TQM programs included their favorable ratings and perceived strategic importance.

Amount of Use. We first studied total quality management in 1990. When we studied it again in 1993, we saw a small amount of growth in its popularity. Our 1996 and 1999 data suggest that this trend has not continued. Indeed, comparing the 1996 and 1999 results suggests that a declining number of companies have TQM programs. What is growing or stable is the use of certain TQM practices among companies who have TQM programs. This trend may suggest that while overall TQM programs may never be adopted on a widespread basis, some of TQM's key practices will be.

Adoption Pattern. As was true with employee involvement, corporations seem to adopt total quality management practices to meet particular competitive challenges and needs. Foreign competition and extreme performance pressures are related particularly strongly to the adoption of certain TQM practices. Also related are key emphases such as being a global company, focusing on customers, and not surprisingly, emphasizing quality for competitive advantage. TQM practices tend to be adopted when organizations have definite, well-developed change strategies. They are also most frequently adopted when an organization is focusing on core competencies and the competencies of its employees.

We seem to be in an era in which the number of companies committed to total quality management programs is constant or declining but a growing number find some TQM practices to be a useful part of their overall approach to organizing. Certain practices from TQM appear to be on the road to being widely accepted as conventional wisdom and good management rather than as part of a specific TQM program. In this respect, TQM may be rated as highly successful, even though as a formal program its adoption is decreasing. Since organizations seem to adopt TQM programs for strategic purposes, there is good reason to believe that such programs will continue to be used by companies whose business strategy they fit.

Reengineering. Reengineering is undoubtedly the most controversial of the organizational improvement efforts that we studied. It is also the one that may be undergoing the most dramatic transformation because of the impact of information technology. The 1999 data showed some interesting results with respect to changes in the adoption of reengineering.

Amount of Use. The use of reengineering programs and practices was not included in our studies before 1996; therefore, we cannot make a definitive statement about their long-term growth. However, the adoption rate we found in 1996 was high, given the short history of process reengineering. The fact that 81 percent of the companies studied had a reengineering program is clear evidence that it has had a wide impact on Fortune 1000 corporations.

The 1999 data show a slight decrease in companies with reengineering programs, to 76 percent. This is still a high number, especially in light of the many criticisms of reengineering programs and the movement of consulting firms away from offering reengineering consulting services. Our results clearly show that the most popular reengineering practices are those that are likely to lead to cost reduction. These include using less supervision, doing the work with fewer individuals, and creating an overall lower cost structure. The next most popular are some of the work structure changes, such as cross-functional units, information system redesign, and process simplification.

Results from the 1999 study show that organizations are using electronic transactions with both suppliers and customers and are doing major redesigns of their information systems. A good guess is that future growth in reengineering will be very strongly tied to the introduction of information technology and the redesign of work processes to accommodate and support e-commerce practices.

Adoption Patterns. It is clear that until now, the major reason for adopting reengineering has been cost reduction. For example, firms that have downsized and removed layers are particularly likely to have adopted reengineering practices. As was true with employee involvement and TQM, the business strategy of the organization seems at least partly to be guiding the adoption of reengineering. Not surprisingly, strategies that lead to the adoption of reengineering include being a low-cost competitor and increasing the speed with which products are brought to market.

Finally, as with EI and TQM, reengineering seems to be adopted when certain improvement strategies are adopted. For example, focusing on core competencies, the adoption of information technology, and an emphasis on the competencies of employees are strongly associated with the adoption of reengineering practices. The adoption of reengineering is also strongly associated with integrated, clearly articulated, and well-developed business and change strategies.

We predict that the term *reengineering* will rapidly disappear from the management literature. But that is not to say that its practices and concepts will disappear. Indeed, quite the opposite may be true. As e-commerce grows, many of the ideas concerned with reengineering, such as lateral processes and work simplification, will increase in use. The difference is that they will be installed under the banner of e-commerce as a part of organizations that are Web-based and provide seamless transactions with customers and vendors.

Knowledge Management. Knowledge management is the least well defined and articulated of the four organizational improvement efforts that we studied. It is also the newest, so we lack historical data on its adoption. Nevertheless, there are some important conclusions that can be reached about its use.

Amount of Use. There appear to many fewer knowledge management programs than there are employee involvement, total quality management, and reengineering programs. Nevertheless, some of the practices that support knowledge management seem to be relatively popular. The most popular is providing access to the Internet for information and knowledge, a result that points to the growing use of information technology in organizations. In addition, there is considerable evidence that organizations do look outside themselves to customers and others for knowledge on how to improve their performance. Thus there is significance evidence that many organizations do spend some time and effort to increase their knowledge assets and manage them effectively. However, in most cases, there is no formal program; only 33 percent of companies have an executive assigned responsibility for knowledge management.

Adoption Pattern. A number of factors seem to be related to the use of knowledge management practices. For example, organizational size is related to the use of a number of knowledge management practices. As was true with the other improvement efforts we looked at, extreme performance pressures and foreign competition tend to be associated with the use of knowledge management practices. Business strategy seems to be one of the best predictors of the use of knowledge management practices, particularly business strategies that have to do with growth, e-commerce, speed of change, and building knowledge and intellectual capital. Finally, the adoption and use of knowledge management practices is strongly related to improvement strategies that focus on creating global business units, outsourcing work, building a team-based organization, and the adoption of new information technology. Overall, the results show that the use of knowledge management practices can be explained by the business situation and the strategy organizations pursue because they are adopted to accomplish very definite business objectives.

Effectiveness. Across the board, virtually every company rates its employee involvement, total quality management, and reengineering efforts as successful. The ratings are more neutral with respect to knowledge management but are still more positive than negative. There is a consistent tendency for a program to be rated as more successful as companies make greater use of the practices associated with that program. For example, in the case of employee involvement, the use of information sharing, knowledge development, rewards, and power-sharing practices are all strongly associated with the perceived success of EI programs.

The reported success of employee involvement programs was unchanged from 1993 to 1999. Organizations consistently rated them highly, and they seem to lead to such direct performance outcomes as productivity and quality. They also tend to have a positive impact on employees. Total quality management programs, like EI programs, are rated as very successful. They are seen as having an impact on direct performance outcomes, profitability, and competitiveness. They are rated as slightly less positive in terms of their impact on employee satisfaction but still get positive scores.

Our surveys revealed that attitudes toward reengineering were more positive in 1999 than in 1996. Although ratings of the effect of reengineering on specific performance outcomes are not as high as they were for EI and TQM, they are still on the positive side. The weak point of reengineering seems to be its impact on employees, a feature that has been widely discussed in the reengineering literature.

Knowledge management programs have by far the most negative ratings. In terms of satisfaction with such programs, ratings are generally neutral but not negative. Ambivalence about knowledge management programs shows up in the ratings of their impact on specific outcomes, which tend to be positive but not as strongly positive as for employee involvement, total quality management, and reengineering. Overall, knowledge management does not seem to be delivering the kinds of results that the other three programs have produced.

The most interesting finding with respect to effectiveness concerns the interaction of EI, TQM, reengineering, and knowledge management. They seem to reinforce each other, one increasing the effectiveness of another. This is reflected in the tendency for the adoption of any one of them to be associated with higher success ratings for the others. There are a number of specific relationships that are worth mentioning. Employee involvement outcomes seem to increase significantly when reengineering and total quality management are used. This may well be because reengineering and total quality management provide important tools that complement the structures and practices of employee involvement. There also seems to be some reciprocity here in the sense that TQM performs better when EI practices are used. Similarly, process reengineering efforts are most successful when they are combined with EI and TQM practices. Finally, knowledge management works best when it is combined with TQM and reengineering practices. These results strongly suggest that the most effective organizational change efforts are those that are able to integrate the practices commonly associated with all four approaches.

Our results also show that a number of factors influence the effectiveness of employee involvement, total quality management, reengineering, and knowledge management programs. One of these, which we studied for the first time in 1996, is the nature of the employee contract. Particularly for EI, TQM, and knowledge management, having the correct employment contract can contribute substantially to success. Emphasizing performance-based rewards and basing continued employment on performance are clearly associated with the effectiveness of these programs.

An organization's change strategy also seems to be a clear determinant of how successful EI, TQM, reengineering, and knowledge management programs are. Change strategies that emphasize integrated programs of change, clearly articulated reasons for the direction of the change, and leadership by top management seem to be the most successful. Since these are complicated programs to administer and implement, it is not surprising that the data provide clear confirmation of the importance of an overall strategic change agenda for a company and of change being led by senior management.

Perhaps the most important finding in the entire study is the relationship between the adoption of employee involvement, total quality management, and reengineering practices and the financial performance of firms. Companies that adopt these approaches perform better, most likely because their adoption helps companies improve their performance. This conclusion is strongly supported by the results of this study, the most extensive ever done on the relationship between these practices and company financial performance. Particularly in the case of employee involvement practices, the performance difference between high and low users is so great that an overwhelming case exists for their adoption. Indeed, the argument can be made that companies that do not adopt employee involvement, total quality management, and reengineering practices are going to be at an increasingly large competitive disadvantage, forgoing millions of dollars in earnings and shareholder value.

Organizing in the Future. Our results leave little doubt that the shape of organizations has changed since 1987. Corporations have reduced layers of management and have adopted a wide variety of practices that are associated with power sharing, quality improvement, and information technology. They have also created new employment contracts. These changes have created a profoundly different work environment for employees. In many cases, these changes have led to a more skilled workforce and to employees becoming more involved in the business. The changes also appear to have led to U.S. organizations becoming more competitive in the global economy.

It is quite likely that we are well on the way to defining a new view of what constitutes effective organizational design and management. This new approach is not made up simply of employee involvement or total quality management or reengineering or knowledge management but rather of an integrated set of practices and structures that draw heavily from these approaches and is enabled by the World Wide Web and company intranets. This new approach will make extensive use of information technology. Information technology seems poised to have a substantial impact on the very nature of how organizations are managed. This has been predicted for years by academics, but only recently has it shown signs of becoming a reality. As IT becomes more pervasive, it promises to change the way organizations think about employee involvement, quality, work design, organization design, information management, and knowledge management.

The data on the strategic nature of organizational change efforts lead us to be hopeful about how change efforts will be managed in the future. We see clear evidence that companies are aligning their business needs with their organizational structures and their management practices. They are increasingly integrating the key technical tools of TQM and reengineering with the employee involvement activities that can make these technical tools effective. They are beginning to use knowledge management practices to build their capabilities and competencies. Thus there is a slow but steady movement toward reshaping organizations to focus more on performance capabilities and strategic directions and less on the creation of burdensome control structures and hierarchies.

We can document tremendous change from 1987 to 1999, but we can also document the fact that a tremendous number of employees are not yet well-trained, well-informed participants in their businesses. We can also document that many of the change activities have been better for the organizations than they have been for the employees, largely because at least two of the major change efforts, total quality management and reengineering, do not seem to improve appreciably the satisfaction and well-being of employees. Organizations that have moved toward the widespread adoption of TQM and reengineering need to pay attention to the human side of the organization. In our opinion, this means focusing on key employee involvement practices and ensuring that the search for efficiency and competitive advantage does not overlook the key human assets that the organization needs to develop and maintain.

One encouraging note with respect to employee well-being is the emphasis that organizations seem to be placing on developing core competencies and the competencies of individuals. This suggests that organizations may be realizing that they have to do a good job of balancing the organizational needs for cost competitiveness and performance with the development of satisfying work relationships that can attract and retain individuals who are the source of competitive advantage.

Information technology is changing the very nature of work and its knowledge requirements. People increasingly possess the critical intellectual capital of the organizations they work for. Thus they may be as important as or even more important than the financial capital of the organization. Because of the increased importance of human capital, organizations are likely to put more and more emphasis on programs that develop human capital, measure its presence in organizations, and help allocate it effectively. Because of this, it is increasingly likely that human resource management systems will make extensive use of information technology and be focused heavily on the competencies and capabilities of individuals.

Because of the relative difficulty of managing change efforts, companies can still gain competitive advantage by being early adopters of integrated management practices that mesh with business strategy and change strategy. We believe that this is where competitive advantage lies in the future. Companies that are able to put together the right pieces are likely to gain a significant long-term competitive advantage. Companies that wish to compete in a global environment must take an integrated total systems approach to management. To do anything less creates a high risk of losing out to companies that are able to master the total systems approach.

Our view of the future is fundamentally optimistic. Our research suggests that firms are increasingly recognizing that how they organize and how they deal with people are crucial sources of competitive advantage. It confirms the accuracy of this view by showing that company financial performance is related to the adoption of EI, TQM, and reengineering. Research and practice are increasingly defining and clarifying the key elements of a high performance approach to management. This approach clearly must include many of the ideas and practices at the core of employee involvement, total quality management, reengineering, and knowledge management.

Our new research findings lead us to revisit a prediction we made in 1998: "It will no longer be the degree to which companies have an effective TQM, EI, or reengineering program that is crucial for their success. Instead, it will be the degree to which they have an effective, integrated set of management practices that support their business strategy and their needs for particular core competencies and organizational capabilities. Indeed, we may be at the end of an era in which employee involvement, total quality management, and reengineering are popular 'programs'" (Lawler, Mohrman, and Ledford, 1998, p. 199). This prediction seems to be coming true more rapidly than we imagined. The focus with respect to organizational effectiveness increasingly seems to be on using information technology and the development of integrated organizational designs and information systems. Organizations are also increasingly focused on their ability to adapt and change as the business environment and technology change. No single program can create an organization that will be successful in today's competitive environment, but the programs that we have studied do suggest important practices and strategies that can contribute to an organization's performing effectively in today's and tomorrow's business environment.

The Questionnaire

THE FIFTH NATIONAL TRIENNIAL SURVEY OF ORGANIZATIONAL PERFORMANCE IMPROVEMENT EFFORTS is being conducted by the University of Southern California. The purpose of this survey is to obtain information on the design, implementation, and operation of a variety of organizational improvement efforts.

This questionnaire is being sent to "Fortune 1000" corporations and should be answered by the CEO or someone else who is familiar with their corporation's management practices and organizational effectiveness efforts. Since this is a corporate wide survey, the respondent may wish to consult key staff familiar with your improvement efforts throughout the corporation. Please answer the questions in terms of **employees in the United States only**. To clarify what is meant by the terms used in this questionnaire, a glossary is included [see Resource B].

Your response will be kept *confidential*. The questionnaire is numbered to aid us in our follow-up efforts and will not be used to single out you or your corporation. Your answers will be combined with those of other respondents and presented only in summary form in our report. Your response is voluntary; however, we urge you to respond since we cannot make a meaningful assessment of the Fortune 1000 without your survey.

This questionnaire should take about 25 minutes to complete. Most of the questions can be quickly answered by checking a box or circling a number. Please return the completed questionnaire in the enclosed postage-paid envelope within *21 days* of receipt. If you have any questions, please call Ed Lawler at (213) 740-9814.

In the event the return envelope is misplaced the address is:

Professor Edward E. Lawler III
Center for Effective Organizations
Marshall School of Business
University of Southern California
Los Angeles, CA 90089-1421

We would like to thank you for your contribution to our study by sending you a complementary book or books. Please indicate which books you want and print your name and complete mailing address or tape your business card below:

☐ Lawler, E., Mohrman, S. and Ledford, G. *Strategies for High Performance Organizations—The CEO Report: Employee Involvement, TQM, and Reengineering Programs in Fortune 1000 Corporations*. San Francisco: Jossey-Bass, 1998. (Report of our 1987, 1990, 1993, and 1996 studies of organizational performance improvement)

☐ Conger, J. A., Spreitzer, G. M., and Lawler, E. E., III. *The Leadership Change Handbook*. San Francisco: Jossey-Bass, 1999. (Leadership experts explain how to lead organizational change efforts)

☐ Lawler, E. E. III. *Rewarding Excellence: Pay Strategies for New Economy*. San Francisco: Jossey-Bass, 2000. (How to pay people in the new global economy)

☐ Mohrman, S. A., Galbraith, J. R., and Lawler, E. E., III. *Tomorrow's Organization: Crafting Winning Capabilities in a Dynamic World* San Francisco: Jossey-Bass, 1998. (Book on organization design)

_____

_____

_____

_____

_____

USC
MARSHALL
SCHOOL OF
BUSINESS

Thank you in advance for your participation in the study.

SECTION A: INFORMATION ON FIRM

1. What is the title or position of the individual completing the majority of this questionnaire? *(Check one.)*

   ☐ 1. Chief Executive Officer, Chief Operating Officer, or President

   ☐ 2. Vice President for Human Resources, Industrial Relations, or Personnel (or equivalent title)

   ☐ 3. Vice President for function other than Human Resources, Industrial Relations, or Personnel (or equivalent title)

   ☐ 4. Corporate Manager for Operations (or equivalent title)

   ☐ 5. Director or Manager of Employee Involvement or Quality (or equivalent title)

   ☐ 6. Other (please specify) _____

2. Of the total number of U.S. employees in your corporation, about what percent fall into each of the following categories? *(Enter approximate percents, which should add to 100%.)*

1. Hourly/clerical	_____%	
2. Technical/professional	_____%	
3. Supervisors/managers	_____%	
4. Other	_____%	
TOTAL	100%	

3. About what percent of your employees work in manufacturing operations? *(Enter percent. If none, enter "0".)*

   _____%

4. About what percent of your corporation's non-managerial employees are represented by labor union(s)? *(Enter percent. If none, enter "0".)*

   _____%

5. About what percent of your corporation's employees are employed in countries other than the United States? *(Enter percent. If none, enter "0".)*

   _____%

6. **Which of the following best describes your company?** (*Check one.*)

☐ 1. Single integrated business

☐ 2. Multiple related businesses with corporate functions providing some integrative support

☐ 3. Several sectors or groups of business units with some corporate functions and support

☐ 4. Multiple unrelated businesses managed independently in a "holding company" fashion

☐ 5. Multiple unrelated businesses actively managed by a corporate office

☐ 6. Other (please specify) _____

7. **Overall, to what extent is your corporation's business environment characterized by the following conditions:**	Little or No Extent	Some Extent	Moderate Extent	Great Extent	Very Great Extent
1. Subject to heavy foreign competition	1	2	3	4	5
2. Rapidly growing market	1	2	3	4	5
3. Shorter product life cycles	1	2	3	4	5
4. Declining markets	1	2	3	4	5
5. Intense quality competition	1	2	3	4	5
6. Intense speed to market competition	1	2	3	4	5
7. Intense cost competition	1	2	3	4	5
8. Rapid change	1	2	3	4	5

8. **To what extent does your corporation's business strategy stress the following:**	Little or No Extent	Some Extent	Moderate Extent	Great Extent	Very Great Extent
1. Increasing the percent of revenue from new products and services	1	2	3	4	5
2. Being a global company	1	2	3	4	5
3. Having a strong customer focus	1	2	3	4	5
4. Increasing the speed with which products are brought to market	1	2	3	4	5
5. Building knowledge and intellectual capital	1	2	3	4	5
6. Being a low cost competitor	1	2	3	4	5
7. Having high levels of quality in everything you do	1	2	3	4	5
8. Responding quickly to changes in the market	1	2	3	4	5
9. Being a technology leader	1	2	3	4	5
10. Entering new businesses	1	2	3	4	5
11. Developing an electronic commerce (E-commerce) capability	1	2	3	4	5

9. **Approximately how much has the size of your domestic (U.S.) workforce changed in the last ten years?** (*Check one.*)

☐ 1. Decreased more than 50%   ☐ 8. Increased less than 20%

☐ 2. Decreased 41 to 50%   ☐ 9. Increased 21 to 40%

☐ 3. Decreased 31 to 40%   ☐ 10. Increased 41 to 60%

☐ 4. Decreased 21 to 30%   ☐ 11. Increased 61 to 80%

☐ 5. Decreased 10 to 20%   ☐ 12. Increased 81 to 100%

☐ 6. Decreased less than 10%   ☐ 13. Increased more than 100%

☐ 7. No change

10. **What were the primary reasons for this change in workforce size?** (*Check one or more.*)

☐ 1. Downsizing

☐ 2. Divestiture

☐ 3. Merger/Acquisition

☐ 4. Growth in Business

☐ 5. Across the Board Layoffs

☐ 6. Outsourcing

☐ 7. Other: _____

11. **Has your corporation removed layers of management during the last ten years?** (*Check one.*)

☐ 1. Yes

☐ 2. No (If no, please go to question 13)

12. **If yes, how many layers of management were removed?** (*Check one.*)

☐ 1. One   ☐ 4. Four

☐ 2. Two   ☐ 5. Five

☐ 3. Three   ☐ 6. Six or More

13. **Does your organization have a formal statement of the social or employment contract that defines what it expects of employees and what they can expect in return?** (*Check one.*)

☐ 1. Yes

☐ 2. No (If no, please go to question 15)

14. If you have a formal written contract, is it . . . (*Pick the most appropriate answer.*)

- ☐ 1. New in the last three years and valid
- ☐ 2. New in the last three years but not valid
- ☐ 3. More than three years old and still valid
- ☐ 4. More than three years old and badly out of date

15. To what extent do the following describe the employment contract your corporation currently operates by (whether written or not)?

	Little or No Extent	Some Extent	Moderate Extent	Great Extent	Very Great Extent
1. Career development is the responsibility of the individual	1	2	3	4	5
2. The continued employment of individuals is based on their performance	1	2	3	4	5
3. The continued employment of individuals is based on their continuing to develop their skills and knowledge	1	2	3	4	5
4. Rewards are tied to seniority	1	2	3	4	5
5. Loyalty to the company is rewarded	1	2	3	4	5
6. Outstanding performers have a job for life	1	2	3	4	5
7. Rewards are tied to individual performance	1	2	3	4	5
8. Rewards are tied to group and/or organization performance	1	2	3	4	5
9. Employees are expected to manage their own performance with a minimum of supervision	1	2	3	4	5
10. No one has a secure job	1	2	3	4	5
11. Fits the corporate business strategy	1	2	3	4	5
12. Is understood by most employees	1	2	3	4	5
13. Employees are satisfied with the employment contract	1	2	3	4	5
14. We are changing direction so fast, it is not clear what the contract is	1	2	3	4	5
15. Supports a balance between work and personal life demands	1	2	3	4	5
16. There are a variety of different contracts in order to accommodate different types of employees	1	2	3	4	5
17. There is a different contract for temporary and part-time employees	1	2	3	4	5

16. Are you currently working on developing a new statement of your corporation's employment contract? (*Check one.*)

- ☐ 1. Yes
- ☐ 2. No
- ☐ 3. Not sure

SECTION B: EMPLOYEE INVOLVEMENT

This section asks questions about your corporation's information sharing, training, reward system, and employee involvement practices. (Items with an asterisk are defined in the glossary.)

• **INFORMATION SHARING**

1. About how many corporation employees are routinely provided with the following types of information?	None (0%)	Almost None (1–20%)	Some (21–40%)	About Half (41–60%)	Most (61–80%)	Almost All (81–99%)	All (100%)
1. Information about the corporation's overall operating results	1	2	3	4	5	6	7
2. Information about their *unit's* operating results	1	2	3	4	5	6	7
3. Advance information on new technologies that may affect them	1	2	3	4	5	6	7
4. Information on business plans/goals	1	2	3	4	5	6	7
5. Information on competitors' relative performance	1	2	3	4	5	6	7

• **TRAINING**

2. About how many corporation employees have received, within the past 3 years, systematic, formal training on the following types of skills?	None (0%)	Almost None (1–20%)	Some (21–40%)	About Half (41–60%)	Most (61–80%)	Almost All (81–99%)	All (100%)
1. Group decision-making/problem-solving skills	1	2	3	4	5	6	7
2. Leadership skills	1	2	3	4	5	6	7
3. Skills in understanding the business (accounting, finance, etc.)	1	2	3	4	5	6	7
4. Quality/statistical analysis skills	1	2	3	4	5	6	7
5. Team building skills	1	2	3	4	5	6	7
6. Job skills training	1	2	3	4	5	6	7
7. Cross training	1	2	3	4	5	6	7
8. Skills in using information technology and computers	1	2	3	4	5	6	7

- **PAY/REWARD SYSTEM**

3. About how many employees are covered by or are eligible for a pay/reward system with each of the following elements?	None (0%)	Almost None (1-20%)	Some (21-40%)	About Half (41-60%)	Most (61-80%)	Almost All (81-99%)	All (100%)
1. All-salaried pay systems*	1	2	3	4	5	6	7
2. Knowledge/skill-based pay*	1	2	3	4	5	6	7
3. Profit sharing*	1	2	3	4	5	6	7
4. Gainsharing*	1	2	3	4	5	6	7
5. Individual incentives*	1	2	3	4	5	6	7
6. Work group or team incentives*	1	2	3	4	5	6	7
7. Non-monetary recognition awards for performance*	1	2	3	4	5	6	7
8. Employee stock ownership plan*	1	2	3	4	5	6	7
9. Flexible, cafeteria-style benefits*	1	2	3	4	5	6	7
10. Employment security*	1	2	3	4	5	6	7
11. Open pay information*	1	2	3	4	5	6	7
12. Stock option plan*	1	2	3	4	5	6	7

- **INVOLVEMENT PRACTICES**

4. About how many of your corporation's employees are currently involved in each of the following activities or programs?	None (0%)	Almost None (1-20%)	Some (21-40%)	About Half (41-60%)	Most (61-80%)	Almost All (81-99%)	All (100%)
1. Suggestion system*	1	2	3	4	5	6	7
2. Survey feedback*	1	2	3	4	5	6	7
3. Job enrichment or redesign*	1	2	3	4	5	6	7
4. Quality circles*	1	2	3	4	5	6	7
5. Employee participation groups other than quality circles*	1	2	3	4	5	6	7
6. Union-management quality of work life (QWL) committees*	1	2	3	4	5	6	7
7. Mini-business units*	1	2	3	4	5	6	7
8. Self-managing work teams*	1	2	3	4	5	6	7
9. Employee committees concerned with policy and/or strategy*	1	2	3	4	5	6	7

SECTION B: EMPLOYEE INVOLVEMENT (CONTINUED)

5. How much of a negative or positive impact, if either, have employee involvement efforts had on each of the following performance indicators in your corporation?

	Very Negative	Negative	Neither	Positive	Very Positive	No Basis to Judge
1. Productivity	1	2	3	4	5	0
2. Quality of product or services	1	2	3	4	5	0
3. Customer service	1	2	3	4	5	0
4. Employee satisfaction	1	2	3	4	5	0
5. Turnover	1	2	3	4	5	0
6. Absenteeism	1	2	3	4	5	0
7. Competitiveness	1	2	3	4	5	0
8. Profitability	1	2	3	4	5	0
9. Employee quality of work life	1	2	3	4	5	0
10. Speed	1	2	3	4	5	0
11. Employee loyalty	1	2	3	4	5	0
12. Knowledge development	1	2	3	4	5	0

6. Overall how positive has your experience been with your employee involvement efforts? (*Check one.*)

☐ 1. Very Negative

☐ 2. Negative

☐ 3. Neither Negative nor Positive

☐ 4. Positive

☐ 5. Very Positive

SECTION C: TOTAL QUALITY MANAGEMENT

This section asks about your total quality efforts.

1. About what percent of employees in your corporation are covered by Total Quality Control (TQC), Total Quality Management (TQM), or similar quality efforts?

_____%

(IF THE ANSWER IS 0, TURN TO PAGE 10)

2. About how many employees work in units that use the following practices?

	None (0%)	Almost None (1–20%)	Some (21–40%)	About Half (41–60%)	Most (61–80%)	Almost All (81–99%)	All (100%)
1. Quality improvement teams	1	2	3	4	5	6	7
2. Quality councils	1	2	3	4	5	6	7
3. Cross-functional planning (e.g., Quality Functional Deployment)	1	2	3	4	5	6	7
4. Direct employee exposure to customers	1	2	3	4	5	6	7
5. Self-inspection	1	2	3	4	5	6	7
6. Work simplification	1	2	3	4	5	6	7
7. Cost of quality monitoring	1	2	3	4	5	6	7
8. Customer satisfaction monitoring	1	2	3	4	5	6	7
9. Collaboration with suppliers in quality efforts	1	2	3	4	5	6	7
10. Just-in-time deliveries	1	2	3	4	5	6	7
11. Work cells or manufacturing cells	1	2	3	4	5	6	7
12. Statistical control methods used by front-line employees	1	2	3	4	5	6	7

3. **How much of a negative or positive impact, if either, have your total quality management efforts had on each of the following performance indicators in your corporation?**

	Very Negative	Negative	Neither	Positive	Very Positive	No Basis to Judge
1. Productivity	1	2	3	4	5	0
2. Quality of product or services	1	2	3	4	5	0
3. Customer service	1	2	3	4	5	0
4. Employee satisfaction	1	2	3	4	5	0
5. Turnover	1	2	3	4	5	0
6. Absenteeism	1	2	3	4	5	0
7. Competitiveness	1	2	3	4	5	0
8. Profitability	1	2	3	4	5	0
9. Employee quality of work life	1	2	3	4	5	0
10. Speed	1	2	3	4	5	0
11. Employee loyalty	1	2	3	4	5	0
12. Knowledge development	1	2	3	4	5	0

4. **Overall how positive has your experience been with your total quality management efforts?** (*Check one.*)

☐ 1. Very Negative

☐ 2. Negative

☐ 3. Neither Negative nor Positive

☐ 4. Positive

☐ 5. Very Positive

SECTION D: WORK PROCESS REENGINEERING

This section asks about your process reengineering activities.

1. About what percent of employees in your corporation work in units that have had process reengineering efforts?

_____%

(IF THE ANSWER IS 0, PLEASE SKIP TO PAGE 12)

2. To what extent, have your process reengineering efforts resulted in the following?	Little or No Extent	Some Extent	Moderate Extent	Great Extent	Very Great Extent
1. Process simplification	1	2	3	4	5
2. The creation of cross-functional units (e.g., departments, customer or product focused units)	1	2	3	4	5
3. Major information system redesign	1	2	3	4	5
4. Enriched multi-skilled *individual* jobs	1	2	3	4	5
5. Multi-skilled *teams*	1	2	3	4	5
6. Doing the same work with fewer people	1	2	3	4	5
7. Doing the same work with less supervision	1	2	3	4	5
8. A lower overall cost structure	1	2	3	4	5
9. Installation of an Enterprise Resource Planning system (ERP)	1	2	3	4	5
10. Electronic transactions with suppliers	1	2	3	4	5
11. Electronic transactions with customers	1	2	3	4	5

SECTION D: WORK PROCESS REENGINEERING (CONTINUED)

> 3. How much of a negative or positive impact, if either, have your process reengineering efforts had on each of the following performance indicators in your corporation?

	Very Negative	Negative	Neither	Positive	Very Positive	No Basis to Judge
1. Productivity	1	2	3	4	5	0
2. Quality of product or services	1	2	3	4	5	0
3. Customer service	1	2	3	4	5	0
4. Employee satisfaction	1	2	3	4	5	0
5. Turnover	1	2	3	4	5	0
6. Absenteeism	1	2	3	4	5	0
7. Competitiveness	1	2	3	4	5	0
8. Profitability	1	2	3	4	5	0
9. Employee quality of work life	1	2	3	4	5	0
10. Speed	1	2	3	4	5	0
11. Employee loyalty	1	2	3	4	5	0
12. Knowledge development	1	2	3	4	5	0

4. Overall how positive has your experience been with your process reengineering efforts? (*Check one.*)

☐ 1. Very Negative

☐ 2. Negative

☐ 3. Neither Negative nor Positive

☐ 4. Positive

☐ 5. Very Positive

SECTION E: KNOWLEDGE MANAGEMENT

This section asks about your use of knowledge management practices.

1. To what extent do you use the following:

	Little or No Extent	Some Extent	Moderate Extent	Great Extent	Very Great Extent
1. Rewards for developing knowledge assets	1	2	3	4	5
2. Rewards for sharing knowledge	1	2	3	4	5
3. Knowledge sharing conferences	1	2	3	4	5
4. Information technology enabled knowledge storing and transfer	1	2	3	4	5
5. External and internal benchmarking	1	2	3	4	5
6. Visits to customers, suppliers and others for learning	1	2	3	4	5
7. Lessons learned or post-mortem reviews for capturing what went well and what went wrong in a project or piece of work	1	2	3	4	5
8. Communities of practice or networks where individuals with a common area of interest can exchange information	1	2	3	4	5
9. Access to the internet for obtaining information and knowledge	1	2	3	4	5
10. External partnerships to develop new knowledge	1	2	3	4	5
11. Rotational assignments for development	1	2	3	4	5

2. Do you have an executive who is in charge of learning and knowledge management?

☐ 1. Yes

☐ 2. No

a. If yes, in what year did you create this position? _____ (year)

b. Is this position part of the HR organization?

☐ 1. Yes

☐ 2. No

c. If no, where is the position located? _____

SECTION E: KNOWLEDGE MANAGEMENT (CONTINUED)

<table>
<tr><td colspan="2">3. How much of a negative or positive impact, if either, have your knowledge management efforts had on each of the following performance indicators in your corporation?</td><td>Very Negative</td><td>Negative</td><td>Neither</td><td>Positive</td><td>Very Positive</td><td>No Basis to Judge</td></tr>
<tr><td>1.</td><td>Productivity</td><td>1</td><td>2</td><td>3</td><td>4</td><td>5</td><td>0</td></tr>
<tr><td>2.</td><td>Quality of product or services</td><td>1</td><td>2</td><td>3</td><td>4</td><td>5</td><td>0</td></tr>
<tr><td>3.</td><td>Customer service</td><td>1</td><td>2</td><td>3</td><td>4</td><td>5</td><td>0</td></tr>
<tr><td>4.</td><td>Employee satisfaction</td><td>1</td><td>2</td><td>3</td><td>4</td><td>5</td><td>0</td></tr>
<tr><td>5.</td><td>Turnover</td><td>1</td><td>2</td><td>3</td><td>4</td><td>5</td><td>0</td></tr>
<tr><td>6.</td><td>Absenteeism</td><td>1</td><td>2</td><td>3</td><td>4</td><td>5</td><td>0</td></tr>
<tr><td>7.</td><td>Competitiveness</td><td>1</td><td>2</td><td>3</td><td>4</td><td>5</td><td>0</td></tr>
<tr><td>8.</td><td>Profitability</td><td>1</td><td>2</td><td>3</td><td>4</td><td>5</td><td>0</td></tr>
<tr><td>9.</td><td>Employee quality of work life</td><td>1</td><td>2</td><td>3</td><td>4</td><td>5</td><td>0</td></tr>
<tr><td>10.</td><td>Speed</td><td>1</td><td>2</td><td>3</td><td>4</td><td>5</td><td>0</td></tr>
<tr><td>11.</td><td>Employee loyalty</td><td>1</td><td>2</td><td>3</td><td>4</td><td>5</td><td>0</td></tr>
<tr><td>12.</td><td>Knowledge development</td><td>1</td><td>2</td><td>3</td><td>4</td><td>5</td><td>0</td></tr>
</table>

4. **Overall how positive has your experience been with knowledge management?** (*Check one.*)

☐ 1. Very Negative

☐ 2. Negative

☐ 3. Neither Negative nor Positive

☐ 4. Positive

☐ 5. Very Positive

SECTION F: PERFORMANCE IMPROVEMENT STRATEGY

This section asks about the overall approach your corporation is taking to performance improvement.

1. To what extent, are you using the following in your organizational performance improvement efforts?	Little or No Extent	Some Extent	Moderate Extent	Great Extent	Very Great Extent
1. Creating global business units	1	2	3	4	5
2. Building a team-based organization	1	2	3	4	5
3. Using temporary project teams to perform core work	1	2	3	4	5
4. Focusing on the company's core competencies	1	2	3	4	5
5. Outsourcing work that is not one of your core competencies or can be done more cheaply externally	1	2	3	4	5
6. Reducing the size of the corporate staff	1	2	3	4	5
7. Introducing new performance measures	1	2	3	4	5
8. Restructuring the corporation by creating new units and eliminating existing ones	1	2	3	4	5
9. Reducing the number of different businesses you are in	1	2	3	4	5
10. Emphasizing the competencies of employees	1	2	3	4	5
11. Significant adoption of new information technology	1	2	3	4	5
12. Initiatives to attract and retain key talent	1	2	3	4	5
13. Developing leadership capability throughout the organization	1	2	3	4	5

2. To what extent are the following descriptive of your organizational performance improvement efforts?	Little or No Extent	Some Extent	Moderate Extent	Great Extent	Very Great Extent
1. Guided by a clearly stated business strategy	1	2	3	4	5
2. Guided by clearly stated beliefs about what makes an organization effective	1	2	3	4	5
3. Integrated company-wide	1	2	3	4	5
4. Occurring quite differently in different business units	1	2	3	4	5
5. Driven by a threat to the organization's survival	1	2	3	4	5
6. Guided by a mission and values statement	1	2	3	4	5
7. Led by top management	1	2	3	4	5
8. Based on a bottom up implementation strategy	1	2	3	4	5
9. The same no matter what country employees work in	1	2	3	4	5
10. Made up of a series of unrelated initiatives	1	2	3	4	5
11. Based on a three or more year plan	1	2	3	4	5
12. Successful in achieving their objectives	1	2	3	4	5

**THANK YOU FOR COMPLETING
THIS QUESTIONNAIRE !!!**

Glossary

PAY/REWARD SYSTEMS

1. **All-salaried pay systems** A system in which all employees are salaried, thus eliminating the distinction between hourly and salaried employees.

2. **Knowledge/skill-based pay** An alternative to traditional job-based pay that sets pay levels based on how many skills employees have or how many jobs they potentially can do, not on the job they are currently holding. Also called pay for skills, pay for knowledge, and competency-based pay.

3. **Profit sharing** A bonus plan that shares some portion of corporation profits with employees. It does not include dividend sharing.

4. **Gainsharing** Gainsharing plans are based on a formula that shares some portion of gains in productivity, quality, cost effectiveness, or other performance indicators. The gains are shared in the form of bonuses with all employees in an organization (such as a plant). It typically includes a system of employee suggestion committees. It differs from profit sharing and an ESOP in that the basis of the formula is some set of local performance measures, not corporation profits. Examples include the Scanlon Plan, the Improshare Plan, the Rucker Plan, and various custom-designed plans.

5. **Individual incentives** Bonuses or other financial compensation tied to short-term or long-term individual performance.

6. **Work group or team incentives** Bonuses or other financial compensation tied to short-term or long-term work group, permanent team, or temporary team performance.

7. **Non-monetary recognition awards for performance** Any non-monetary reward (including gifts, publicity, dinners, etc.) for individual or group performance.

8. **Employee stock ownership plan** A credit mechanism that enables employees to buy their employer's stock, thus giving them

an ownership stake in the corporation; the stock is held in trust until employees quit or retire.

9. Flexible, cafeteria-style benefits A plan that gives employees choices in the types and amounts of various fringe benefits they receive.

10. Employment security Corporation policy designed to prevent layoffs.

11. Open pay information A communication program that gives employees information about pay policies, ranges, increase amounts, bonus amounts, and job or skill evaluation systems. May or may not include information about what specific individuals are paid.

12. Stock option plan A plan that gives employees the opportunity to purchase company stock at a previously established price.

INVOLVEMENT PRACTICES

1. Suggestion system A program that elicits individual employee suggestions on improving work or the work environment.

2. Survey feedback Use of employee attitude survey results, not simply as an employee opinion poll, but rather as part of a larger problem-solving process in which survey data are used to encourage, structure, and measure the effectiveness of employee participation.

3. Job enrichment or redesign Design of work that is intended to increase worker performance and job satisfaction by increasing skill variety, autonomy, significance and identity of the task, and performance feedback.

4. Quality circles Structured type of employee participation groups in which groups of volunteers from a particular work area meet regularly to identify and suggest improvements to work-related problems. The goals of QCs are improved quality and productivity; there are no direct rewards for circle activity, group problem-solving training is provided, and the groups' only power is to suggest changes to management.

5. Employee participation groups other than quality circles Any employee participation group, such as task teams or employee work councils, that does not fall within the definitions of either self-managing work teams or quality circles.

6. Union-management quality of work life (QWL) Joint union-management committees, usually existing at multiple organizational levels, alongside the established union and management relationships and collective bargaining committees. QWL committees usually are prohibited from directly addressing contractual issues such as pay, and are charged with developing changes that improve both organizational performance and employee quality of work life.

7. Mini-business units Relatively small, self-contained, organizational unit (perhaps smaller than the plant level) that produces its own product of service and operates in a decentralized, partly autonomous fashion as a small business.

8. Self-managing work teams Also termed autonomous work groups, semi-autonomous work groups, self-regulating work teams, or simply work teams. The work group (in some cases, acting without a supervisor) is responsible for a whole product or service and makes decisions about task assignments and work methods. The team may be responsible for its own support services such as maintenance, purchasing, and quality control and may perform certain personnel functions such as hiring and firing team members and determining pay increases.

9. Employee committees concerned with policy and/or strategy Any group or committee that includes non-management employees that is created to comment on, offer advice on, or determine major corporation policies and/or business strategies.

Beginning in Section 10, we present results based on index scores for employee involvement and each element of employee involvement (information sharing, knowledge, rewards, and power sharing). We also present results based on index scores for total quality management, reengineering, and knowledge management. This resource provides additional information about how the indices were constructed and calculated. Our description is aimed at interested readers who want enough information to understand our procedures but not at academic colleagues who are interested in highly technical statistical details about the indices.

Our indices of management practices are somewhat different from standard survey scales, such as job satisfaction, pay equity, or work group conflict. These measures typically are constituted of multiple survey items. Researchers use statistical tests, such as factor analysis and internal consistency reliability analysis, to demonstrate that these items are reliable indicators of the same underlying construct. The items in the measure covary; that is, the scores on all items are highly correlated. Management practices are different because they are partly substitutable. For example, an organization that includes all employees in quality circles probably will not also include all employees in participation groups or union-management QWL committees. However, other practices, such as the communication of different kinds of information, may covary as in a traditional survey scale.

We therefore used a three-step procedure to develop appropriate indices. First, we used standard statistical procedures (factor analysis and internal consistency reliability analysis) to discover practices that, when combined, represented different indicators of the same underlying construct. The information-sharing practices, for instance, all loaded highly on the same factor and had a high reliability score. The same is true for three social skills training items: training in group decision-making and problem-solving skills, training in leadership skills, and training in team-building skills. Items with these characteristics were averaged into scales or subscales.

Second, we used items relevant to each of the four major constructs that were strongly relevant theoretically and that were at least to some extent related statistically to other items in that index.

Finally, we made sure that our measures of power, rewards, information, and knowledge were the same in all five time periods (1987, 1990, 1993, 1996, and 1999). Because we were interested in examining changes over time, we did not include in the EI indices items that were not in the 1990 survey. These included stock option plans and employee committees concerned with policy or strategy.

The indices reported in this book are slightly different from those we reported in our study of the 1990 data (Lawler, Mohrman, and Ledford, 1992). We dropped the weightings used for some items in order to simplify the indices. Changes in the mix of practices that companies used in 1993 led to new patterns in the relationship of practices within each index. We also revised the indices so that they would be both meaningful and consistent across all five time periods.

Employee Involvement Indices. We calculated the *information* index score for each company that was the average of the company's scores for all information-sharing practices. These are the same items that we used for the information index in previous years.

We calculated a *knowledge* index score for each firm that averaged the scores for the social skills training subscale, training in skills in understanding the business, quality/statistical analysis, job skills, and cross-training. We used all of these items in the knowledge indices we constructed in previous years, although we used a different formula for combining these items.

We calculated a *rewards* index score for each firm that averaged scores for four key reward practices that research has indicated are related both to other employee involvement practices and to organizational effectiveness. These reward practices were knowledge- or skill-based pay, profit sharing, gainsharing, and employee stock ownership plans. We did not use two items that were not used in the 1987 survey (work group or team incentives and nonmonetary awards), one practice that research has not clearly demonstrated to affect organizational effectiveness (all-salaried pay systems), and one practice that is important but is not necessarily supportive of employee involvement efforts (individual incentives).

We calculated a *power* index score for each firm that averaged the firm's scores on survey feedback, job enrichment, quality circles, participation groups, union-management QWL committees, minibusiness units, and self-managing work teams. In 1993, we dropped the use of two subscales present in our prior study because a different pattern emerged in the data. We excluded suggestion systems from the index on statistical grounds. We excluded employee policy and strategy committees because this was a new item in 1993.

The *employee involvement index* score was obtained by averaging the index scores for each of the four constituent elements of employee involvement: information, knowledge, rewards, and power. Each of the four indices was weighted equally.

Total Quality Management Indices. Our statistical analyses indicated that there were two meaningful TQM scales. *Core practices* consisted of quality improvement teams, quality councils, cross-functional planning, customer satisfaction monitoring, collaboration with suppliers in quality efforts, and direct employee exposure to customers. *Production-oriented* practices consisted of statistical control methods used by front-line employees, self-inspection, and work or manufacturing scales. Two single items did not fit with either scale: just-in-time deliveries and work simplification.

Reengineering Indices. Our statistical analyses indicated that there were three meaningful reengineering scales. The *work structure* index included five items, all of which describe approaches to organization and work designs. The *cost reengineering* index contained three items, two of which involved eliminating employees and one that referred to other cost reductions. The *e-commerce* index contained three items, all of which are concerned with electronic transactions. The response scales for these items were extent-of-use ratings ranging from 1 (little or none) to 5 (great). Thus a high score means extensive use.

Knowledge Management Indices. Our statistical analysis indicated that there were two meaningful knowledge management scales. The *management practices* index included nine items, all of which describe organization practices and policies that develop and move knowledge within an organization. The *rewards* index included two items, which describe how behavior with respect to knowledge is rewarded. The response scale for these items was extent-of-use rating, ranging from 1 (little or none) to 5 (great). Thus a high score means heavy use.

References

Becker, B. B., and Huselid, M. A. "High Performance Work Systems and Firm Performance: A Synthesis of Research on Managerial Implications." *Personnel and Human Resources Management,* 1998, *16,* 53–101.

Beer, M., and Nohria, N. *Breaking the Code of Change.* Boston: Harvard Business School Press, 2000.

Blasi, J. R. *Employee Ownership: Revolution or Rip-Off?* New York: Ballinger, 1988.

Blinder, A. S. *Paying for Productivity.* Washington, D.C.: Brookings Institution, 1990.

Brown, J. S., and Duguid, P. *The Social Life of Information.* Boston: Harvard Business School Press, 2000.

Cappelli, P. *The New Deal at Work.* Boston: Harvard Business School Press, 1999.

Cole, R. E. *Managing Quality Fads.* New York: Oxford University Press, 1999.

Collins, J. C., and Porras, J. I. *Built to Last.* New York: Harper-Business, 1994.

Commission on the Skills of the American Workforce. *America's Choice: High Skill or Low Wages!* Rochester, N.Y.: National Center on Education and the Economy, 1990.

Conger, J. A., Lawler, E. E., III, and Finegold, D. L. *Corporate Boards: Strategies for Adding Value at the Top.* San Francisco: Jossey-Bass, 2001.

Conger, J. A., Spreitzer, G. M., and Lawler, E. E., III. *The Leadership Change Handbook.* San Francisco: Jossey-Bass, 1999.

Cotton, J. L., Vollrath, D. A., Froggatt, K. L., Lengnick-Hall, M. L., and Jennings, K. R. "Employee Participation: Diverse Forms and Different Outcomes." *Academy of Management Review,* 1988, *13*(1), 8–22.

Davenport, T. H. *Process Innovation: Reengineering Work Through Information Technology.* Boston: Harvard Business School Press, 1993.

Davenport, T. H., and Prusak, L. *Working Knowledge: How Organizations Manage What They Know.* Boston: Harvard Business School Press, 1998.

Deming, W. E. *Out of the Crisis.* Cambridge, Mass.: MIT Press, 1986.

Denison, D. R. *Corporate Culture and Organizational Effectiveness.* New York: Wiley, 1990.

Easton, G. S., and Jarrell, S. L. "The Effects of Total Quality Management on Corporate Performance: An Empirical Investigation." *Journal of Business,* 1998, *71,* 253–307.

Golembiewski, R. T., and Sun, G. "QWL Improves Worksite Quality: Success Rates in a Large Pool of Studies." *Human Resource Development Quarterly,* 1990, *1*(1), 35–44.

Hackett, B. *Beyond Knowledge Management: New Ways to Work and Learn.* New York: Conference Board, 2000.

Hackman, J. R., and Oldham, G. R. *Work Redesign.* Reading, Mass.: Addison-Wesley, 1980.

Hamel, G. "The Concept of Core Competence." In G. Hamel and A. Heene (eds.), *Competence-Based Competition.* New York: Wiley, 1994.

Hammer, M. "Reengineering Work: Don't Automate, Obliterate." *Harvard Business Review,* 1990, *90*(4), 104–113.

Hammer, M., and Champy, J. *Reengineering the Corporation.* New York: HarperBusiness, 1993.

Hansen, G. S., and Wernerfelt, B. "Determinants of Firm Performance: The Relative Importance of Economic and Organizational Factors." *Strategic Management Journal,* 1989, *10,* 399–411.

Herzberg, F. *Work and The Nature of Man.* Orlando, Fla.: Harcourt Brace, 1966.

Huselid, M. A. "The Impact of Human Resources Management Practices on Turnover, Productivity, and Corporate Financial Performance." *Academy of Management Journal,* 1995, *38,* 635–672.

Huselid, M. A., and Becker, B. B. "Methodological Issues in Cross-Sectional and Panel Estimates of the Human Resources–Firm Performance Link." *Industrial Relations,* 1996, *35,* 400–422.

Ichniowski, C., Kochan, T. A., Levine, D., Olson, C., and Strauss, G. "What Works at Work." *Industrial Relations,* 1996, *35,* 299–333.

Juran, J. M. *Juran on Leadership for Quality.* New York: Free Press, 1989.

Kochan, T. A., and Osterman, P. *The Mutual Gains Enterprise.* Boston: Harvard Business School Press, 1994.

Kotter, J. P., and Heskett, J. L. *Corporate Culture and Performance.* New York: Free Press, 1992.

Lawler, E. E., III. *High-Involvement Management: Participative Strategies for Improving Organizational Performance.* San Francisco: Jossey-Bass, 1986.

Lawler, E. E., III. *The Ultimate Advantage: Creating the High-Involvement Organization.* San Francisco: Jossey-Bass, 1992.

Lawler, E. E., III. "Total Quality Management and Employee Involvement: Are They Compatible?" *Academy of Management Executive,* 1994, *8*(1), 68–76.

Lawler, E. E., III. *From the Ground Up: Six Principles for Creating New Logic Organizations.* San Francisco: Jossey-Bass, 1996.

Lawler, E. E., III. *Rewarding Excellence: Pay Strategies for the New Economy.* San Francisco: Jossey-Bass, 2000.

Lawler, E. E., III, Ledford, G. E., Jr., and Mohrman, S. A. *Employee Involvement in America: A Study of Contemporary Practice.* Houston: American Productivity and Quality Center, 1989.

Lawler, E. E., III, and Mohrman, S. A. "Quality Circles After the Fad." *Harvard Business Review,* 1985, *63*(1), 64–71.

Lawler, E. E., III, Mohrman, S. A., and Ledford, G. E., Jr. *Employee Involvement and Total Quality Management: Practices and Results in Fortune 1000 Companies.* San Francisco: Jossey-Bass, 1992.

Lawler, E. E., III, Mohrman, S. A., and Ledford, G. E., Jr. *Creating High Performance Organizations: Practices and Results of Employee Involvement and TQM in Fortune 1000 Companies.* San Francisco: Jossey-Bass, 1995.

Lawler, E. E., III, Mohrman, S. A., and Ledford, G. E., Jr. *Strategies for High Performance Organizations—The CEO Report: Employee Involvement, TQM, and Reengineering Programs in Fortune 1000 Corporations.* San Francisco: Jossey-Bass, 1998.

Ledford, G. E., Jr., Lawler, E. E., III, and Mohrman, S. A. "The Quality Circle and Its Variations." In J. P. Campbell, R. J. Campbell, and Associates, *Productivity in Organizations: New Perspectives from Industrial and Organizational Psychology.* San Francisco: Jossey-Bass, 1988.

MacDuffie, J. P., and Krafcik, J. F. "Integrating Technology and Human Resources for High Performance Manufacturing: Evidence from the International Auto Industry." In T. A. Kochan and Michael Useem (eds.), *Transforming Organizations.* New York: Oxford University Press, 1992.

Mohrman, A. M., Jr., Mohrman, S. A., Ledford, G. E., Jr., Cummings, T. G., Lawler, E. E., III, and Associates. *Large-Scale Organizational Change.* San Francisco: Jossey-Bass, 1989.

Mohrman, S. A., Cohen, S. G., and Mohrman, A. M., Jr. *Designing Team-Based Organizations: New Forms for Knowledge Work.* San Francisco: Jossey-Bass, 1995.

Mohrman, S. A., Galbraith, J. R., and Lawler, E. E., III. *Tomorrow's Organization: Crafting Winning Capabilities in a Dynamic World.* San Francisco: Jossey-Bass, 1998.

Mohrman, S. A., Tenkasi, R. V., and Mohrman, A. M., Jr. "Learning and Knowledge Management in Team-Based New Product

Development Organizations." In M. M. Beyerlin, D. A. Johnson, and S. T. Beyerlin (eds.), *Advances in Interdisciplinary Studies of Work Teams,* 1999, *5,* 63–88.

Moran, L., Hogeveen, J., Latham, J. and Ross-Eft, D. *Winning Competitive Advantage: A Blended Strategy Works Best.* Cupertino, Calif.: Zenger-Miller, 1994.

Nadler, D. A., Shaw, R. B., Walton, A. E., and Associates. *Discontinuous Change: Leading Organizational Transformation.* San Francisco: Jossey-Bass, 1995.

O'Toole, J. *Leadership A to Z: A Guide for the Appropriately Ambitious.* San Francisco: Jossey-Bass, 1999.

Peters, T. J., and Waterman, R. H. *In Search of Excellence.* New York: HarperCollins, 1982.

Pfeffer, J. *Competitive Advantage Through People.* Boston: Harvard Business School Press, 1994.

Prahalad, C. K., and Hamel, G. "The Core Competence of the Corporation." *Harvard Business Review,* 1990, *68*(3), 79–91.

Rogers, E. M. *Diffusion of Innovations.* (3rd ed.) New York: Free Press, 1983.

Rosen, C., Klein, K. J., and Young, K. M. *Employee Ownership in America.* San Francisco: New Lexington Press, 1986.

Rousseau, D. M. *Psychological Contracts in Organizations: Written and Unwritten Agreements.* Thousand Oaks, Calif.: Sage, 1995.

Rousseau, D. M., and Schalk, R. *Psychological Contorts in Employment.* Thousand Oaks, Calif.: Sage, 2000.

Rumelt, R. P. "Foreword." In G. Hamel and A. Heene (eds.), *Competence-Based Competition.* New York: Wiley, 1994.

Senge, P. M. *The Fifth Discipline.* New York: Doubleday, 1990.

Staw, B. M., and Epstein, L. D. "What Bandwagons Bring: Effects of Popular Management Techniques on Corporate Performance, Reputation, and CEO Pay." *Administrative Science Quarterly,* 2000, *45,* 523–556.

Tichy, N. M. *The Leadership Engine.* New York: HarperBusiness, 1997.

Whyte, W. H. *The Organization Man.* New York: Simon & Schuster, 1956.

Womack, J. P., Jones, D. T., and Roos, D. *The Machine That Changed the World.* Old Tappan, N.J.: Macmillan, 1990.

Zingheim, P. K., and Schuster, J. R. *Pay People Right! Breakthrough Reward Strategies to Create Great Companies.* San Francisco: Jossey-Bass, 2000.

Zuboff, S. *In the Age of the Smart Machine: The Future of Work and Power.* New York: Basic Books, 1988.

Index

Note: Page references to tables are noted in italics.

60; financial effects of use of, *157, 159*; and knowledge management, 79; questionnaire, 225–226; and reengineering outcomes, 132–133, 132–*133*; and reengineering practices, 77–79; relationship of, to employee involvement, 71–73; use of, *57–63*, 207–208

Total quality management (TQM) outcomes: and change strategy, 124–125; and employee involvement, 117–119; and employment contract, 121, *123–124*; experience with, *114*; and extent of adoption of practices, *118–119*; and knowledge management, 120–121, *122*; on performance, *115–116*; and reengineering, 119–120

Toyota, 93

Training. *See* Skills training

U

Union-management quality of work-life (QWL). *See* Quality-of-work-life (QWL) committees

United States General Accounting Office (GAO), 22–24

University of Southern California, 22, 23, 217; Marshall School of Business, Center for Effective Organizations, 22, 217

U.S. Baldrige National Quality Award, 58

V

Vollrath, D. A., 149

W

Wall Street Journal, 3

Walton, A. E., 19

Waterman, R. H., 3, 90

Wernerfelt, B., 149

Westinghouse, 90

Whyte, W. H., 85

Womack, J. P., 6

Work cells, 61

Work design practices, *50–53*; percentage of employees covered by, *51. See also* Power sharing

Work simplification, 61

Work structure index, 238

World Wide Web, growing use of, 6, 69

Y

Y2K, 94

Young, K. M., 43

Z

Zingheim, P. K., 40, 42, 43

Zuboff, S., 10

How to Use the CD-ROM

System Requirements

Windows PC

- 486 or Pentium processor-based personal computer

- Microsoft Windows 95 or Windows NT 3.51 or later

- Minimum RAM: 8 MB for Windows 95 and NT

- Available space on hard disk: 8 MB Windows 95 and NT

- 2X speed CD-ROM drive or faster

- Netscape 4.0 or higher browser or MS Internet Explorer 4.0 or higher

Macintosh

- Macintosh with a 68020 or higher processor or Power Macintosh

- Apple OS version 7.0 or later

- Minimum RAM: 12 MB for Macintosh

- Available space on hard disk: 6MB Macintosh

- 2X speed CD-ROM drive or faster

- Netscape 4.0 or higher browser or MS Internet Explorer 4.0 or higher

NOTE: This CD requires Netscape 4.0 or MS Internet Explorer 4.0 or higher. It also uses the free Acrobat reader. You can download these products using the links below:

http://www.netscape.com/download/index.html
http://www.microsoft.com/windows/ie/download/default.asp
http://www.adobe.com/products/acrobat/readstep.html

Getting Started

Insert the CD-ROM into your drive. The CD-ROM will usually launch automatically. If it does not, click on the CD-ROM drive on your computer to launch. You will see an opening page. You can click on this page or wait for it to fade to the Copyright Page. After you click to agree to the terms of the Copyright Page, the Home Page will appear.

Moving Around

Use the buttons at the left of each screen or at the bottom of each screen to move among the menu pages. To view a document listed on one of the menu pages, simply click on the name of the document. To quit a document at any time, click the box at the upper right-hand corner of the screen.

Use the scrollbar at the right of the screen to scroll up and down each page.

To quit the CD-ROM, you can click the Quit option at the bottom of each menu page, hit Control-Q, or click the box at the upper right-hand corner of the screen.

In Case of Trouble

If you experience difficulty using the *Organizing for High Performance* CD-ROM, please follow these steps:

1. Make sure your hardware and systems configurations conform to the systems requirements noted under "Systems Requirements" above.

2. Review the installation procedure for your type of hardware and operating system. It is possible to reinstall the software if necessary.

3. You may call Jossey-Bass Customer Service at (415) 433-1740 between the hours of 8 A.M. and 5 P.M. Pacific Time, and ask for Jossey-Bass CD-ROM Technical Support.

Please have the following information available:

- Type of computer and operating system
- Version of Windows or Mac OS being used
- Any error messages displayed
- Complete description of the problem.

(It is best if you are sitting at your computer when making the call.)